BUCKET
~ TO ~
# GREECE

Volume 17

V.D. BUCKET

Copyright © 2025 V.D. Bucket
All rights reserved.

No part of this publication may be reproduced, distributed, or transmitted in any form or by any means, including photocopying, recording, or other electronic or mechanical methods, without the prior written permission of the publisher, except in the case of brief quotations embodied in critical reviews and certain other non-commercial uses permitted by copyright law.

All names have been changed to spare my wife embarrassment.

Editor: James Scraper
Proofreader: Alan Wood
Cover Designer: German Creative
Interior Formatting: The Book Khaleesi

Other Books in the Bucket to Greece Series

Bucket to Greece Volume 1
Bucket to Greece Volume 2
Bucket to Greece Volume 3
Bucket to Greece Volume 4
Bucket to Greece Volume 5
Bucket to Greece Volume 6
Bucket to Greece Volume 7
Bucket to Greece Volume 8
Bucket to Greece Volume 9
Bucket to Greece Volume 10
Bucket to Greece Volume 11
Bucket to Greece Volume 12
Bucket to Greece Volume 13
Bucket to Greece Volume 14
Bucket to Greece Volume 15
Bucket to Greece Volume 16

Bucket to Greece Collection Vols 1-3
Bucket to Greece Collection Vols 4-6
Bucket to Greece Collection Vols 7-9
Bucket to Greece Collection Vols 10-12
Bucket to Greece Collection Vols 13-15

Bucket to Greece Short 1
Bucket to Greece Short 2

Chapter 1

Between a Bucket and a Hosepipe

Creeping as stealthily as I could in my stocking feet, I dragged my weary frame across to the kitchen sink. In desperate need of a quick cooling off, I stuck my head directly under the tap. To say I was an overheated sweaty mess would be an understatement: it came nowhere near to describing my transformation into a rather pungent, bedraggled wet rag in need of a good wringing out. Turning the tap on, I groaned in frustration when nothing came out.

"There's no water, lad."

Jolted by the unexpected sound of Violet Burke's voice in my kitchen, the top of my scalp slammed painfully into the useless tap, threatening to leave a prominent dent in my pate. "For goodness' sake, Mother. Must you sneak up on me like that?"

Was it really too much to expect the house to be free of uninvited relatives when all I yearned for was a bit of peace and quiet on returning home from a hard day's repping on Pegasus? My patience had been stretched to the limit by the air conditioning in the Punto malfunctioning and blasting hot air all over my clammy body, non-stop for the last hour.

Moreover, I was almost at breaking point from having Sherry tag along for the day: as if watching her making cow eyes at Captain Vasos whilst manically braying wasn't bad enough, I had been forced to listen to her twittering on about compost and the biodegradable qualities of coffee grinds, egg shells, and, to my absolute horror, pubic hairs, all the way home. If it hadn't been for the certain knowledge that I would incur Marigold's wrath, I would have given in to temptation and happily ditched Sherry by the side of the road a good hour back.

"It looked to me as if you were doing some skulking about yourself, Son." Violet Burke's observation was spot on. Having no wish to alert Marigold to my presence, I had snuck in as silently as possible. I knew that as soon as my wife got wind of my return, I would be subjected to a relentless grilling, Marigold just itching to know if there was the slightest sign of a romance blossoming between the good *Kapetanios* and her horsey friend.

"Your shirt's fair dripping, lad."

"It's that vile modacrylic-mix the tour company insist on us wearing," I said, too bone-tired to come up with a witty quip playing on dripping and lard. Massaging my battered scalp, it occurred to me that even if the water was off yet again, there should be an ample flow from the back-up tank.

As though reading my mind, Violet Burke volunteered, "The pump for the water is down 'cos the leccy's off. Here, you can get yourself sluiced off in this bucket of water."

Turning around, I noticed my mother appeared a tad dishevelled. Weighed down with a bucket, its precious contents slopping over the sides and creating a potentially lethal slip hazard on the kitchen tiles.

"I carted it up from the spring water tap in the village for your Marigold, but I reckon your need might be greater."

Doubting that she'd managed to stash the heavy bucket in the basket on the front of her bicycle, I cautioned her, "You shouldn't be hauling around full buckets of water in this heat, Mother. Not at your age."

"Get away with you. I'm nowt but a spring chicken." I have to say that the vigour Violet Burke displayed as she gave me a crafty wink, belied the reality of her octogenarian status. "I had to do summat to shut your Marigold up. She can't half mither on. She was fair doing my head in. I can tell you now, lad, that wife of yours is not a happy camper."

"Why ever not?"

"She was in the shower when the water ran dry. You should have heard her screaming like a banshee when she saw the state of her hair; all clogged up with shampoo that she can't rinse out. You can tell by the amount of shampoo your Marigold slaps on that she never had to put up with rationing."

Appearing suddenly lost in thought, my mother turned momentarily silent. I'd have put good money on her casting her mind back to her wartime encounters with my limping soap-salesman of a father, Vic. As she'd told me many times, Violet Burke had been rather free with her favours in exchange for a bar of soap, not even holding out for the good stuff. Vic had seduced Violet with huge slabs of cheap laundry soap which gave her terrible dandruff.

Shaking her head as though coming out of a trance, Vi continued, "Mind you, your Marigold did have a point. She looked a right sight and no mistake. Not a good look for someone as vain as your wife."

Too tired to bother arguing that Marigold wasn't in the slightest bit vain, I allowed Violet Burke to have the last word. Although generally, I always pride myself on being a selfless husband, considerate to a fault in putting my wife's needs before my own, I made a grab for the bucket. Knowing full well that I was depriving Marigold of the means to rinse the dried-in suds from her clogged up hair, I leant over the sink, tipped the bucket over my head and indulged in a thoroughly good sluicing.

Rationalising that my need was indeed greater than that of my wife, I made no attempt to ration the precious water. I had been exposed to the intolerable heat for hours on end, working my fingers to the bone herding a group of tourists that included a particularly cantankerous couple from Crewe. Marigold had probably indulged in nothing more taxing than lounging around for the day like a consumptive heroine, her nose buried in the latest exclamation mark ridden moving abroad book, whilst sipping a cool drink and nibbling sickly-sweet *halva*.

Nothing had ever felt so refreshingly good as the blast of cold water over my head. Throwing all decent norms to the wind, I ripped off the sodden flame-retardant acrylic and grabbed a tea towel. Dipping it in the remaining remnants of water in the bucket, I added a generous squirt of washing up liquid before wiping the wet cloth over my glowing armpits.

"You mucky bugger," Vi grumbled in a disapproving tone, lowering her considerable frame onto a kitchen chair. "That tea towel's going to be fit for nowt now, except for wiping down the chicken house. Speaking of tea towels..."

"I think I can stretch to some new ones..."

"What, and loosen your wallet?" Vi scoffed.

Moseying over to me, Catastrophe rubbed itself against my leg. After one sniff, the disloyal feline stuck its nose in the air and abandoned me, taking up residence on Violet Burke's lap.

"Speaking of tea towels, Dina's in such a state that she's fit for nowt but blowing her nose in a drying up cloth and having a crying jag."

Grabbing a cold bottle of sparkling water from the rapidly defrosting fridge, I sat down opposite my mother, her worried tone sparking my concern for Dina.

"Why? What's happened?"

"Eleni's only gone and upped and left. She packed her bags and is planning to move back in with her parents up in town. She's taken little Nikoleta and the new baby with her."

"Not again. What's Kostis been up to this time?"

"The usual. Dina reckoned Eleni caught him red-handed, playing around again. If you want my opinion, Eleni did the right thing in leaving him; she's given that philandering loafer too many chances as it is. He wants his marbles testing does that Kostis. Fancy risking losing such a lovely little family over a bit of tourist skirt."

"I'm surprised Eleni didn't take off the last time he played away…"

"Aye, she was a right mug for having him back. This time is different, lad, for sure. Kostis got all riled up, yelling Eleni was nagging him something rotten and needed shutting up." My mother visibly shuddered, her voice dripping with angry indignation as she continued. "He only went and give her a right clout. You should see the shiner he's given the poor lass. Dina's that ashamed of Kostis."

"That's dreadful. There's no excuse for a man to ever hit a woman."

I gave my mother's hand a gentle squeeze, knowing that talk of Kostis belting Eleni would have brought back painful memories of Reginald Slack, Violet Burke's wife-beating second husband. Having no truck with such behaviour, my mother had taken off after a public bashing, never giving the offending Slack so much as a whiff of a second chance. If nothing else, Violet Burke was made of strong stuff and always stood her ground.

"And can you imagine, it's not ten minutes since Kostis was giving Eleni grief because the new baby wasn't a boy? I told him straight, there's no point in blaming Eleni when it was your sperm that was responsible for determining the baby's sex."

"Kostis has never struck me as the brightest bulb in the box."

"Anyhow, Dina's taken Eleni going right hard."

"I can imagine," I sympathised. Dina lived for her grandchildren and loved Eleni like a daughter. The whole village would feel their loss. Eleni was popular with the local clientele that frequented the taverna and little Nikoleta was the favourite playmate of my adorable two-year-old niece, Anastasia.

"Nikos blew his top when he heard Kostis had been playing away again. When he got wind of Eleni's black eye, he finally snapped and chucked his waste of space of a son out on his ear."

"That must have been hard on Dina."

In typical Greek fashion, Dina doted on her son, putting him on a pedestal and worshipping the ground he walked on, fussing over him as though he was a veritable Greek god rather than an idle lummox. Perchance these latest antics would open Dina's eyes to Kostis' feet of clay.

"When did all this happen?" I asked.

"Late this afternoon. I had a ringside seat while I was peeling the spuds for tonight's chips. It was nearly as entertaining as Corrie, in a horrible car crash way."

"Poor Dina."

"Aye. Nikos reckons Dina will have to stay well away from doing the salads. He said her tears will water the olive oil down."

BUCKET TO GREECE (VOL.17)

The thought of Dina weeping and distraught, prompted me to reiterate my words, "Poor Dina. I really do feel for her."

"I knew you would, lad. That's why I told her you'd do the taverna kitchen for her tonight."

"You volunteered my services..." I spluttered in disbelief. It seemed that Violet Burke had clearly overstepped the mark.

"It's just for a night or two, till Dina feels a bit more up to facing things," Vi added blithely as though standing in for Dina was a walk in the park. Preparing salads, frying chips, and serving food to a taverna full of customers struck me as hard graft, especially as I'd already put in a full day repping on top of a three-hour drive.

"Since you're so keen on volunteering, Mother, why didn't you volunteer yourself?"

"What, me? I'm an old pensioner and I've been working my fingers to the bone all day..."

"So have I. And technically, I'm retired," I fired back, thinking it was amazing how quickly Violet Burke could morph from 'nowt but a spring chicken' into a feeble pensioner, when it suited.

"Swanning around on a yacht with my old mucker, Vasos, is hardly the same as scrubbing lavs. I was that booked solid today that I hardly had chance to draw breath, what with doing for the *kafenion* and then Gordon Strange wanting a good bottoming as soon as Moira left for England. He's that particular but Moira's middle name is messy. I can't say I'm taken with my newest client."

"Who's that?"

"That John Macey fella. I don't reckon he's normal for a bloke…"

"How so?" I felt genuinely intrigued by my mother's observation.

"He's too tidy by half. I'd swear he went round with a duster before I arrived." My mother absent-mindedly stroked Catastrophe's belly as she spoke. Ever since giving a home to Petey, she'd become more tolerant of Marigold's pampered pets.

"Surely, that's a good thing," I said, rather deflated that Violet Burke's interpretation of not normal was something as inconsequential as keeping a neat house.

"The cheeky bugger only tried to dock half-an-hour off my pay …"

"Surely he didn't catch you idling."

"Not likely. The place gave me the shivers so I stepped up my pace and was done thirty minutes early."

"It seems a tad pedantic of Macey."

"'Ere, you'll never guess. He had that smug Bessie round at his place. You know, her that was knocking around with that gormless Norman at my Hungarian dinner party. I reckon it was her what put Macey up to trying to short-change me. He doesn't strike me as the type with enough gumption to have come up with it himself."

"Oh, good grief. I'd hoped we'd seen the last of smug Bessie in the village. Have you told Marigold? She'll be all agog at the news. You know what she's like if there's a hint of romance in the air."

"I don't reckon that Bessie has got it in her to be romantic. Her whole demeanour is more plodding than siren. 'Appen she's more the type to lead a fella by the nose…"

Vi's words were interrupted by Marigold padding into the kitchen, asking, "Have you told me what?"

Clad in a light silk robe, my wife's glorious Titian locks were wrapped in a towel. Catching sight of me, Marigold immediately lost interest in discovering what she may or may not have been told, instead focusing on my ill-mannered display of lounging around topless, my hair still sopping wet from a good sluicing.

"Really, Victor. It's most indecorous of you to be half-naked in the kitchen. What if one of our neighbours happens to drop by unannounced? And why are you dripping?" A sudden realisation hit my wife, a look of palpable relief sweeping across her face as she eagerly asked, "Is the water back on?"

"He's that sweaty that even after a good rinsing, the lad still pongs. And the water's still off," Vi apprised my wife.

Marigold's face fell. Pulling a fabric fan from the pocket of her robe, she fanned herself vigorously. The kitchen was stifling without electricity to power the ceiling fan.

"Sweating all over my new seat cushions. Really, Victor."

"Sorry. I was dangerously overheated. The car's air con is on the blink. It refuses to send out anything other than hot air. I'll ask Giannis if he can take a look at it but there's no guarantee he won't have other things lined up."

Marigold appeared to be listening with only half-an-ear. As her gaze settled on the empty bucket, she gasped. "Don't say you've taken all the water, Victor."

"I'll go out and get you some more in a minute," I offered, grabbing a second bottle of cold water to slake my thirst.

"I'll probably need more than one bucket to get all this gunk out of my hair," Marigold said. "I can't believe that I'm reduced to rinsing my hair from a bucket. If I can't get all the shampoo out, I'll have to wear a sunhat this evening which would be a terrible fashion faux-pas after sunset."

"I'm sure no one will notice," I said, earning myself a withering look from my wife. "You could always pop down to the garden and use Guzim's hosepipe. His water supply should be fine; it's only ours that needs electricity to power the pump."

"Don't be ridiculous," Marigold countered.

Belatedly, something else that Marigold had said resonated with me, prompting me to query, "You mentioned this evening?"

"Yes. Didn't I say that we've got plans? I ran into that charming young couple in the shop and they invited the two of us to join them for dinner this evening."

"What charming couple?"

"Toby and Felicity. You know, the couple staying at Sofia's. I think they were a bit shy to go in the local taverna on their own. It can be quite daunting if one isn't used to the way the locals tend to stare at strangers."

"My mother has volunteered my services to run the taverna kitchen this evening for Dina…"

"Oh, no. That won't do at all, not at all. You must get

out of it, Victor. It's going to look a bit peculiar if you have to keep jumping up from the table to serve salads and fry chips."

"I can't let Dina down now that Vi has volunteered my services…"

"Really, Vi. You can't just go around volunteering Victor willy-nilly," Marigold objected.

"It's no more than you did yourself," I reminded Marigold, thinking back to our first winter in the village when I had practically taken up residence in the taverna kitchen whilst Dina rested up with a broken arm. Although in retrospect I was grateful for the experience and the way it helped me to integrate into village life, at the time I had been none-too-pleased with Marigold for offering my services. "Anyway, you'll have to dine with them without me. Dina needs me."

Once Violet Burke had explained why she had taken it upon herself to say that I'd help out, I was up for the challenge. Being particularly fond of Dina, I would happily do anything I could to help ease her distress. It wouldn't kill me to step back into my cheffing role for a couple of nights.

Looking at Marigold, I could tell from the way her expression softened that she was going to try and wear me down with a spot of wheedling. Fortunately, I was saved by the bell when my mobile phone rang. As I answered Cynthia's call, Marigold tutted at the water spilt over the floor tiles before busying herself by mopping it up: her unprompted action disproving Violet Burke's constant assertion that my wife is a lazy mare.

I was happy to assure Cynthia that Marigold and I

would be delighted to babysit Anastasia the next day, both of us enjoying a day with our niece. Finding a regular babysitter to replace Sofia had presented Barry and Cynthia with a challenge whilst Sampaguita was away in the Philippines.

Marigold's face fell when she realised that she already had firm plans for the next day, having arranged to go into town with Athena for a mosey around the shops. I found the very notion that my wife could restrain herself to a bit of window shopping patently absurd; the pair of them were clearly intending to go on a shopping spree, Athena apparently addicted to buying up cheap bling.

"What a blow. It would have been such a pleasure to have Anastasia for the day. Will you be able to manage on your own, Victor?"

"Of course. I'm more than capable of looking after one small child. The two of us will be sure to have a marvellous day which is more than you'll have, if you plan on going to town in the Punto."

"You mean because of the air con? Can't you fix it, Victor?"

"What do you think?" Naturally, my question was rhetorical. The very notion that I could fix anything that had gone wrong with the Punto, laughably absurd.

Wringing the mop out, Marigold was suddenly all smiles as she said, "Now, do tell me all about how Sherry got along with Vasos? Did you detect a hint of romance in the air?"

Reluctant to face an interrogation, I promised Marigold that I would fill her in later. "Right now, I need to fill up this bucket so you can sort your hair out. Come on, Mother. I'll walk you down." My words weren't so much an invitation for Violet Burke to join me, as a plea for her to leave.

No sooner had I spoken than it occurred to me that my joshing comment about Marigold swilling herself down under Guzim's hosepipe had more legs than a throwaway quip. Rather than trawling all the way to the village tap to fill my bucket, I would simply avail myself of Guzim's hosepipe. Grabbing a clean pair of shorts and the bottle of washing up liquid, I ushered my mother down, promising to deliver a bucket of water to the *apothiki* in a jiffy.

Chapter 2

A Bit of an Exhibitionist

Heading across the garden to Guzim's pink palace of love, I was relieved to see no evidence of the Albanian shed dweller lurking; perchance he was still hard at work helping Yiota on the farm. Shamelessly stripping down to my Y-fronts, I doused myself in washing-up liquid before picking up the hosepipe. No sooner had my hands connected with the rubber pipe than the door to Guzim's hovel was thrust open, leaving me caught out in a very compromising position. The surge of heat in my cheeks gave me a clue that I was blushing like an overripe tomato.

Clad in a pair of baggy and grubby, grey jogging trousers, the elastic waistband noticeably sagging, paired with a garish orange pullover most unsuited to the summer temperature, Guzim dispensed with the usual pleasantries. Without so much as a civil hello, he demanded to know what I was doing with his hose. *"Ti kaneis me to lasticho mou?"*

"Syngnomi. Eprepe na rotiso. Den echoume nero." Apologising, I told Guzim I should have asked before presuming to use it, explaining we had no water.

"Kanena provlima." Assuring me it was no problem, Guzim went on to say I could avail myself of his water whenever I fancied. Turning the water on, Guzim's wide rictus grin displayed his almost toothless gums as he asked me, with a completely straight face, if I'd like him to scrub my back. *"Tha itheles na sou tripso tin plati?"*

Robustly declining Guzim's generous offer, I reflected that when Guzim had been incapacitated in the Bucket spare bedroom following his release from hospital back in January, I hadn't given him so much as a swipe with a wet cloth. Instead, Violet Burke had been the one to administer a bed bath, giving a mortified Guzim a thoroughly good bottoming, much to the Albanian's chagrin.

Directing the flow of water over my body, I revelled in the welcome water, pleasantly warm because the hosepipe had been left lying around in the direct sun. I found hosing myself down to be almost enjoyable, certainly preferable to the alternative of remaining intolerably sweaty. Of course, it wouldn't be an experience I would wish to replicate in winter.

"Koita." Calling on me to look, Guzim didn't bother to specify what exactly he wanted me to look at. I soon

caught on as the sound of a grotesque cackle filtering across my garden drew my attention to Kyria Maria standing at her open bedroom window, seemingly highly amused at the sight of my taking a public shower: thank goodness I hadn't thrown caution to the wind and stripped off my undies or she'd likely have me done for indecent exposure. My embarrassment was compounded when Papas Andreas joined his mother at the window, making not the slightest attempt to conceal his laughter.

The rather unnerving experience of being spied on by Kyria Maria and her son afforded me an inkling of what Guzim must be forced to endure when the likes of Marigold's friend Geraldine and other visitors gawked at him from the Bucket spare room when he showered. I made a mental note to have a word with Doreen and see if she could rig up another shower curtain for the hapless Albanian: the original one which she and Marigold had installed during the great shed makeover, intended to preserve Guzim's modesty, had long since succumbed to the elements.

With my ablutions complete, I once again thanked Guzim for the use of his hosepipe before filling up my bucket with water for Marigold. Once I had lugged the overflowing bucket up the outside stairs, I siphoned the contents into various jugs and empty bottles to make things easier for my wife to handle. With Marigold sorted with enough water to hopefully free her Titian tresses from the caked-in sludge of excessive shampoo, I headed back down to Guzim's hosepipe to once again fill the bucket up, this time for my mother.

BUCKET TO GREECE (VOL.17)

By the time the bucket was full and I had heaved the heavy receptacle back through the garden, I had managed to work up another film of cloying sweat. Much as I was tempted to hot-foot it back to the hosepipe, I really didn't fancy treating Kyria Maria to another peep show. Making do with a top and tail administered by a wet cloth, would have to suffice before my shift in the taverna kitchen.

Approaching the *apothiki*, I spotted Panos' brother Hal hammering on my mother's door. Once again, I was taken aback by Hal's uncanny resemblance to my late friend. Greeting me bombastically as though we'd been great friends for years, Hal stepped to one side as Violet Burke threw the door open.

"'Ere, watch where you're slopping that water, Victor. I'm in no mood to start mopping again," Vi barked. "Don't go bringing that bucket in here. The leccy has just come back on so I'll have no need of that water."

"Have you checked the water is definitely flowing?"

"Well, I was just about to when you came hammering fit to knock my door down."

"That was Hal, not me." Pathetic as it may sound for me to unashamedly dob Hal in, I often find that whenever Violet Burke's voice took on a certain tone, I seemed to shrink inside to a young boy eager to win his mother's approval. I'm pretty sure my reaction is some kind of psychological hangover from being abandoned in a coal-smeared bucket. Embarrassed by my knee-jerk response, I pushed past my mother, telling her, "I'll just pop in and check your flow."

As the water gushed into the kitchen sink with a sight

more pressure than we were used to upstairs, I could hear Violet Burke giving Hal a somewhat frosty reception, reminding him yet again that her name was Mrs Burke and she didn't appreciate him taking liberties by addressing her as Violet.

Returning to the living room, I saw that my mother had reluctantly granted Hal admittance, no doubt in exchange for the pair of handsome free fish he was proffering.

"So, what breed is this, then?" Vi demanded, staring suspiciously at the fish as though they were of dubious origin.

"*Sargos*. I caught them myself," Hal proudly declared.

"*Sargos*. What's that translate to in English when it's at home?"

"It's white sea bream," I told her.

"Is it good for battering?"

Hal looked momentarily confused, no doubt attempting to process the notion that Violet Burke intended to give the already dead fish a good walloping.

"She means does it do well cooked in batter," I explained.

Confirming my instincts, Hal admitted, "Ah, I thought Mrs Burke was planning to give the fish a good thrashing."

"You daft 'apeth," Vi said with a chuckle, finally bestowing the semblance of a smile on Hal.

"I believe that *sargos* is best chargrilled or baked in the oven with tomatoes and garlic," I told Vi.

"'Appen I'll take it round to Maria's and she can do

the two of us a right nice fish supper. She's got the art of gutting the beggars down to a fine art."

"I suppose there wasn't much call for gutting frozen cod or plaice in the chippy..."

"Aye, you're right there, lad," Vi agreed. "It'll be grand to have some company and Maria's right partial to a nice bit of fresh fish."

"There's nothing like enjoying fresh fish in good company," Hal said, clearly angling for an invite. However, an invitation to join Vi and Maria was not forthcoming. In my mother's defence, it was hardly her place to extend an invitation for Hal to dine at her neighbour's home; she hadn't even got around to inviting herself yet.

"Victor, you must come by tomorrow when the new donkey I have bought for Yiota will be delivered," Hal said.

"I have my little niece for the day tomorrow. Can I bring her along too? She'll just love meeting the donkey."

"Of course. Come at noon. I'll make lunch for three," Hal invited. "You are most welcome to join us too, Mrs Burke."

"Do I look like one of them bone-idle ladies that have time to lunch? I'll have you know, some of us have to work for a living."

Whilst Hal simply gaped at my mother's snappy response, I reflected that Violet Burke gave off more of a dinner lady vibe rather than that of a lady who lunched.

Much as I would have loved to linger and observe the interaction between Hal and my mother, I was eager to hop in the shower before heading to the taverna to stand in for Dina. I must confess to feeling just a tad peeved when my announcement that I must leave was met with complete indifference by the two of them. Nor did it escape my notice that my mother didn't tell Hal to sling his hook as I exited stage left.

Stepping outside, I spotted Giannis the bee man approaching on a push bike, not his usual mode of transport, his glossy black curls unconstrained by anything so mundane as a cycling helmet. Jumping on such a fortuitous opportunity, I flagged him down, explaining there was a problem with the Punto's air con and asking him if he could spare a moment to take a quick look.

Dismounting, Giannis told me he was giving the bicycle a test drive, being in the midst of trying to fix a bent out-of-shape diamond frame for Frank over in Nektar. Giannis went on to say that I would most likely need someone more expert than him to check for a refrigerator leak. It appeared we were talking at cross purposes, no doubt the result of a linguistic error: I had certainly not asked Giannis to pop up to the kitchen to fix my fridge. Indeed, the Greek word for fridge, *psygeio*, had not even passed my lips.

Despite his obsession with my fridge, Giannis nevertheless slipped into the driver's seat and fiddled with the air con knob. Within thirty seconds, he pronounced the problem solved: passing me a sticky and crumpled sweet wrapper, he explained it had been jamming the heat knob, *"To koumpi thermotitas itan kollimeno me afto."*

Feeling about two inches tall, my mind immediately conjured up an image of Sherry guzzling a bag of wrapped sweets on the way back from town. Not only had the annoying woman nearly driven me insane with her inane blather, she had also been responsible for my being fried by the heater.

Appearing more than a tad bemused by my utter incompetence in failing to spot the actual problem, Giannis shrugged off my attempt to compensate him for his effort. As I assured him that there really was no need for him to trouble himself by popping upstairs to check my fridge out, he burst into laughter, explaining that the car's air-conditioning unit contains a refrigerator, though obviously a tad smaller than the one currently defrosting all over my kitchen floor.

Hoping he wouldn't blab to the whole village about how utterly dense I'd been, I determined to repay his kindness with some of the bounty from my garden. Marigold would be over the moon when I told her she would be able to enjoy a sweat-free drive to town the next day but likely disappointed that she'd missed the chance to fawn over the local pin-up.

Giannis appeared to be keen to get away, directing worried glances at Violet Burke's front door. Asking him if he was trying to avoid my mother, Giannis emitted a long-drawn-out sigh before confiding that Ioanna, his mother, was away on a two-week holiday. Since the moment she left, all the village ladies had never been off his doorstep, popping round to thrust casseroles and pans of soup on him. It appeared that Giannis expected Violet Burke to open her front door and shower him with unwanted food dripping in lard.

"*I Yiota mou eipe oti i Kyria Burke troei pites se tenekedes.*" Giannis visibly shuddered as he said that Yiota had told him Mrs Burke eats pies in tins.

His words reminded me of the time when Marigold had been back in England and all the village ladies had landed on my doorstep with homemade food. Whilst I was more than capable of attending to my own needs, Giannis was, by his own admission, totally clueless when it came to finding his way around a kitchen.

Feeling it prudent to warn Giannis not to eat any of Athena's octopus if she turned up with anything concocted from the eight-legged mollusc, I was alarmed when he told me he'd tucked into that very dish prepared by Athena's hands, the previous evening, finding it most enjoyable. Since I harboured grave doubts about Athena's tendency to re-freeze defrosted octopus, I was relieved to see that Giannis didn't appear to be suffering any of the visible signs of food poisoning.

Giannis admitted he had gorged himself silly on quite the feast, courtesy of the village ladies' largesse. He heaped praise on Litsa's *fava* topped with caramelised onions and revealed he had polished off every last meatball in the pasta dish cooked by my neighbour, Kyria Maria. He had been fit to burst by the time he'd made headway with the aromatic *pastitsio* which Apostolos' wife had popped by with. If the donated dishes continued to flow in Giannis' direction, his toned and muscular frame could be in danger of turning to flab.

Nevertheless, Giannis admitted that although he had thoroughly enjoyed all the food, he would have preferred to eat at the taverna or have Yiota invite him over for a homecooked meal. Asking him why, he told me that he felt obligated to scrub all the dishes before handing them back. Totally unfamiliar with the concept of washing up, he had found the mundane chore a Herculean task. I found it quite mind boggling to think anyone could reach their thirties without ever washing a single dish.

As the young man remounted the bicycle, I once again showered him with profuse thanks for fixing the air con. Before he pedalled away, I gave him a helpful tip, advising he really ought to wear a cycling helmet as a safety measure. Although he promised to take my advice, I considered his promise a tad insincere, merely going along with my suggestion for a quiet life.

Waving Giannis away, I headed indoors. Marigold emerged from the bathroom, her wet locks, thankfully free of shampoo, glistening with what she informed me was some stuff called leave-in-conditioner. Filling my wife in on my chat with Giannis, Marigold gasped in horror.

"Oh, goodness. I do believe I have committed a dreadful social faux pas which could reduce my standing in the village..."

"How so?"

"I should have taken a homecooked meal round to Giannis. After all, it is the expected thing."

"It sounds as though he has plenty of food to keep him going," I argued.

"That's hardly the point, Victor. I ought to have popped by with something." Watching as Marigold chewed her lip in consternation, I assumed her annoyance had nothing to do with Giannis' possible hunger pangs: rather, her annoyance was directed at herself for missing an opportunity to land on Giannis' doorstep and dazzle the lad with her cooking.

"There's really no need to beat yourself up about it," I reassured my wife. "You probably didn't even realise that Ioanna had left Giannis home alone to fend for himself."

If Marigold detected the hint of sarcasm in my words, she ignored it. "If I had known, I'd have knocked up one of my trifles for him."

"Well, he did say that Ioanna is away for a fortnight so you still have plenty of opportunity to impress him with your trifle. With the amount of food he apparently put away last night, I doubt he'd have been able to do justice to one of your custardy delights."

"I'll do him a trifle tomorrow when I get back from town," Marigold declared. The fanciful gleam in her eyes made me speculate that she was fantasising about timing her trifle delivery for the end of Giannis' work day. No doubt, if she timed her delivery just right, she could disturb his ablutions and have Giannis appear at the door in nothing more than a towel. Having the knack of being able to read my wife like a book, I imagined she would be desperate to find a new frock in town, something suitably sparkly for delivering trifle in.

Changing the subject, Marigold breezily announced that she'd managed to replace me for dinner, having persuaded Barry to join her in the taverna with Toby and Felicity. I guessed my wife had used quite a bit of arm-twisting to persuade her brother to act as my stand-in.

"Do try not to embarrass me, Victor. I don't know how I'm going to explain that you'll be our waiter."

"Just promote me to the role of head chef," I quipped.

BUCKET TO GREECE (VOL.17)

"I do hope your mother did a good job with the cleaning there. I'd hate for our paying guests to get the idea the taverna is a bit spit and sawdust."

"That was our first impression and it certainly never put us off from going back," I reminded Marigold. There was no need for my wife to assume anyone new to the taverna would harbour a snobbish attitude towards it, at least once they'd tasted the food on offer. Whilst not being fancy or pretentious, the food was as good as any that one could hope to find in the finest five-star establishment, whilst the basic setting was offset by the friendliness of the hosts.

Mightily relieved that I was able to grab a quick shower away from the gaze of Maria next door, I hoped that word didn't get back to Marigold about my impromptu hosepipe shower. She would most certainly have a negative opinion about my potentially embarrassing her by turning into an exhibitionist.

Refreshed and dressed in a short-sleeved button-down paired with smart slacks, ready for my cheffing stint, I decided to throw caution to the wind and go tieless, the early evening heat inspiring my casual choice. As an aside, I should explain that the longer we lived in Greece, the more inclined I was to adopt a more informal attitude to my dress, slowly unburdening myself of the stuffed-shirt constraints I had adhered to back in England.

About to head out to the taverna, I was delayed by a telephone call from one of my old work colleagues back in Manchester. The call from Pelham took me completely by surprise since we hadn't kept in touch after I'd taken early retirement. After exchanging pleasantries, Pel cut to the chase, telling me that James Scraper, our old boss at the Food Standards Agency, had updated him on our latest venture into rental accommodation.

"I'm with Bill...the two of us are taking a holiday in Greece. We're in Athens at the moment but fancy somewhere well away from the beaten track that isn't overrun with tourist hordes. I wondered if you possibly had a vacancy?"

"For when?"

"As soon as possible. It's too hot for us here and there are too many people. A remote mountain village sounds just the ticket, a welcome escape from the busy city." About to assure him that they were most welcome to stay in the currently unoccupied downstairs apartment, I hesitated, wondering if he was possibly angling for a freebie. My fear was immediately dispelled when Pelham went on to add, "And before you say anything, I absolutely insist on paying the full whack. It wouldn't do if word got out that I was taking advantage of our professional relationship to procure a preferential rate."

Since I'd had no intention of offering him a discount, I simply told him that I understood his position and wouldn't dream of insulting him by offering a knockdown rate that might tarnish his well-deserved reputation for integrity, if word got out. I recalled that back on the job in Manchester, even the hint of a freebie would freak Pelham out. If a restaurant owner so much as offered him a coffee on the house, Pel would issue a severe warning about the consequences of attempting to bribe a public official.

BUCKET TO GREECE (VOL.17)

Personally, I often accepted a coffee on the house, providing said house passed scrutiny and met with my exacting hygiene standards. It had not taken me long in my glittering role of public health inspector to cotton on that the jar of cheap instant coffee most restaurateurs left next to the kettle was not intended for human consumption: it was only prominently positioned there as a decoy in case the taxman came calling. Without the bona fide evidence of instant, the taxman would presume the restaurateur was drinking the expensive filter stuff and add an appropriate charge to the tax return.

Agreeing to have the apartment ready for Pelham by the next evening, I was grateful that everything was ship-shape and gleaming, only a welcome basket needed. Moreover, I experienced a frisson of excitement at the prospect of hobnobbing with my former colleague who was still on the job; at least when he wasn't holidaying in my adopted country. Rubbing my hands together with excited glee, I looked forward to hearing all about the latest public health violations that had cropped up on my former turf since I'd hung up my hairnet.

As Marigold tried on a variety of outfits to find something suitable for her evening out, I filled her in on the news that we would soon have paying guests in both apartments.

"Pelham?" Marigold's brow furrowed in a slight frown as she mulled the name over in her mind. "The name rings a bell."

"He's generally known as Pel but he's very pedantic and never fails to correct anyone that shortens his name."

Marigold raised an eyebrow. "A bit like you then if people call you Vic. I think I remember him now. Didn't we go to his place for dinner with him and his wife...what was her name?"

"Lydia."

"That's right, Lydia. We had dinner at their place but they always had some feeble excuse whenever we invited them back. She was a strange one as I recall."

"How so?"

"Don't you remember, she was so thin she made anorexics look fat..."

"Ah, yes. She didn't like to eat." A vision of an anxious, stick-thin woman came to mind. I recalled Lydia pushing a teaspoon of cottage cheese and a few chunks of tinned pineapple around her plate whilst the rest of us tucked into steak in a rich peppercorn sauce, served with chips and grilled mushrooms. "Apparently, she'd had a perfectly healthy relationship with food until she married Pelham. He told her so many tales of kitchen filth that she practically gave up eating, convinced one of any number of bacterial horrors could be lurking in every bite and might finish her off. It was most irresponsible of Pelham to be so free with the details to a layman. Not everyone can come to terms with the many perils inherent in food prepared in a filthy environment."

"Well, you certainly never held back when describing the places you inspected," Marigold countered.

"Yes, but you never really listened. Benjamin was the one who lapped up all the gory details of unfiltered grime and rancid sauces..."

"Well, you did put him off chips for life..."

"Only restaurant fries. He can't get enough of his granny's chips."

"Are you sure it's wise to rent the apartment to Pelham and Lydia? What if she's one of those bulimics who's constantly purging? It could play havoc with the enamel on the bowl of the new toilet."

"Pelham wanted the booking for two people but he didn't mention Lydia. He said he was in Athens with a fella called Bill."

"Do you suppose Lydia knows he's holidaying with *another* man?"

The way in which Marigold gave such weight to the word *another* alerted me to her thinking.

"Really, Marigold. Is that where your mind is going? There's probably a very simple explanation. You wouldn't think anything of it if I took a holiday with Barry..."

"I most certainly would," Marigold argued. "I'd want to know why you were holidaying with my brother and excluding me. You know how much I enjoy a good holiday..."

"The point is entirely moot, Marigold, since I'm not actually planning a holiday without you. I was simply citing it as an example to demonstrate that it doesn't mean Pel is up to anything out of the ordinary with this Bill chap."

Completely ignoring my rational thinking, Marigold mused, "Do you suppose that Pelham has been gay all along and just didn't feel comfortable coming out of the closet? It might explain his marrying that stick insect. Lydia could be one of those sideburns."

"I think you'll find the word you're groping for is beard. Your mind works in most peculiar ways, darling. It is likely nothing more than two friends enjoying a Greek break."

"Did you tell Pelham that there's only one double bed in the apartment?" Clearly, I hadn't managed to convince my wife that Pel's relationship with Bill was anything but innocent.

"Well, the couch folds out. They don't call them sofa beds for nothing."

Chapter 3

Victor is Invited on a Date

The taverna was empty when I rolled up for my shift. The shade inside offered a welcome escape from the still hot rays of the evening sun, the sun at this time of the year hanging around until close to nine o'clock when it put in a spectacular display of bedding down for the night. The light filtering in through the windows highlighted the basic décor, lacking the pretentiousness of any fancy touches. At least one could guarantee the place was always sparkling clean since Violet Burke had an impeccable charring reputation to maintain.

Casually discarded on the floor, a child's doll missing an arm and a dog-eared teddy bear with the stuffing spilling out of one ear, might make the uninitiated wonder if they had wandered into someone's rather scruffy home. Considering the doll and teddy may well act as a poignant reminder to Dina, of her grandchildren, I picked them up, shoving them out of sight amidst some other random clutter in a battered cardboard box tucked away in a dark corner.

Despite the warmth of the evening, I grabbed a paper tablecloth, claiming a table inside for Marigold, certain my wife and brother-in-law would prefer to dine indoors since I was on duty.

The sound of sobbing coming from the kitchen alerted me that Dina was on the premises. Catching sight of me, a warm, though somewhat forced smile, brightened Dina's features, visible tear trails evident on her lined face.

"*Victor, agori mou,*" Dina cried out, referring to me as her boy as I swept her off her feet and twirled her around. Dina went on to say that it had lessened her sadness when Violet told her that I would come along to help her out in the kitchen. Reaching up to pinch my cheeks as though I was a cute baby, Dina gushed that I was such a good boy, "*Toso kalo paidi.*"

I expressed my surprise at finding Dina in the taverna, having presumed she would be too upset to see anyone.

"*Den antexa na eimai moni epano,*" Dina said, telling me that she couldn't face being alone upstairs. Adding that she thought of me as a second son, "*Se skeftomai os deftero gio,*" Dina was overcome with a bout of weeping.

Between wiping her eyes and blowing her nose, Dina

told me that even though she was so ashamed of Kostis, she couldn't stop worrying about him. Guiding her into a chair in a corner of the kitchen, I popped the *briki* on to make Dina a coffee, adding a dash of *Metaxa* to the brew to calm her nerves. As I set to slicing cucumber and green peppers for the salads, Dina sipped the brandy-laced coffee, confiding that she had no idea where Kostis had gone after Nikos threw him out.

Suggesting to Dina that maybe her son had taken to the mountains for a spot of illegal hunting, illegal since it was out of season, I didn't voice my thought that perchance Kostis may well be shacking up with his latest conquest. There was no point in needlessly adding to Dina's sorrow when she was mourning the physical absence of her two granddaughters and her daughter-in-law, Eleni.

It seemed like only yesterday when we had all attended the happy occasion of the christening of the new baby, Dina, named in honour of her paternal grandmother. In retrospect, Kostis' surly demeanour, precipitated by his disappointment in Eleni not producing a boy, had cast a shadow over the celebration. It seemed none of us had anticipated that the shadow would prove to be a harbinger of a shattered family.

As the two of us chatted, I was relieved to see that Dina appeared to derive some comfort from my presence, though I knew that nothing could take away the ache she was carrying. For Dina's sake, I crossed everything that I had in the hope that Eleni would once again forgive Kostis, take him back, and return to Meli with the children.

A couple of local old-timers filtered in, reminding me that in addition to cheffing for the evening, I was expected to play the part of a general dogsbody and waiter. Leaping into the fray, I busied myself delivering bread, olive oil and drinks to their table.

Marigold was the next to arrive, roping her brother along. I barely recognised Barry, done up in a suit and tie: his wedding suit no less. He looked most uncomfortable as he hissed in my ear that he felt like "a right wally" having succumbed to Marigold's nagging him into dressing up like the dog's dinner.

Tugging at the knot in his tie to loosen it, Barry confided, "Marigold reckoned that with you embarrassing her by playing at being a waiter, I had to take one for the team."

Overhearing Barry's remark, Marigold complained, "Victor, what on earth are you thinking? You're not wearing a tie. I rather got the impression the couple we're meeting are quite refined."

"Victor can have mine," Barry volunteered, ripping the tie off and undoing his collar button.

"Have you any idea how hot it will get in the kitchen once I start frying chips?" I responded.

Completely ignoring my question, Marigold continued, "I can't believe that you chose this evening to let your standards slip when we've paying guests to impress."

"Granted, we want the apartments to impress so that we'll get repeat bookings and happy customers will rave about Sofia's to their friends and family... but personally speaking, I don't have the slightest interest in impressing anyone."

BUCKET TO GREECE (VOL.17)

"Barry. Must you?" Marigold took umbrage with Barry rolling up his trouser legs and rubbing vinegar into the flesh above his ankles.

"Mosquitoes," Barry replied.

Pouring Marigold a glass of Nikos' *spitiko* wine, I remembered how when the couple had stayed in the *apothiki*, Felicity had audaciously wandered around in front of me in her bra as though it was perfectly normal. Considering her boldness, I didn't suppose either of them were particularly keen on standing on formality. They probably wouldn't even bat an eyelid if Barry topped up his wine with vinegar.

Popping into the kitchen, I asked Dina if she knew where Nikos had got to. A couple more tables were being claimed and the outside grill needed firing up. Shrugging wearily, Dina said she had no idea where Nikos could be; she hadn't seen him since he stormed off after chucking Kostis out on his ear. I decided to give him another half-hour before tackling the grill myself. Although I had managed to reach a stage of competence when it came to grilling the meat, I didn't have the same natural touch as Nikos with his lifetime of experience. As an aside, Nikos wouldn't have a clue where to start when it came to knocking up a decent curry.

After serving the rest of the customers with drinks, bread, salad, and cheese slathered with olive oil, I decided to pull up a pew with Marigold and Barry. Inviting Dina to join us, she brushed me off, saying she couldn't face everyone fussing and she'd rather sit quietly in the kitchen.

I suspected she was feeling increasingly anxious

about her husband; ever the doting grandfather, Nikos would also be feeling more than a little letdown by his son's antics.

Still tired from my long day in the heat, I sank into the chair beside Marigold. My wife immediately began to grill me again on the likelihood of any romance blossoming between Sherry and *Kapetanios* Vasos.

"I was working, you know. I was too busy to study every little nuance of their interactions..."

"Just spill, Victor," Marigold persisted. "Did they appear to be getting on, or was their connection at the expat dinner party just a fluke?"

"Well, you'll be pleased to hear that for once, Vasos had actually made a real effort with his appearance. He didn't reek of sweat as he usually does; in fact, he walked around in a suffocating cloud of Old Spice and minty fresh toothpaste...and he hadn't been gargling with *ouzo*."

"Ooh, that sounds promising." There was nothing like the prospect of a successful coupling to put a spring into Marigold's step. "What else, Victor?"

"Let me see. Vasos had gelled his hair down and he'd paired his shorts with that dusky pink velvet jacket that he wore for Barry's wedding..."

"Oh, I remember that." A dramatic eye roll accompanied Barry's words.

"Indeed, it is indelibly etched in my memory too," I said. "Guzim was very taken with it despite his usual opinion that pink is for sissies."

Throwing her arms in the air in exasperation, Marigold said, "Never mind dragging Guzim into it. I want to hear more about Sherry and Vasos."

"Well, Sherry was wearing some yellow kaftan thing…"

"I know perfectly well what Sherry wore. I popped round the evening before to help her choose the perfect outfit…"

"You picked out that tent?" If nothing else, my wife usually has impeccable taste in clothes.

"It's not easy for Sherry to find things that flatter…there's a multitude of things she's self-conscious about and prefers to hide. She claims she has abnormally large shoulders and very thick thighs."

"I suppose that Heinrich the hippie harped on about any supposed physical imperfections until she believed she actually had problem areas," I suggested.

"That's exactly what I said to Sherry," Marigold said, a surprised expression on her face. "I didn't expect you to be so perceptive, darling."

"Victor being perceptive will be handy for his book. Character observation and all that," Barry chortled.

"Heinrich was a terrible person," I declared, recalling the nasty streak he had demonstrated when he and Sherry had gate-crashed our romantic dinner in Monemvasia, seemingly revelling in belittling Sherry at every turn whilst effectively fleecing her.

"Then, of course, Sherry is very sensitive about any wobbly bits," Marigold continued.

"She hides them well under those billowing kaftans," Barry acknowledged. "I could well adopt that fashion myself if I ever balloon from eating too many of Dina's wonderful chips."

"If you grow a beard to go with the kaftan, you'd end

up looking like a British Demis Roussos," I said, my quip earning me a look of derision from Marigold.

"Anyway, Sherry is very keen that we get the new Slimming Club started..."

"A fat club," Barry snorted.

"No, it's a weight loss club, Marigold insisted. "It was Doreen's idea..."

"You don't need to join a slimming club, darling. Your figure is perfect," I said, mentally clocking up my brownie points."

"I've put a couple of kilos on," Marigold said, her tone indicating she had been rather surprised when her weight registered on the scales. Considering she seemed to consume the equivalent of her own body weight in cloyingly sweet pistachio *halva*, she had got off lightly by gaining nothing more than a couple of indiscernible kilos. Chewing her lip reflectively, Marigold decided, "Perhaps I'll give the chips a miss tonight. They won't be as good as Dina's anyway."

"Or as Vi's," Barry added.

"Charming, I'm sure." Bridling at the double insult, I was sorely tempted to flounce off. "Anything else the pair of you would like to criticise my skills in or are you drawing the line at the deep fat fryer?"

"Vi's chips are a close second to Dina's chips and Dina's chips are the best in the world. Just think of yourself as a bronze medallist in the fried potato stakes," Barry urged. Taking third place when there were only three contenders was, to my mind, a tad demoralising. Still, I was pretty sure that neither my mother nor Dina could knock out a decent curry.

BUCKET TO GREECE (VOL.17)

I did recall Violet Burke cooking up a packet of dehydrated Vesta curry packed full of flavour enhancers, the packet discovered in Harold's cupboard.

It was a nostalgic moment for Barry when he tucked into Vi's dish, having been a real aficionado of a Vesta curry back in the days when he boasted a mullet and moustache. I can even remember him borrowing our Manchester kitchen back when we were still newlyweds, to knock up a Vesta in an attempt to impress a girl with his sophisticated ways. Since it was the first time the girl had sampled anything foreign, she had considered Barry to be daring and adventurous, at least in the kitchen.

As I recall, the second time Barry prepared dinner, the girl was less than impressed, not even bothering to pretend to tuck into a plate of raw tripe and onions practically drowning in malt vinegar. Needless to say, there was no third dinner. Barry would have been better served by taking his date to the local pub for half a shandy and a bag of pork scratchings.

"I don't know how we veered off the subject at hand," Marigold interjected. "Victor, do tell us more about Sherry and Vasos."

Emitting a weary sigh, I realised Marigold had no intention of letting the matter drop until she'd wrung every last detail out of me. Mentally willing Toby and Felicity to arrive and distract my wife, I launched into an account of the day.

"If I'm being honest, today's trip on Pegasus was a nightmare. Rather than being left in peace to get on with my job, which, I might add, can be very taxing, not a minute went by without Vasos or Sherry demanding that I translate for them."

"I'm sure you exaggerate, Victor," Marigold scoffed.

"I can assure you that Vasos was constantly in my ear, wanting me to turn his Greek compliments into English ones. The whole situation was perfectly ridiculous. Can you imagine how embarrassed I felt when Vasos expected me to tell Sherry that ever since the moment they first met, he dreamt of resting his head on the soft cushion of her ample bosom? I drew the line at telling her that he couldn't wait for her to strip off her dress..."

"You can be such a prude, Victor," Barry scoffed. "He probably meant so that she could enjoy a swim. Lots of people wear a swimming cossie under their clothes when they go on a boat trip."

"Well, I just wouldn't have felt comfortable saying it. It may have all got so confusing that Sherry may have jumped to the deluded assumption that the risqué comments that I was parroting in translation were actually mine, rather than Vasos' hyperbolic compliments."

"Are you never going to let it drop, Victor?" Marigold dramatically rolled her eyes.

"Let what drop?" Barry's interest had clearly been piqued.

"That Sherry threw herself at Victor's head..."

"Oh, I remember that," Barry snorted. "I still find it hard to believe...Victor just isn't the type to have women making advances towards him."

"For goodness' sake, keep it under your hat, Barry. If word got out, Sherry would be mortified."

"And she only ever did it the once..." Marigold piped up in defence of her friend.

"And she wasn't exactly sober at the time" I added.

"You do realise that Litsa's brother can hear you?" Barry gesticulated towards Mathias, the elderly gent concentrating on slicing a head of raw garlic and adding it to a thick wedge of Dina's homemade, oil-soaked bread.

"Sherry's secret is safe. Mathias can't understand a word of English," I pointed out.

"Or maybe that's just what he wants us to think," my brother-in-law posited. Tapping his nose with one finger, Barry resembled a sage philosopher. It really was most remarkable the effect a simple change of clothes can have: Barry never looks remotely sage in his grimy builder's overalls.

Noticing Marigold was getting impatient, I continued recounting the interactions I had been party to between Vasos and Sherry.

"Fortunately, I had plenty of work to do, enabling me to avoid the pair of them to a certain extent. Just before we moored up for the day, Vasos wanted me to ask Sherry out on a date...with him, not me," I hastened to add. "He suggested coming up to Meli one evening and meeting Sherry in the taverna for dinner. Sherry overplayed her hand by eagerly accepting immediately. There was none of that playing hard to get as there was back in our day..."

"You never once played hard to get, Victor," Marigold said, bestowing a tender look in my direction.

"And then Vasos only went and invited me along on their date..."

"You're having a larf." Barry creased up with laughter.

"Ridiculous though it may sound, it is true. Vasos wanted me to go along on their date so that I could translate for the pair of them."

"I don't think Sherry would be too keen on having you along as a third wheel," Marigold said. "Your presence would surely put the kibosh on any romance developing."

"Since I put my foot down and flatly refused to join them, you can assure Sherry that I won't be tagging along as a gooseberry…"

"Oh, that's Sherry now," Marigold said as her mobile trilled.

Answering her phone, Marigold stood up to take the call outside. As she stepped away from the table, I could hear Sherry braying down the telephone line at fifty paces. It appeared that Marigold demonstrated complete kindness towards her friend by letting Sherry tell her all about her day on the water with Vasos, rather than revealing I had already filled her in. Admittedly, there had been a large number of gaps in my recounting since I had spent the best part of the day using any excuse to avoid being stuck with the pair of them at the same time, Sherry having pretty much taken up residence in the wheelhouse.

Whilst Marigold chatted away to Sherry outside, Barry thanked me profusely for having Anastasia the next day.

"The pleasure is all mine, Barry. I'm looking forward to it. Ana and I always have a delightful time together."

"Any plans for the day?"

"We'll be confined to the village as Marigold has the Punto. Hal has invited us to pop by for a visit with the new donkey that's being delivered tomorrow."

"Ana will just adore that, a donkey and her favourite Uncle Victor," Barry said. "It will certainly make a change from frogs and stick insects."

Chapter 4

Turning More Greek by the Day

Wandering back inside, Marigold looked around the taverna, musing, "I wonder what's happened to that young couple? They're terribly late."

"They could have adopted Greek time," Barry suggested.

"Much as I abhor tardiness, it is probably just as well that Toby and Felicity are running late as Nikos still hasn't turned up to fire the grill," I observed.

"I wish he'd get a move on. I'm starving," Barry complained over the sound of his stomach rumbling. "You could always make a start on the grill, Victor."

"I'll give it another half hour."

BUCKET TO GREECE (VOL.17)

"That's what you said half an hour ago," Barry reminded me. "If you hadn't insisted on dragging me out, Sis, I could be tucking into a Fray Bentos at home."

"Really, Barry. Tinned pies are not a healthy option," Marigold chided.

"You have tasted my wife's cooking?" Barry's words reminded me of Cynthia's proclivity for turning out woefully inadequate dishes comprising anaemic-looking processed sausages in brine from Lidl. Cynthia's heart just wasn't in the kitchen.

"Sherry was just telling me that she's signed up for a beginner's course in Greek so she can master the lingo and communicate with her new boyfriend," Marigold told us.

"Boyfriend," Barry scoffed. "She's a bit quick off the mark. She hasn't even been on a date with Vasos yet."

"I imagine Vasos would consider that point redundant. If he twigs that Sherry thinks of herself as his girlfriend, he'll be hopping around like an over-excited four-year-old boy who's just discovered the delights of digging up worms," I said. "And the sooner Sherry can master the odd sentence in Greek, the happier I will be since it should render my translating services superfluous to requirements."

"I can meet up with Sherry and give her some pointers with her Greek if it will help to facilitate the smoothness of their romance," Marigold said.

"I hardly ever hear you using Greek," Barry said to his sister.

"Actually, Marigold is quite proficient in the language," I said proudly. "She rarely uses it when the two of us are out and about together since it makes her feel hideously self-conscious."

"Not to mention there's the constant worry that I might make some simple mistake in the language which will make me a laughing stock," Marigold confessed. Looking at me, my wife didn't need to add the words *like you*: I could read it in her eyes. Fortunately, it was like water off a duck's back to me since I knew my efforts to communicate in the local tongue were at least appreciated, even when I bodged it.

"Victor. *Douleveis i apla kathesai ston kolo sou?*" Mathias called over, asking if I was working or just sitting around on my backside.

"*Doulevo.*" Confirming I was working, I went over to tend to his requirements. The natives were getting restless waiting for their meat. If Nikos didn't put in an appearance soon, Mathias may be forced to share his bulb of garlic.

Stepping into the kitchen to throw some more salads together for the hungry patrons, I watched in horror as Dina blew her nose in a tea towel before using the same soggy rag to wipe down the chopping board. Springing into action, I immediately divested Dina of the cloth, chucking it in the rubbish with no compunction. About to sanitise the chopping board, I realised there was no point. After witnessing Dina smearing the contents of her nose across said board, I tossed it in the rubbish, knowing I would never be able to chop anything on it again with a clear conscience.

Not wishing to upset Dina further, I adopted the most tactful tone I could muster to give her a dressing down about the necessity of always adhering to hygienic practices in the food preparation area. I didn't flinch from informing Dina that her thoughtless actions could have brought down half of Meli with an outbreak of something nasty. Amazingly, rather than my reprimand prompting another bout of weeping, Dina squared her shoulders and apologised profusely, mortified that she had been so careless. In fairness to Dina, even though she loathes cleaning in general and was delighted to pass the baton, or mop, to Violet Burke, she is usually very scrupulous in ensuring she keeps a clean kitchen: at least, for the most part.

Dina's face brightened considerably when Nikos strode through the taverna; noticeably, his handsome features were troubled, no doubt the ruckus Kostis had caused weighing heavily on Nikos' mind. Unusually, Nikos didn't stop to greet the customers, instead heading straight for the kitchen where he folded his wife in a tender embrace. Leaving them to enjoy a few quiet moments together, I grabbed another half-kilo of *spitiko krasi* for Mathias' table, noticing that Marigold and Barry had now been joined by the young English couple, Toby and Felicity, our resident paying guests in the Sofia Apartments.

When the two newcomers stood up to greet me, I couldn't help but be a tad tickled by their appearance: instead of dressing down for the local spit and sawdust taverna, the pair of them were more suitably attired for a night at the opera, having pulled out all the stops. Clad in a smart black suit with a pristine white shirt and black bow tie, Toby managed to make more of a waiter-like impression than the actual waiter; which would be me. Felicity looked pretty in a midi-length floral pink silk number boasting what, I have on good authority, were something known as puffed sleeves: naturally, I defer to Marigold when describing women's clothes since she proclaims to be something of an expert.

After my earlier bout with unrelenting sweat, I felt for the poor girl as I watched Felicity attempt to discreetly dab up the pooling perspiration seeping through the silk. It really was far too humid to have one's armpits encased if one wasn't somewhat acclimatised to the temperature; sweating in silk does leave such an unsightly stain. Tempted though I was to proffer some pertinent advice on how to remove sweat stains from silk, I knew Marigold would have my head if I dared to be so bold with Felicity. I suppose no woman wants to hear that their problem perspiration is both unfragrant and flagrantly visible.

After enquiring about Violet Burke's health and declaring her to be quite the character, Toby said, "Marigold was just telling us that you're actually working here tonight to help out a friend in need. We think that's marvellous, don't we sweetie?"

"Not marvellous that you're working, but marvellous the way that the people in these small communities always rally around to help one another out," Felicity clarified. "We barely know our neighbours in Chelsea, do we darling?"

"I can't say we do," Toby agreed.

"Do call me Flick," Felicity insisted as she gushed with genuine enthusiasm about the apartment. Taking

Toby's hand, she proclaimed, "Sofia's is just perfect, isn't it, darling? It's just what we needed, so peaceful. Can you imagine how jolly fabulous it is to wake to the sound of birds singing rather than the noise of a busy London street?"

As Felicity spoke, she reminded me of Sherry with their mutual jolly-hockey-sticks attitude. Fortunately, for the younger woman, she wasn't reliant on dentures yet, nor had she acquired a braying laugh.

"The peaceful environ of Meli is just wonderful," Toby concurred.

"I rather imagined that Chelsea would be a quiet neighbourhood to live in," Marigold said without mentioning her assumption was based on its reputation for being upmarket.

"Oh, good grief, no. There's always something making a din; barking dogs, some thoughtless idiot playing loud music at all hours..."

"And it's not the type of music we want to listen to, is it, sweetie? That's why Meli is such an oasis to us. I can't believe how lucky we are to have discovered this village; it's our ideal spot for a holiday. It was such a disappointment when we found there was nowhere for tourists to stay, short of turfing your charming mother out of her home, and then we lucked out again by hearing you'd turned some old wreck into apartments to rent," Toby said.

"The apartment is so comfortable and the décor just so tasteful," Flick enthused. "And relaxing in the outdoor space is just splendid, not to mention the views are to die for."

"I'd be tempted to prolong our booking for another couple of weeks," Toby added, practically giving me palpitations at the thought of an extended booking. "It's impossible though due to work commitments and the lack of Internet in the apartment. If it wasn't for that, I'd be able to work out here for a couple of weeks."

"We have a request in with Otenet for them to connect the apartment to the Internet," Barry said. "The only problem is, they're not exactly known for providing a quick service. How many weeks did they say it would be, Victor, the last time you called?"

"They promised it would be up and running in six weeks but I'm taking that with a pinch of salt," I said, making a mental note to start harassing the telephone company on a daily basis until it was sorted, having no compunction about making a total nuisance of myself if necessary. As an aside, it would be easy to harass the Otenet staff relentlessly since they offered the option of an English-speaking operative via their telephone service line, even providing free calls to their number from our landline. Of course, one had to go through the usual hoops of pressing numbered options for the service required and suffer through the inevitable holding stage of ghastly canned music, but otherwise, they were quite painless to deal with. "The connection in our house is excellent. It's that all-day sort, not the dial-up type that costs a small fortune."

"Maybe we can take another break in the autumn if the Wi-Fi is connected by then," Felicity suggested.

"What about you, Flick?" Marigold asked. "Do you need to rush back to work once your holiday is over?"

"Oh, I can work anywhere."

"What is it that you do, dear?" Marigold pressed.

"I'm an author…"

"Flick writes bonkbusters," Toby proudly announced.

"Like Jilly Cooper?" Marigold said.

"Yes, but I'm a small fish, not wildly successful like Jilly…"

"Not yet, sweetie, but I'm sure that one day your titles will be rubbing noses on airport shelves with Jilly's paperbacks."

"Felicity, do you find writing books is lucrative?" Marigold asked, her question eliciting astonished gasps from both Barry and I.

"You can't ask that," Barry told his sister.

As Marigold flushed at the realisation she had dropped a social clanger, I hurriedly explained to the young couple, "My wife is turning more Greek by the day. Unlike the British who tend to be more reserved, the Greeks will bombard anyone they meet with personal questions which may be considered inappropriate…"

"That's right," Barry concurred. "I've lost count of the amount of times practical strangers have wanted to know how much I earn or how much I paid for the house…"

"Well, us Brits are never shy when it comes to boasting about house prices," Toby said, attempting to ease Marigold's embarrassment. "But I can see what you mean about the Greeks. We got chatting to a man in the shop earlier and when we told him where we were staying, he was quite blunt in questioning how much we were paying for the apartment."

"Toby, I don't think he was Greek..."

"Well, he was speaking Greek before he started chatting to us," Toby pointed out.

"Toby, he was definitely English," Flick argued. "You must have spotted he wore socks and sandals."

Wondering which expat had the nerve to pry into the financial side of our holiday rental business, I attempted to hide the curiosity in my voice as I asked, "Did he give a name?"

"No. He was tall with grey hair and very prominent eyebrows..."

"A bit sluggish?" I pressed.

"Not really, he didn't appear to be lacking energy..."

"I meant his eyebrows...did his eyebrows resemble two fat slugs?"

"Ah, now you come to mention it..." Toby chortled.

"John Macey," I declared. "Darn cheek of the fellow prying into things that are none of his business."

Placing her hand on Flick's arm, Marigold leaned in close, apologetically saying, "Victor's right. I must be turning Greek. I really shouldn't have asked you if writing was lucrative."

"I didn't mind. Personally, I do wish there was more transparency about authors' incomes," Flick jumped in. "Unless one is a household name like Jilly, there's not a lot of money in it. I couldn't survive on the royalties my publisher pays me...I have to churn out regular Mills & Boon romances as a side gig."

Clearly impressed to be breaking bread with a

published author, my wife sent a questioning look in my direction which I responded to with an imperceptible shake of my head; Marigold immediately acknowledged my gesture. Although she was tempted to mention my own literary endeavour and perhaps seek advice on publishing from Felicity, we had a pact to keep my scribblings top secret and retain the anonymity of the Bucket name. It really wouldn't do for my identity to get out if my book ever took off, the two of us valuing our privacy and reluctant to be turned into a pair of laughing stocks.

"We have a resident author here in Meli," Barry piped up to Marigold's consternation. Flushing to the roots of her hair, the daggers-drawn look she directed at her brother served as a warning to keep his mouth shut about buckets. Nevertheless, Barry couldn't resist opening his big mouth, fortunately sparing my blushes when he said, "We have an old expat living in Meli who writes porn."

"Erotica, Barry, erotica," Marigold corrected in a strident tone, not wishing to have her reputation tarred by association with a purveyor of porn.

"Blimey, Sis, I've never heard you use erotica to describe Milton's smut before."

Noticing Marigold was getting decidedly hot beneath the collar, I butted in, reminding Barry, "Milton prefers to go by Scarlett Bottom."

"With a pseudonym like that, I'd put money on him having a sexy lead called Brandy," Toby joshed, reducing the rest of us to tears of laughter. After all, Milton's smutty scribblings were nothing if not ridden with predictable cliches.

Chapter 5

A Cat with Seven Lives

With Flick filling Marigold in on the rather racy plot of her work in progress, I excused myself, asking Barry to grab some bread and wine from the kitchen for Toby and Flick whilst I had a quick word with Nikos. After consoling his wife, Nikos had headed directly outside to fire up the grill. Hovering over the grill, evidence of his foul temper was written all over his face, his frown marring his usual handsome looks as he cursed his useless son, Kostis, relentlessly. Despite the obvious irritability which he made no attempt to hide, Nikos took the time to deposit a couple of kisses on my cheeks and thank me profusely for supporting Dina.

"Ah, Victor, what to say? If it not the enough that the Kostis break the Dina's heart, some vandal has to spray paint the *kokoras*. Not the word to Dina, Victor. I not want to add to her the upset."

"My lips are sealed," I promised. "But who in their right mind goes around spray painting roosters?"

Even as I asked the question, I had a ridiculous vision of milliners perhaps marking a cockerel's feathers with vibrant paint before plucking them to embellish fashionable hats. Violet Burke would certainly snap them up if she tired of plastic fruit adorning her hat brims.

"They not to spray paint the *kokoras*, Victor. They spray paint the word *kokoras* all over one of my olive grove walls. The big ugly letters in the red and green."

Since Nikos' clarification still made not an iota of sense to me, I pressed the issue. "But why would someone paint the word *kokoras* on your wall?"

"It is the insult, Victor. They to call me the, how to say in English, the *delios?*"

"A coward. That sounds a bit off-the-wall, Niko," I said, belatedly realising I could have chosen my words better. "Perchance it was an indiscriminate vandal who targeted your wall at random."

"It is much the work to remove the obscenity…"

"The obscenity?"

"As well as the insult *kokoras*, the vandal spray the *prosvlitikes lexeis.*"

"Spraying expletives on a wall is the height of moronic behaviour," I said earnestly, wondering if Barry's Greek reading comprehension was up to filling me in on exactly which words had Nikos so riled up. A sudden thought occurred to me. Considering it a tad delicate, I pondered the wisdom of mentioning it before blurting out, "Do you think it could possibly be the work of Kostis, taking some form of petty vengeance against you for throwing him out?"

After ruminating for a moment, Nikos was firm in voicing his opinion that he didn't think Kostis could be responsible. "No, I cannot to believe the Kostis would to do it. He would know how much it would to hurt the Dina."

I raised an eyebrow; Kostis hadn't cared two hoots that by cheating on Eleni he had hurt not only his lovely wife, but his adoring mother.

"And I not to think the Kostis will be to hang around in the village. No, knowing my son, I think he will be on the coast to chase the, how to say, the tourist dress?"

"Skirt," I corrected him, thinking Nikos was probably right. After all, my own first instinct had been to guess that Kostis may have already moved on to another woman, a woman with half of her bed conveniently going begging.

Giving me a gentle nudge, Nikos reminded me that I was being derelict in my duties. With the grill about ready to receive the meat, there were chips to be fried. Having used me as a sounding board, Nikos appeared in a somewhat improved mood but I very much doubted he would be putting on a spontaneous show with his *bouzouki* later.

The next hour flew by in a whirl of activity as I served the customers with fresh salad and feta cheese in a pool of olive oil, topped up empty *kanatas* of Nikos' *spitiko* wine, and busied myself frying chips to accompany the succulent lamb chops hot from the grill.

After having a quiet moment with her husband, Dina appeared in better form, even up to mucking in with the frying. Pointedly, she restricted herself to only blowing her nose into sheets of paper kitchen roll, thus averting an outbreak of food poisoning. With everyone served and the hum of lively conversation in the air, I once again joined Marigold and the others, finally free to tuck into the plate of delectable lamb chops which Nikos served me, fresh from the grill.

Toby and Flick raved about the food, seemingly completely nonplussed by the spit and sawdust aspect of the taverna, instead appreciating the simple pleasures of the fare on offer. Moreover, to their credit, they took their overdressed state in their very best holiday togs, completely in their stride, never deigning to cast dismissive looks in the direction of the garlic-eating pensioner. Mathias. The veritable poster boy for the cliché of an elderly Greek peasant, Mathias had turned out in crumpled black slacks with a bit of old rope serving as a makeshift belt, paired with a frayed checked fleece shirt that had seen better days.

Talk around the table took a surprising turn when Marigold announced that Manolis had treated Doreen to a brand-new moped, a cute little 50cc model, perfect for flitting about the village.

"Doreen on a moped. That I have to see." Barry's eagerness was evident in his wide-eyed look.

"You'll have to wait until she's passed the test and

V.D. BUCKET

has an official diploma in her hand," Marigold told us. "She's been cramming for the test all day and yes, before you ask, Victor, Doreen will of course wear a helmet."

"That perm of hers should soften her landing if she goes over the handlebars without a helmet," Barry joshed.

"Really, Barry, you shouldn't make jokes at Doreen's expense. You know how fond I am of her," Marigold chided her brother. It struck me that Marigold really had grown fond of Doreen. When Moira Strange had moved to the village, I had rather assumed that Marigold might drop Doreen in favour of a new bestie, but Moira spent more time in England than she did in Greece, taking every photographic ear assignment she could get before her shell likes visibly aged. Even though I suspected that the friendship between Marigold and Doreen had been born out of convenience, the two of them were now happily glued together. As long as Doreen didn't take it upon herself to move back into the Bucket residence, I admit to finding her passably tolerable these days.

"When does Doreen take the moped test?" I asked.

"The day after tomorrow. She has to go to the main police station in town. It's a two-parter, a written test followed by a practical one."

"I expect the practical test will involve weaving around strategically placed traffic cones," Barry quipped.

Along with Marigold, I burst into laughter, to the utter confusion of Toby and Flick.

"Doreen's estranged husband collects traffic cones

as a hobby..." Barry revealed. Despite his explanation, the irony appeared to go over the heads of the young couple: perchance one needed to be acquainted with the dull-as-porridge Norman and his obsession with traffic cones, to get the joke.

Marigold surprised me by expressing the sentiment that she really hoped Doreen passed the test. I should hasten to add that my surprise was nothing to do with Marigold peevishly hoping that Doreen would fail, but because Marigold has always been dead against mopeds and motorcycles, dismissing them as dangerous contraptions and a noisy nuisance to boot, to be avoided at all costs. I attributed Marigold's change of heart to her recent experience of wrapping her arms tightly around the local pin-up, Giannis, as she rode pillion on his motorcycle when the Punto had broken down on the way to Kyria Kompogiannopoulou's funeral. I doubt her opinion would have changed if instead of Giannis, Marigold had been reduced to clinging onto Guzim and riding pillion on the Albanian shed dweller's decrepit moped.

Spiros entered the taverna apparently deep in thought, hesitating for just a moment before he joined us. Resuming my role as waiter, I brought him bread, wine, and virgin oil, before adopting my role of kitchen dogsbody by throwing a salad together and then popping outside to tell Nikos we needed another plate of his mouthwatering chops.

"The Spiros came out to chat me and his lamb is already to cooking," Nikos informed me, a fresh look of despondency on his face.

As I took my seat with the others, Spiros told me, "I have the word with the Nikos. I had to tell him that some the mindless moron to dump the big pile of the rubbish in the Nikos' olive grove."

"That's disgraceful. Probably someone too lazy to make it all the way to the bins," I guessed.

"It is the worse," Spiros said. "They empty the rubbish bag. There is the food and plastic to make the horrid mess that the Nikos must to clean up."

"I see what you mean about a mindless moron," Barry agreed. "Cynthia will have kittens if she gets wind of this. You know how obsessive she gets about environmental issues."

"And with good cause," I said. "Randomly dumping the contents of bin bags is thoughtless and destructive."

"And a potential choking hazard for any wild-life," Marigold added.

"I wonder if it's just a coincidence that the rubbish was scattered in Nikos' olive grove so soon after his wall was vandalised with spray-painted insults," I mused.

"Insults?" Barry queried.

"*Kokoras*," I clarified. "Along with a string of Greek obscenities that are more up your alley than mine."

"The Kostis has to took the gun from upstairs so I offer the shotgun to the Nikos. He may to need the protection." Spiros absently mindedly stroked his bushy eyebrows. With narrowed eyes, he waited for the implication of his words to sink in.

"The shotgun?" Barry parroted, peering at Spiros intensely.

"Would that be the same gun that nearly blasted Blat to oblivion when he unearthed it from under the toilet? The one you were going to pass onto the police?" I realised that once Spiros had relieved us of the gun, I, for one, had not given it a second thought, presuming the matter had been taken care of in a responsible manner.

"You never to know when the shotgun will come in the handy," Spiros replied, his tone indicating the subject was closed. His rather tight-lipped approach suited me since I had no desire to become embroiled in anything involving weapons. On occasion, I am quite content to go along with the old adage, ignorance is bliss.

"Any other news, Spiro?" Barry asked, perchance hoping the conversation would take a lighter turn.

"The Sampaguita return home the *avrio*. I go the morning to the airport in the *Athina*." Just saying his wife's name made Spiros' eyes light up: he had sorely missed his fragrant Filipina flower. "*Avrio* the night, I take the beautiful Sampaguita out for the romantic dinner under the star…"

"Have you anywhere particular in mind?" I asked.

"I think to take her to that restaurant that have the curtain instead of the paper…"

"You've lost me."

"The place the four of us went together, you and the Marigold, the Sampaguita and me," Spiros clarified.

Marigold started laughing. I couldn't imagine what had set her off until she managed to say between giggles, "They weren't curtains, Spiro. You are talking about tablecloths made from fabric rather than paper."

Taking Marigold's hand, Spiros affectionately said,

"Some the time you can be the very difficult woman. I remember you send the food back because it wasn't hot..."

Rushing to my wife's defence, I said, "That strikes me as eminently reasonable. Marigold expects her hot food to be hot, and only her salads cold."

"The Greek would not to do that and cause so much the trouble..."

"It's hardly a lot of trouble to bung something in the microwave for thirty seconds to make it hot..."

"The Greek would not to do it," Spiros reiterated.

As Spiros spoke, Marigold appeared distracted, pulling a pen and paper out of her handbag. In answer to my raised eyebrows, she volunteered, "I'm just adding a new alarm clock to my shopping list for tomorrow."

"A new alarm clock?" I queried.

"I told you the snooze button is broken. Sometimes, I think that you never listen to a word that I say, Victor."

"The snooze button?" Spiros appeared baffled. "I never to hear of such the thing."

"It's a button one presses when the alarm goes off and you fancy another ten minutes," Marigold explained. Since Spiros still appeared somewhat confused, Marigold added, "You can press it several times when you need a bit longer in bed."

"I cannot to understand," Spiros replied. "When the alarm ring, you get up. If you not want to get up, why to set the alarm in the first place?"

"Well, one intends to get up when one sets it, but the alarm is such a rude awakening that one often fancies just a few more minutes," Marigold said.

"You should get up when the alarm goes off," Spiros insisted.

"My wife is very fond of a lie-in," I revealed.

"It makes no sense to set the alarm and then not to get up," Spiros stubbornly persisted.

"I'm with you, Spiro," I said. "When the alarm goes off, I spring out of bed instantly…"

"I'm with Marigold," Flick said. "Snooze buttons are one of life's greatest inventions."

"I find it hard to believe that you've never heard of such a thing, Spiro," Marigold scoffed. "After all, the alarm clock I need to replace is a Greek one." Because of the erratic nature of our unreliable electricity, we had binned the radio alarm clock we'd carted over from England, replacing it with a battery powered clock with an annoying tick, purchased from the One Euro shop.

Clearly not won over by Marigold's argument, Spiros called out to Dina, asking if she'd ever heard of a snooze button. *"Akousate pote gia ena koumpi anavolis?"*

"O Kostis chrismopolise ena. Misei na sikonetai," Dina called back, saying Kostis used one, adding he hates getting up.

"It is not manly," Spiros decreed with a shrug before changing the topic of conversation. "I think the new doctor will to move to the village."

"Ah, the one you told me about who had his eye on the house that needed the renovation work," I said.

"No. It is the another doctor and the different house. I think the doctor is very rich. I show him the house the five time already. I hope he will to buy because I invest the much time. Last night, I show the house very late.

The doctor to want to get the feel for the house in the dark."

"What makes you say he is rich?" I asked.

"The doctor to drive the brand-new car and even though the house is the much expensive, he would to pay cash."

"Which house, Spiro?" Marigold asked.

"The house on the square with the blue door..."

"That narrows it down. Half the houses in the area have blue doors," Barry pointed out. "Ah, is it the house that belonged to Kyria Kompogiannopoulou?"

"No, the Sofia leave her the house to the five-year the old grandson. I think it will stay the empty because the Sofia's daughter, he much the prefer to live in the town, not the village."

Attempting to fathom Spiros' words, Toby and Flick exchanged a confused glance. Unlike those of us who were well acquainted with the Greek tendency to mix up the genders when speaking in English, they must have found Spiros' reference to Sofia's daughter as he, a tad mind boggling. Perchance they misinterpreted and jumped to the conclusion that Sofia's daughter was a man in a dress. Unaware that our fellow diners were struggling to make sense of his line of chat, Spiros continued, "The house the doctor to look at is the big house set back from the church."

"The big detached house purportedly owned by an elusive Athenian who has never set foot in Meli since we've been here?" Barry questioned.

"Yes. The old man to die and the nephew inherit. The nephew not want the expense of the upkeep of the second house. She to sell it with all the furniture, all the everything, the cooker and the wash machine. The nephew want the money to put the swim pool in the house in the *Athina*."

"Does it need renovating inside?" Barry asked hopefully.

"There will be much the work before she to fill it with water…"

"Not the pool, the house in the village," Barry interrupted.

"It is in the, how you to say, in the prissy condition…"

"Pristine," I corrected.

"Every year, two times, the man from the *Athina* send some the one to do any the odd job, cut the vegetation and clean the place. It is so the prissy, the doctor can to move in the straight."

"I take it you'll earn a nice little commission, Spiro, if you manage to flog it," I ventured.

"Yes. It will be, how the Violet Burke to say, not too shabby. The doctor to think to open the surgery in the village. I think the house will need the one room downstair to be convert for the doctor to see the patient."

"So, he's thinking of practising in the village itself," Marigold said. "I think the prospect of having a doctor resident in the village is marvellous?"

"Most definitely," Barry agreed.

"It will certainly be handy for you to have a medical professional close by, Barry. There are many dangers in your line of work," I pointed out.

"Dangers?" Marigold's voice took on a worried tone.

"Barry's job involves scaling rather suspect scaffolding and handling lethal tools," I said. Not wishing to alarm Marigold unduly, I added, "But naturally, Barry abides by all the relevant health and safety edicts."

At least my brother-in-law had the grace to blush, no doubt recalling the many occasions I had called him out for blatantly flouting said safety requirements. I hoped that by making my observation in front of his sister, I could guilt him into adhering to the rules.

"Is the doctor married?" Barry's question was an obvious attempt to change the subject and one he knew would pique Marigold's interest.

"I not to know," Spiros replied, his answer immediately resonating with my wife: even before the poor chap had taken up residence in the village, Marigold was matchmaking in her mind. "The doctor like to keep the cards close to his breasts."

"Chest," I corrected.

Spiros' mobile phone began to vibrate on the table. Taking the call, Spiros remained in his seat rather than politely popping outside. Whilst Marigold and Barry chatted quietly with Flick and Toby, I engaged in a spot of unabashed earwigging, feeling rather smug that I was able to understand most of Spiros' Greek words. Spiros was telling the caller, whom he addressed as Alex, that Alex's cat, which had been on the missing list for a couple of days, had been spotted on the roof of a house in Nektar by a neighbour. Spiros told Alex that he had rushed over to feed it but there was no sign of it when he arrived, reassuring Alex that he had left some food for the feline. Spiros then told Alex to ring again the next day when hopefully he would have more news about the missing cat.

In response to my raised eyebrows, Spiros looked a tad sheepish as he told me, "Next time the Alex to phone me, I will to tell him the cat to fall off the roof."

"Did the cat fall off the roof?" I asked sceptically.

"No, but the tomorrow I will tell him it did."

Experiencing a *eureka* moment, I asked, "Were you talking about the same cat that I caught you slinging in the bins earlier in the week?"

Running into Spiros at the bins a couple of days ago, I had made no bones about expressing my disgust at this deplorable local habit of casting dead cats in the rubbish, a habit which some of the Greeks engaged in as an alternative to burial: considering Spiros' occupation, I found it particular egregious that he would dispose of a dead cat in such a shameful manner rather than arranging a burial. He hadn't even gone to the trouble of stashing the cat in a black bin bag.

"Yes, the same cat," Spiros confirmed. "You know the Kyrios Alexandros from Nektar? He is the more than ninety year with the white hair."

"I don't think so…"

"He not to get out much. He go to the *Athina* to stay with the daughter for two the week and I promise to him to feed the cat. He only gone two the day when I find the cat dead."

"So why did you tell him that the cat had been spotted by the neighbour?" I asked, beginning to feel understandably confused as to whether or not the cat had met its end by falling from the roof. Spiros appeared to have form when it came to things in his orbit plunging from a roof: after all, the only reason we had our home in Meli is because Spiros' uncle plummeted from the roof.

"Victor, think. The Alex love the cat very much. I cannot to blurt out to the Alex that his cat is dead: it might to give him the heart attack. I must to build up to it *siga siga*. Tomorrow, when I to tell him the cat fall off the roof, I will tell him the vet is still hope that the cat can recover."

I conceded that Spiros may well have a point about not blurting out bad news to an aged pensioner, instead, gradually working up to deliver the worst. Nevertheless, I would never accept such a casual disposal of a domestic pet. Saying that, when my chicken, Fix, had popped her clogs earlier this year, Guzim had been the one to reveal his sensitive side by insisting that we bury Fix at the bottom of the garden: in his mind, there had never been any question of chucking her in the bins as I had suggested, though naturally I had intended to triple-bag her first. Of course, if Marigold had her way, poor dead Fix would have been bunged in the oven and served up for Sunday lunch.

"You'd better hope that your old fellow doesn't want to bury his cat when you finally tell him it is dead. The bins were emptied yesterday." Visibly paling as my words sank in, Spiros made the sign of the cross in front of his chest as it dawned on him that there was no getting the cat back if Alex did indeed wish to bury it.

Hearing the tail end of our conversation, Marigold exclaimed, "Please tell me that Tesco isn't dead."

Spiros hastily reassured my wife that Tesco, the spawn of Cynthia's vile cat and the brother of Pickles, was still alive and kicking. Moreover, Spiros declared that he was looking after Tesco very well during Sampaguita's absence.

"When the Alex call again, I will to remind him that the cat have the seven life..." Spiros continued.

"Nine," I corrected. "Cats have nine lives."

"What piddle is this, Victor? The cat have the seven life."

"It's definitely nine," I argued.

"Victor is right. Cats have nine lives," Flick jumped in.

"*Apostoli, poses zoes echoun oi gates?*" Spiros called out to the local barber, asking him how many lives cats have.

"*Epta.*" Without hesitating, Apostoli replied with the number seven.

"*O Victor einai o vlakas. Leei i gata echei tin ennia zoi,*" Spiros called back, declaring I was a fool for saying that cats had nine lives.

Bristling with indignation at being branded a fool, I jumped on my high-horse. "You are the fool, Spiro. The myth of cats having nine lives originated in ancient Egypt..."

"No, no. The seven life start in the ancient Greece..." Spiros argued as the taverna descended into a vociferous spat on sectarian lines, the British born among us all insisting that cats had nine lives, the Greeks all backing Spiros' ridiculous claim that cats had seven lives. Surprisingly, Barry was the one to restore calm to the room, pointing out in both English and Greek that it was totally ridiculous to fall out over such a stupid argument since, all myths aside, it was indisputable that cats only lived one life.

With peace restored, I endured a bone crushing embrace from Spiros before beginning to clear the tables. As I worked, I couldn't help but notice that Toby and Flick appeared to have tuned out of the conversation, instead engaging in some rather overt romantic eye contact. As Flick intercepted a wink from her man with a telling blush, Toby declared that they'd both had a top-class evening but it was time for them to call it a night. Toby insisted on settling the bill before they left, reminding us that he'd been the one to invite us to join them.

With Nikos summoned to tally the bill, I told the young couple that the downstairs apartment would be occupied from the next evening, happy to assure them that they needn't expect any din from below as Pelham was a very respectable type. I even went so far as personally vouching for Pelham's good character since he had been a former colleague of mine at the Food Standards Agency. Remarkably, Marigold demonstrated great restraint in keeping her own counsel about Pelham bringing a chap along as his holiday companion, instead of his wife.

Nikos tallied up the bill by jotting the prices down on the paper tablecloth. Even though my friend was not his usual self, he went through the customary spiel he invariably used to impress newcomers to the taverna, boasting that everything they had eaten was either home-reared or home-grown, excepting the water for which he took no responsibility. The Chelsea pair duly chuckled in response, their reaction clearly helping to lift Nikos out of the doldrums he had been sunk in all evening. Hearing that Toby and Flick were staying in Meli for a fortnight, Nikos promised to give them a performance on his *bouzouki* if they returned. Naturally, they assured him they'd be back, having relished every bite of the wonderful food amid the convivial company.

Chapter 6

A Curse on Nikos

It was an unspeakably early hour for Marigold to be up and about as I waved her and Athena off in the Punto when they set off for their shopping spree in town. They had planned their departure with military precision, their arrival in town synchronised to time with the opening of the clothes shops, both of them hating to try outfits on when the changing rooms reached an oppressively hot temperature. Even though she was out with her hairdresser friend, Marigold's day would be ruined if her hair started sweating mid-change.

Heading on foot through the village to Barry's place to collect Anastasia for the day, I basked in the delightfully cool breeze, well aware it would undoubtedly dissipate once the sun came up. The prospect of spending a leisurely day with my adorable niece not only filled me with the joys of spring, but put a spring in my step.

Anastasia was always such a delight to be around, full of lively curiosity and effervescent cheer. At just twenty-eight months of age, her keen intelligence was reflected in her precocious vocabulary: having mastered the art of chattering away in both English and Greek, her bilingual skills put me, along with the rest of the extended Bucket family, to shame.

Strolling past one of Nikos' many fields, I spotted the taverna owner knee-deep in a pile of festering rubbish, a look of fury on his face as he bundled something into a black bin bag. Dispensing with the usual pleasantries, Nikos spat, "This is too much, Victor, too much. Look what the vandal do now."

"Dumping all that rubbish in your field is disgraceful," I concurred. "Any idea who could be responsible?"

"I must to have the enemy," Nikos shouted, his face red with anger as he lobbed an empty *ouzo* bottle and a rancid-looking yoghurt container into the bag. "It is not just the rubbish that you see..."

"Have they dumped something else?"

"The *peristeri*, how to say in English?"

"A pigeon..."

"Yes, they to throw the dead pigeon on top of the rubbish."

"Perhaps it flew there and met an untimely end by hitting its head," I suggested, recalling how a blackbird had stunned itself by flying slap-bang into our closed balcony doors.

"You to think the pigeon missing the head can fly, Victor?"

"Missing its head?"

"Yes, look," Nikos entreated, delving into the bin bag.

"Really, I'd rather not. I've no stomach for that," I protested. With my breakfast barely digested, just the thought of encountering a decapitated pigeon made me feel queasy.

Ignoring my protest, Nikos brandished a yoghurt-smeared, headless pigeon corpse with a flourish. "See, the dead *peristeri.*"

"You really shouldn't be handling it with bare hands, Niko," I advised. "Pigeons are the most unhygienic species of bird. That thing could be riddled with communicable diseases."

"I not to know if it have the disease but I know that to find the dead pigeon is unlucky. It mean someone to put the curse on me…"

"A curse?" I parroted, considering Nikos' claim a tad far-fetched. Proffering the bottle of hand sanitiser which I had slipped in my pocket, a necessary precaution when about to take charge of an infant for the day, I advised Nikos, "Chuck the pigeon back in that bin bag, Niko, and scrub your hands with this. One can pick up all sorts of lurgies from pigeon droppings…"

"This dead pigeon is not going to be dropping any droppings," Nikos pointed out whilst waving the stiff remains around.

Nikos' anger struck me as completely justified. If dumping rubbish in his field wasn't bad enough, deliberately decapitating a pigeon indicated a level of malevolence that was hard to fathom.

"Climb over the wall, Victor, and give me a hand to clean this mess up," Nikos barked.

"Sorry, Niko, no can do. As much as I'd like to stay and help you out, it's not possible. I'm on my way to collect Ana. I'm on babysitting duty for the day."

"If you to pass the taverna, take little Anastasia in to see the Dina. She cry much over the loss of the Nikoleta," Nikos said, his angry expression giving way to a wistful look. "But not the word to Dina about the rubbish. She have enough the upset already. If she hear about the pigeon curse, she will be the weep all day."

"My lips are sealed," I promised.

Continuing on my way, I pondered the possibility of who the likely culprit could be who was targeting Nikos by spray painting his wall and emptying bags of rubbish in his fields. No one in particular sprang to mind. Generally liked in the village, Nikos had no enemies that I was aware of.

Of course, it was possible that someone with a years-old grudge was engaged in some petty vengeance: the slain pigeon on his land clearly indicated the targeting of Nikos was personal.

Striding across the village square, the movement of a white cotton cutwork curtain with handmade lace at the downstairs window of what had been Kyria Kompogiannopoulou's house, caught my eye. Pausing for a moment, I wondered if the movement had been a trick of my imagination since the house now stood empty. Shrugging it off as a trick of the light, I continued towards my destination, eager to see my niece.

"Victor, I can't tell you how much I appreciate this," Cynthia said in greeting, little Ana balanced on her hip. "As soon as Sampaguita gets back from the Philippines, she is going to take care of Ana on the days that I work."

"Ana will be in good hands with Sampaguita, not to mention it will be good for Spiros' wife to mind a child rather than a cranky old man."

"Cranky and old aren't the first words to spring to mind about you, Victor..."

"I was referring to Sampaguita's last charge, Haralambos," I said in exasperation.

Smiling coyly, Cynthia backtracked. "Anastasia is just so excited to spend the day with her favourite uncle. She insisted on wearing her prettiest dress."

"Daisies," Ana said, drawing my attention to her lovely pale lemon frock adorned with printed white daisies.

"It's very pretty, Ana," I said. "But Cynthia, it's hardly practical..."

"You told me the two of you had a lunch date..."

"Indeed, but it's at Yiota's farm, not Fortnum & Mason. I'd hate for Ana's frock to get all mucky."

"Oh, how you fuss, Victor. We do have one of those new-fangled things known as a washing machine, you know."

"Fine. Just don't give me a lecture if I return Ana to you covered in donkey hairs."

"Come on through, Victor. Barry's already left but

I've still got a couple of minutes before I need to go. We were just identifying some of the pond life," Cynthia said, passing Ana to me. Cooing with delight, my infant niece showered my cheek with sloppy kisses.

"Frogs?"

"Yes, frogs, but there's other things too. Look, there's a Balkan Green Lizard just emerging from that crevice in the wall," Cynthia trilled, pointing to a vibrantly bright green lizard as Ana clapped her hands in excitement. "They like to hide from predators in nooks and crannies when they sleep. Now the sun is coming out, it will probably laze around, snacking on insects."

"You really have created a blissful spot with your ecological pond," I praised. The colourful hydrangeas which Cynthia had planted served as an excellent cover for the sturdy wooden fence which Barry had erected to prevent Anastasia from falling into the water: the floral touch meant that the fence now blended into the natural environment without detracting from the beauty of the idyllically peaceful setting, a haven for wildlife and a welcome spot for relaxation. "Such an improvement on Harold's pool."

"It gives Anastasia her very own nature class right on our doorstep."

"Indeed. Even Marigold, who isn't keen on things like lizards and frogs, admits the pond has great educational value for Ana."

Something slithering through the weeds caught my eye. I stepped backwards, warning Cynthia, "I think there's a snake."

"The thing with brown stripes? No need to be such

a worrywart, Victor, it isn't a snake. It's a legless glass lizard…perfectly harmless."

"A legless lizard? I never heard of such a thing."

"They're actually quite common. They are often mistaken for snakes by people who don't know that legless lizards are a thing," Cynthia schooled me. "Glass lizards are insectivores, feeding on things such as grasshoppers, spiders and beetles."

No sooner had the word beetles passed Cynthia's lips, than the legless lizard undulated forward with a smooth and stealthy motion, targeting what appeared to be a huge brown beetle as its prey. As quick as lightning, the lizard extended its tongue and grabbed the beetle, its jaws closing around the insect like a deadly vice as it made quick work of its breakfast.

"Oh, what a shame," Cynthia said. "I think that was a Great Diving Beetle. Well, I'd best be off. What's your agenda for you and Ana for the day?"

"I thought we could drop in on the chickens when we leave here and then, of course, we're off to visit Hal to see the new donkey that arrives today."

Smothering Anastasia in kisses, Cynthia reluctantly departed, at least reassured that she was leaving her darling daughter in more than capable hands. As I gathered Anastasia's things together, my niece distracted me by replicating the croaking sound of a frog. Peering attentively into the pond, Ana grabbed my sleeve. "A frog," she squealed in delight.

Squinting through the by-now bright sunlight, I focused on the Muddy Stream Frog, muddy in colour that is, rather than muddy from rolling around in the mud:

the lack of a distinct colour served as an effective camouflage against predators. The frog appeared content to stay in one place, its bulging eyes providing a panoramic 360-degree view of its surroundings whilst its throat vibrated in a move that Cynthia had assured me was known as buccal pumping. It turned out that Ana wasn't the only one to benefit from the educational qualities of the ecological pond: I was also acquiring some useful tit-bits about the local wildlife.

Instead of hurrying to leave, the two of us settled down for a spot of wildlife gazing, Anastasia babbling on about nothing of any consequence in a mix of English and Greek.

Unwittingly, Ana was able to help me fine-tune my Greek pronunciation by giving me the correct translation of a frog, *enas vatrachos*, a beetle, *ena skathari*, and a legless lizard, *mia savra choris podia*. Not only was Anastasia's Greek accent perfect, she apparently knew the grammatically correct gender of said frogs, beetles and lizards, as though she had absorbed the knowledge through osmosis. All credit must go to the Greek village ladies for Ana's faultless accent and proficiency in Greek, the hours they had spent visiting or babysitting rubbing off on the child.

Confident that by now, I would be spared being pestered by Guzim since he should have left my garden and gone to work in Yiota's fields, I suggested to Anastasia that we make tracks and visit my chickens. Strapping her securely into the pushchair, I stroked the soft skin of her dimpled cheeks and ruffled her riot of glossy curls before plonking a sunhat on her head.

"Are you looking forward to seeing the chickens?" I asked.

"Chuckies and soldiers," Ana replied enthusiastically, prompting me to promise that as soon as we'd collected the morning's eggs, I would soft boil a couple of them and serve them up with buttered soldiers. With enough practice, I hoped that one day my chuckies and soldiers would be as good as those turned out by Violet Burke.

Anastasia, preferring to walk, demonstrated her impatience with being pushed through the village square by kicking her heels. Since it was difficult to manoeuvre the pushchair whilst holding onto Ana's hand, I told her she could run off her energy in the garden as soon as we reached the Bucket residence. Arriving home, I secured the rarely used ornate gate and freed Ana. She was more than happy to toddle along beside me as we headed over to the chicken coop, helping me to dig up and pocket some carrots to take along for Hal's donkey from the vegetable patch, keeping hold of some carrot tops to feed to my flock.

With many visits to the chickens under her belt, Anastasia was familiar with them all, correctly identifying my brood by name. At that current moment in time, the Bucket chicken population comprised six fine specimens: Mythos, Dionysus, Mastika, Baileys, Nano, and Raki: if one wished to be pedantic, it could be argued that it was a bit of a stretch to refer to Raki as a fine specimen on account of her gammy leg. Nevertheless, after overcoming the traumatic ordeal of being snatched by a hawk, she remained not only a good layer, but my favourite chick of the bunch. Unfortunately, Fix had become egg-bound earlier that year: succumbing to the condition, she had passed away. My plan to replace her with a rooster had been overruled by Marigold who was convinced she'd never get another lie-in with a resident rooster in the garden.

As Anastasia ran around inside the chicken run, calling out the chickens by name as she chased after them, I reconsidered Marigold's suggestion that we should rename the hens. Marigold was firmly of the opinion that it wasn't appropriate for a two-year-old child to be calling out the name of alcoholic beverages. Only Nano, whom Guzim had named after the former Albanian Prime Minister, Fatos Nano, evaded the drunken vibe of the other chickens. Even though I could definitely see Marigold's point, I remained convinced that renaming the birds would confuse them: the last thing I wanted was a bunch of bewildered hens on my hands, with Guzim nagging me to send them to a therapist.

Anastasia appeared confused by Mastika's visible lack of feathers, giving the chicken an oven-ready look. Although I explained the moulting process to Ana, telling her that it was perfectly natural for the hens to lose their feathers every twelve to eighteen months, I had a feeling it went over her head. I must confess that the very first time I spotted one of my chickens had not only shed her feathers but had stopped laying, my immediate reaction was to presume the chicken needed a trip to the veterinarian: without the bulk of her feathery padding, the hen looked visibly scrawny.

Guzim had soon set me straight, absolutely revelling in his superior knowledge of chickens by telling me it was a perfectly normal process, assuring me that the feathers would soon grow back and the hen would resume laying. Even now, when one of my chicks starts losing her feathers, it takes me by surprise: but rather than thinking the hen is sickly, I wonder if Violet Burke has been plucking the bird to add some feathers to her cap.

Having worn out her little legs by running around, Anastasia accompanied me into the chicken coop where the two of us collected the still-warm eggs, freshly laid that morning. Wandering back through the garden, I picked some fresh apricots from the tree. Not only would they be a tasty accompaniment for Ana's eggs, I needed to add some to Pelham's welcome basket.

Once indoors, I carefully timed the soft-boiled eggs and buttered the soldiers. Anastasia played with the cats, even though Catastrophe and Clawsome were rather reluctant to be played with. Fortunately, Pickles put in a rare appearance, showing much more willingness to engage with the child than either of Marigold's pampered imported domestics demonstrated. I didn't tell Anastasia that her mother's vile cat, Kouneli, had fathered Pickles because I wouldn't be able to say no to my darling niece if she clamoured to take Pickles home with her to live with its mutant father. Although I would never admit it, I had developed a particular soft spot for Kouneli's offspring and was quite keen to hang on to it.

Chapter 7

A Frosty Reception

Anastasia had just finished polishing off her chuckies and soldiers when Spiros phoned. Without any preamble, Spiros pleaded, "Victor, I must to need the help."

"Name it," I told him, always happy to repay one of the numerous favours Spiros had done for me. Even as I selflessly volunteered for whatever my friend had in mind, I hoped beyond hope that whatever it was didn't involve one of his corpses.

"I must to leave for the *Athina* airport to pick up the Sampaguita. The rich doctor telephone and want to make the another view of the house. Can you to show it?"

V.D. BUCKET

"When?"

"Now...the ten minute."

"No problem, Spiro. I'll wait outside my house so you can give me the key."

"You must to, how to say, smear, the doctor..."

"Smear the doctor? You've lost me, Spiro." My mind boggled as I tried to decipher if Spiros wanted me to slander the reputation of the medic or spread him on a soldier.

"Smear, schmeer, schmaltz..."

I might have been slow on the uptake but I finally cottoned on. "Ah, you want me to schmooze him? Oil the wheels for a sale."

"Yes, the exactly. Make to him lots of the schmoozing and schmaltzy, Victor. You must to charm the doctor. I expect him to make the offer soon. And Victor..."

"Yes..."

"Make sure to put on the good dress and the tie. The doctor expect the professional. I tell him, you are my the colleague in the real estate."

"No problem. Give me a couple of minutes to change and I'll meet you downstairs," I told Spiros. Dashing through to the bedroom, I hastily threw on a smart suit and tie, reflecting that Spiros must be taking this client very seriously.

"Come on, Anastasia. We need to pop downstairs to see Uncle Spiros."

Having left the pushchair at the bottom of the stairs, I picked Ana up to carry her down, the outdoor stairs still a challenge for her chubby little legs. "What on earth? Why are you so sticky, Anastasia?"

Batting her eyelashes in a trick she'd picked up from her Aunty Marigold, Anastasia revealed that she'd been feeding the cats with the apricots intended for Pelham's welcome basket.

"You shouldn't feed the cats apricots," I chided, clueless if cats could safely eat them or not, Marigold being the Bucket expert on feline dietary matters. Grabbing the kitchen sponge, I hurriedly wiped Anastasia's face and hands, telling myself that any germs on the sponge would help to strengthen my niece's immune system. Since there was no time to deal with the sticky paw marks the cats were leaving all over my pristine kitchen floor, I made a mental note to slop the mop around on my return.

Anastasia squealed in delight when Spiros pulled up in the hearse but, alas, there was no time for the two of them to schmooze since Spiros had a plane to meet. Chucking the house key out of the hearse's window, Spiros thanked me profusely before driving away. Watching as the hearse disappeared, I realised that Spiros had neglected to tell me the name of the potential house buyer. I decided the best thing to do was to rush over to the house and be there when the doctor arrived.

As I wheeled the pushchair at speed towards the village square, Ana gabbled away to herself. I apologised to the Greek neighbours I passed, each of them keen to linger to cluck over Anastasia, telling them I had no time to stop. No doubt word would get around the village that I had been tearing along in charge of a pushchair; I imagined that speculation would be rife as to the nature of my emergency.

V.D. BUCKET

By the time I reached the large house on the village square, Anastasia had fallen asleep. Despite scouring her face with the kitchen sponge, I had failed to clean up the eggy mess on her chin where she had dribbled the yellow yolk. Not wishing to disturb her slumber, I left it to coagulate whilst she slept.

Situated on the village square, the house certainly enjoyed a prime position in real estate terms, though its proximity to the church would be a blasted nuisance when Papas Andreas engaged in a spot of bell ringing: perchance the doctor didn't share the Buckets' distaste for the excessive clanging of bells first thing on a Sunday morning. Set back behind a high stone wall, the house didn't directly abut the square. Well-established trees stood sentinel-like between the wall and the house, offering welcome shade without detracting from the splendid sea view afforded from the first-floor balcony.

Trying out the key that Spiros had given me, I sighed in relief when the front door opened at once, reassured there would be no worries about gaining access once the doctor arrived. Although I was naturally keen to explore inside the house, I decided it would be prudent to wait on the doorstep until Spiros' client turned up. As I waited, I turned to examine the ornate copper door knocker fashioned in the shape of a hand, albeit a hand missing a thumb. It struck me that the hand was feminine in design, the copper slightly tarnished in contrast to the door which had recently been treated to a new coat of glossy blue paint, matching exactly the colour of the rather elaborate balcony railings. With my interest piqued, I was keen to look inside.

BUCKET TO GREECE (VOL.17)

I watched as a brand-new, grey Ford Focus pulled into the square and parked up. A woman dressed in a drab grey skirt suit and low-heeled shoes alighted the car. Even though she appeared to be heading purposefully towards me, I dismissed the woman since Spiros had alluded to the doctor as he. Thus, I was rather taken aback when she reached my side and addressed me, saying in a crisp no-nonsense tone, "Mr Bucket?"

"*Nai, pragmati. Kai prepei na eisai i giatri,*" I told her, confirming my identity and saying she must be the doctor. I really could have swung for Spiros for being so remiss in failing to furnish me with her name.

"Yes," she replied in English. "Doctor Fotoula Papadima."

Switching to English, I parroted like a fool, "Ah, yes. Doctor Papadima." Failing to look convinced that I was familiar with her name, I could see her visibly sizing me up. Unfortunately, the conclusion written on her face appeared to be that I fell rather short of the professionalism she considered her due.

Extending my hand for her to shake, I realised that once again, Spiros must have mixed up his genders when speaking in English. There was certainly nothing sexist in my assumption that I had been expecting a male doctor: Spiros must have referred to her as 'he' at least twenty times the previous evening.

After rather reluctantly shaking my hand, Doctor Papadima earned a couple of brownie points in my book by taking a moment to slather her hands in sanitiser: whilst a lesser man may have taken offence, I applauded her rigorous adherence to hygiene. As the doctor took a step back to study the exterior of the house, I took a moment to study her. My first impression was that she was unremarkable, someone who would blend seamlessly in with the crowd. She appeared to be of indeterminate age; at a guess, I would hazard she could be anything between thirty and fifty. Even to my untrained eye, she appeared to be devoid of any dress sense, having paired her drab grey suit with sheer black pop socks, something I had heard Marigold observe was a fashion faux pas too far. Of average stature, her figure appeared neat and trim, her hair short and dark, not a trace of make-up adding a dash of colour to her unnaturally pale face. If it wasn't for the fact that I have just described the doctor, I would most definitely lean towards the descriptive of nondescript.

"Would you like to go inside?" I invited.

"Of course." Her clipped words indicated she was not a fan of the blatantly obvious.

"Spiros said you've already seen the property a number of times," I said, opening the front door and indicating she should enter before me.

"Purchasing a house is not a decision to be taken lightly," she informed me as though schooling a dolt. I noticed the doctor's English was impeccable but her words were spoken with a heavy Greek accent, her unnecessary use of a superfluous stress accent on English words, very marked.

"Are you from this area?" I asked.

"No."

"So, what attracted you to the village…"

Interrupting my question, the doctor indicated she

had no interest in small talk. "There is no need to show me around. I would prefer no distractions while I judge if the house is suitable." That was me firmly put in my place, practically reduced to the role of nothing more than a blithering nuisance.

Fotoula Papadima immediately disappeared through the door directly to the left of the entrance, leaving me to cool my heels in the large and impressive foyer.

My first impression on viewing the interior was a resounding wow, the huge space in immaculate condition, the foyer boasting a magnificent blue and white tiled floor which immediately caught my eye. The different designs of the tiles blended floral and abstract patterns, reminding me of swirling images viewed through a kaleidoscope.

An impressive staircase, curving upwards, took centre place. Opening the door directly opposite the one the doctor had entered revealed a stunning living room featuring elaborate cornices, a high ceiling, and a marble floor. Making my way inside, I admired the exposed stone wall serving as a backdrop to the gigantic fireplace, big enough to spit-roast a whole wild boar: masses of cushions piled atop the built-in stone seating in the fireside nook made it a particularly inviting spot to sink into with a good book.

The sheer scale and size of the rather majestic living room put our own grand salon to shame. I instantly knew that Marigold would go mad for this house: alas, Spiros had informed me how much the property was going for and it was well out of the Bucket price range. The doctor must indeed be loaded if she could contemplate buying the property as a cash purchase.

"Mr Bucket." Feeling a tad guilty, almost as though I'd been caught snooping, I jumped to it when the doctor called my name. The room to the left of the entranceway appeared equally grand, an apparent combination of library and study, an antique desk taking pride of place in front of the window. With the doctor demanding my attention, I forced myself to focus on her question rather than the room. "The estate agent mentioned there were some local builders capable of making the renovations to the high standard."

Pausing for a moment to ponder who the estate agent could be, it dawned on me that she was referring to Spiros.

"Indeed. I can personally give the local builders the highest recommendation. What sort of renovation work are you thinking of?"

"I would need to turn this room into my surgery."

"Ah, so you're planning to practise medicine in the village?"

Completely ignoring my question, she continued, "It will need a separate entrance creating from outside. I will also need a waiting room and toilet facilities."

Glancing around, I noted the room was certainly large enough to be divided into a surgery and a waiting room, with plenty of space to spare. In addition, she told me the door leading to the foyer would need to be sealed off as it wouldn't do to have patients wandering freely in her private quarters. When I made the suggestion that she simply keep the door locked rather than sealing it off, her look indicated it might not be sensible to dismiss me out of hand, after all. She had clearly overlooked the obvious solution to prevent random patients gaining free access to her home. "Could you telephone the builders and ask them to come over and see if the work I have in the mind is viable?"

"When would it suit you to meet them?"

"Now?" Although she didn't snap her fingers, her tone was laden with 'hop to it.' "I don't want to have to return later."

"Have you got far to come?"

Once again ignoring my question, her eyes bore into me, willing me to get on with it and stop wasting her precious time.

"Certainly," I said, sharing her preference not to return later. "I'll just step outside to make the call."

When it came to sizing up building jobs and offering quotes, Vangelis and Barry had a failproof system in place. If the person requiring work done on a property was Greek, Vangelis would turn up to deal with the initial discussions; if the person was English or non-Greek speaking, Barry would be the one to attend.

"I will take another look upstairs. Call me when the builder arrives," Doctor Papadima demanded, her tone making it clear she didn't expect me to join her. I felt a stab of disappointment that I wouldn't have the chance to have a quick poke around upstairs since I was curious to view the rest of the house.

"He should be here any moment," I told her since Vangelis had told me he was close by, enjoying a coffee break in the *kafenion*. Wondering if I ought to advise him to turn up in a suit and tie, I decided against it as it would likely delay his arrival. Presuming the doctor's dismissive attitude towards me may well be because I was foreign, I hoped her icy manner would thaw a little in Vangelis' capable Greek hands.

My friend arrived in the blink of an eye. Speaking in a whisper, I warned Vangelis to expect a frosty reception before giving him the lowdown on the work needed. With Vangelis up to speed, I called up to announce his arrival to the doctor. As I had anticipated, the doctor was all business when she apprised Vangelis of the work required. Ever the consummate professional, Vangelis was able to provide an estimate on the spot. Confirming she would be in touch with Vangelis, the doctor reluctantly shook his hand before instantly reaching for the hand sanitiser again. She then informed me that she had made a decision and would purchase the house, telling me she would be in touch with my boss to set the ball rolling. I bit my lip to prevent a chuckle escaping; I found it quite amusing that I had been mistaken for Spiros' underling.

Glancing down at the still sleeping Anastasia in her pushchair, a half-smile graced the doctor's lips and she deigned to ask me a personal question. "Your granddaughter?"

"My niece," I said, taking no offence at the presumption that I looked old enough to be mistaken for a grandfather.

"*I Anastasia einai vaftistira mou.*" Vangelis' features took on a look of doting pride as he announced Anastasia was his goddaughter.

BUCKET TO GREECE (VOL.17)

Tutting loudly, Doctor Fournas bent down and wiped the toddler's egg-smeared chin with a dab of sanitiser and a tissue. I could only hope that her bedside manner was a tad mellower where actual patients were involved.

Chapter 8

Alienating the Regulars

Eager to spend some time with his goddaughter, Vangelis persuaded me to join him for a quick coffee in the *kafenion* before he rushed back to work. Settling the pushchair in a shady spot in the courtyard, I left Anastasia with her doting *nonos* whilst I popped inside to place our coffee order. Unusually, the courtyard was dotted with the usual old-timers who more typically enjoyed their coffees inside. Weaving my way between the tables, I nodded in greeting, surprised when a few of the elderly men muttered, "*Kali tychi,*" meaning good luck, as I passed them.

I was rather taken aback to discover the *kafenion* deserted bar a complete stranger behind the kitchen counter. The unknown woman ignored my approach. Peering intently into a magnifying mirror balanced on the work surface, she wielded a pair of tweezers in close proximity to the food preparation area: short of squeezing her spots or shaving her legs, it would be hard to think of a more disgusting practice to engage in around food than plucking her eyebrows.

Even though I had never set eyes on the woman before, I immediately assumed my old and familiar mantle of public health inspector, snapping, "You can't do that in here. It is most insanitary."

Considering I had used my most authoritative tone, I had expected her to react with something more than an expression of complete boredom.

Briefly suspending her tweezing activity, the woman yelled, "Christo," before fingering the tweezers again.

"You have to stop that," I ordered, knowing such a violation of the food hygiene laws could get the *kafenion* closed down again. The only response the woman gave was a shrug. As it dawned on me that perhaps she didn't understand English, I repeated my demand in Greek, "*Prepei na to stamatiseis afto…*"

My diktat tapered off as I spotted a multi-legged, big black bug on the counter, no doubt attracted by the woman's unhygienic carryings on. Without further ado, I smashed my fist down on the bug, my action leaving a sticky residue across the side of my hand.

Finally reacting, the woman came out from behind the counter, the scent of stale tobacco and cheap perfume practically asphyxiating me.

Frowning at me, the lines on her forehead stood out as deep furrows, indicating her miserable expression was her standard look as she stomped across the room. Opening the door leading into the *apothiki*, she yelled Christos' name several times over, making me ponder, *what is it with stroppy women today?*

Never having laid eyes on the woman before, I had no clue who she was though she would certainly be hard to miss, dressed in a short, black leather mini skirt. Her low-cut top revealed far too much cleavage for it to be considered polite before luncheon. The dark roots topping her yellow, straw-like hair, screamed she wasn't a natural blonde and her leathery, tanned skin more than hinted that she spent a lot of time on a sunlounger without applying appropriate sun protection.

Emerging from the *apothiki*, Christos shook his head in a sign of agreement as the woman pointed at me and muttered something. Whilst I was unable to catch the full gist of what she was saying, I did detect a number of Greek expletives coming out of her unnaturally crimson mouth.

The woman, looking indifferent when Christos playfully slapped her backside, disappeared into the *apothiki*.

In turn, Christos took her place in the kitchen. As he stroked his moustache, I noticed it was missing its usual lustre. When he asked what he could get me, I detected his voice lacked his usual exuberance: in fact, I would hazard that Christos appeared to have mislaid his customary get-up-and-go. On the plus side, without it, he appeared less slimy than his norm.

Refusing to allow Christos to turn a blind eye to what

had been going on in his kitchen, I told him, "That woman was plucking her eyebrows over the counter. You can't allow things like that to go on in your kitchen."

"She wasn't plucking," Christos responded. Using the discarded tweezers, he picked up the bug I had flattened with my impetuous thump. "She was about to glue these false eyelashes in place."

"False eyelashes. It can't be. It looks more like a house centipede," I said. Staring in disbelief at the squashed creature, I realised the sticky mess on my hand was glue, rather than what I had presumed to be the gunky insides of a bug.

As I hastily rubbed at my hand with a sanitiser loaded handkerchief, a half-smile crossed Christos' features. "Ah, I can see the resemble to a centipede. In Chicago, we call them the bathtub bug."

"Well, whatever it is, you can't allow random women to go around glueing them on in your kitchen. It just isn't on…"

Shrugging, Christos responded by saying, "Maria like to look good," as if that explained her deplorable kitchen habits.

Quite whether she had achieved her aim was certainly open to debate: I, for one, did not think she looked attractive, her style bordering on tarty and a tad too much in one's face.

"Well, you need to have a firm word with your employee," I advised.

"Maria doesn't work here. She is my girlfriend."

The heavy sigh that accompanied Christos' words hinted at a troubled relationship. It was no secret that

Christos had been seeing a woman who lived close to the *Dimarcheio* down on the coast, but beyond that I hadn't paid much attention to the rumours concerning his love life, my natural assumption being that whoever took up with the slimy Greek must be either visually impaired or not quite the full shilling.

The convenient upside to his liaison was that his hands were too full for him to fawn over my wife.

Fingering his lacklustre pornstache, Christos admitted, "Maria has many moods. She is much work and the customers haven't taken to her."

"Ah, is that why your usual customers are all sitting outside?"

Spooning Greek coffee into a *briki*, Christos grunted in the affirmative.

Still, I reasoned, whatever personal problems Christos was having with his girlfriend, didn't excuse his lackadaisical approach to hygiene. As the joint owner of the place, it was his responsibility to lead by example.

"The kitchen needs a thorough cleaning before Thanasis turns up and shuts the place down again," I snapped. "You really shouldn't let anyone in the kitchen who hasn't got a food hygiene certificate."

Striding determinedly across the *kafenion*, Christos stuck his head through the *apothiki* door and hollered, "Mrs Burke."

Emerging from the *apothiki* with a face like thunder, Violet Burke complained, "No need to blast my ear drums."

"The kitchen needs cleaning," Christos told her, his tone abrupt.

"There's no need to talk to me like I'm your skivvy," Violet Burke exploded, her nostrils visibly flaring. "A bit of respect wouldn't go amiss."

"I pay you to clean..." Christos spluttered.

"That's it. I'm done," Violet Burke announced, making a song and dance of stripping off her pinny and freeing her unnaturally bright crimson hair from the confines of her headscarf. It appeared that something had been brewing between the two of them; whatever it was had reached breaking point.

"But it is not the done time. What about the kitchen? It needs cleaning." Christos' tone had unmistakably morphed from authoritative to wheedling, his facial expression switching from indifferent to shocked.

"You'd best find some other mug to do it then. I quit," Vi snapped.

"You can't quit," Christos protested, his voice raised in alarm.

"I can and I am. And don't say I didn't give you fair warning. It's bad enough having two bosses here but I refuse to take orders from that right mucky cow, Maria. I told you straight after the last time she stopped over, I'm not taking orders from that impertinent floozy," Violet Burke chuntered. "As if it's not bad enough cleaning up after you and Manolis in that pigsty upstairs...that fancy woman of yours takes the biscuit. She's as common as muck and needs to go on a course to learn some manners."

"Are you really quitting?" I asked my mother.

"That I am, lad," she replied, giving me a broad wink as she pushed past me and stormed out, calling out to Christos over her shoulder with a final shot, "You can send over my money what's owed."

"What am I supposed to do now?" Christos bemoaned. "I need your mother, Victor. Can you have a word?"

"My mother can be stubborn beyond belief," I told Christos. "If she has really made up her mind to quit, I doubt I would be able to influence her decision. What on earth did your girlfriend do to get her so riled up?"

"I don't know, Victor. If I must to choose between Maria and Mrs Burke, there is nothing else for it. I will have to break up with Maria. Manolis will go crazy if Maria costs us your mother. Manolis is always saying that no one gives a good bottoming like Violet Burke."

"It seems a tad drastic," I opined, thinking he could just carry on with his girlfriend well away from the *kafenion*, instead of rubbing Maria in my mother's face. On balance, I reflected it personally suited me well if Christos had a woman on the go. If he was about to become footloose and fancy-free again, no doubt he would end up sniffing around after my wife once more.

"Victor, can you to serve for ten minutes? I must to break up with Maria now before I lose the nerve." Christos stared longingly at a bottle of *Metaxa*, presumably contemplating taking a shot of Dutch courage.

"No, I can't," I stated emphatically, having no wish to be drawn into Christos' mess: it was, after all, a mess of his own making. "I'm looking after my niece. And, I'm with Vangelis and we still haven't ordered our coffees."

"I'll get Apostolos to do your coffees," Christos countered, downing a shot of neat brandy straight from the bottle. Following me out to the courtyard, he pleaded with the local barber to knock up the coffees whilst he took care of some personal business.

Looking around for my niece, I spotted her patting the ornamental stone Cockapoo, now painted a gaudy orange, which Milton had rescued from the bins.

"What's going on?" Vangelis asked me, sweeping Anastasia up and bouncing her on his knee.

"Christos is about to dump his girlfriend, Maria."

"Good riddance." Vangelis' grin indicated he was all in favour of the move.

"I must be late to the party," I said. "I've never come across this Maria person before."

"That's because you not to spend half your day drinking coffee in here. The Maria is not the popular. She is the lazy and rude. The Manolis hate it when the Christos bring her here. He say it not good for the business."

"She has deplorable hygiene habits," I shared with Vangelis. "I dread to think what Pelham would think if he was to walk in on this Maria…"

"Pelham?"

"An old colleague of mine from the Food Standards Agency. He's arriving later today to stay in the downstairs Sofia apartment."

"Barry must be much the pleased to have the booking."

"Indeed. We both are. In fact, I've managed to secure another few bookings through July and August. It was a worrying time when it looked as though the apartments would be empty after we'd invested so much time and money in the project. By the way, the doctor confirmed she is going to buy the house. It looks as though you'll have some local work there once the sale goes through."

"Excellent news," Vangelis said with a grin.

Recalling how Athena had been dead set against a doctor moving into the village due to some superstitious nonsense about killing off pensioners, I asked Vangelis how his wife would likely react.

"I think because the doctor is the young woman, the Athena might to accept it," Vangelis ruminated.

"I wonder how this lot will take it," I said, gesticulating towards the elderly men mopping their sweaty foreheads, resigned to sitting outdoors in the heat to avoid Christos' girlfriend.

"I think they would to prefer the man. They are the old-fashioned," Vangelis said as Apostolos arrived bearing our coffees. Placing our cups on the table, Apostolos turned to Mathias, asking, *"Eisai etoimi gia to kourema sou?"* meaning, 'Are you ready for your haircut?'

"Den tha pao mesa mechri na fygei i Maria." Shuddering, Mathias replied he wasn't going inside until Maria left. It seemed that not only had Christos' girlfriend precipitated my mother jacking in her job, she had certainly done a good job of alienating the regulars.

"O Christos chorizei me ti Maria tora," I said, telling the others that Christos was breaking up with Maria now.

My announcement was met with cheery faces and cries of *"Bravo."* Apostolos and Mathias practically outdid themselves in genuflecting and making the sign of the cross, the barber even declaring he would buy a round of *ouzo* for all the customers and raise a toast of good riddance to Maria.

BUCKET TO GREECE (VOL.17)

I couldn't help but wonder if I should have bitten my tongue rather than impetuously informing everyone that Christos was dumping his girlfriend. Likely the slimy Greek was so weak-willed that a flash of Maria's cleavage would be enough to tempt him from his avowed path of ditching her. If he failed to follow through, I would look like an idiot and gain a reputation as a feckless and ineffectual gossipmonger.

"*Apostoli, fere mou ena potiri nero*," Mathias said, requesting the barber bring him a glass of water.

"*Echeis paratisei to ouzo?*" I quipped, asking Mathias if he had given up *ouzo*.

"*Prepei na paro skoni*." Mathias' reply that he must take dust rather threw me.

"*Skoni?*" I queried, certain I must have misheard. Turning to Vangelis, I asked, "Why on earth does Mathias want to take dust?"

"*Skoni* is not just the dust. It is the Greek word for powder too," Vangelis clarified.

"*Nai, skoni*," Mathias confirmed, digging a packet of soluble pills out of his pocket.

"Ah, *einai dialyta chapia*," I said, furnishing an alternative Greek way of saying soluble pills.

In addition to flashing his packet of pills, Mathias waved a tube in my face, announcing to the clientele at large without a trace of embarrassment, "*Echo afti tin krema gia tis aimorroides.*"

It was way too much information; I really didn't need to know that he had cream for his haemorrhoids. Mathias' confession instigated a loud discussion amongst the old-timers about their various medical complaints, confirming my belief that Greece was a nation of hypochondriacs.

Apostolos appeared bearing a tumbler of water for Mathias, Christos following in his wake with a bottle of *ouzo* and glasses.

Filling the glasses with the clear liquor that would turn cloudy the moment water was added, Christos slumped into a chair, announcing, "It's done. I told Maria we are finished."

"How did she take it?" I asked.

"Not well. She threw the fry pan at me. If I hadn't ducked, it could have killed me. As soon as Manolis gets here, I must drive Maria home."

I didn't envy Christos being stuck in a vehicle with a frying pan throwing jilted harpy.

"You must stick firm, Christo. Don't let the Maria to charm you," Vangelis advised. I stifled a laugh at his words, very much doubting that charm of any description would be in Maria's bag of tricks.

"Victor, you think your mother will come back?" Christos asked.

"She can be very obstinate once her mind is made up. I imagine it will take quite a bit of grovelling and the offer of a decent pay rise."

"*Yamas*," Mathias called out. Toasting us with his fizzing glass of pills, I took advantage of the distraction to pour my own unwanted glass of *ouzo* into the nearest plant pot.

"Perhaps I should find the wife who will work here for free and be nice to the customers," Christos mused.

"Just don't go around proposing to my mother or

you'll never see hide nor hair of Violet Burke again," I warned.

Chapter 9

Germy Cats and Graffiti

Anastasia gabbled continuously as I wheeled her along in her pushchair, a sun shade protecting her delicate skin from the sun's rays. Pointing animatedly to one side, Anastasia cried out, "Lizard," my cue for slowing down so she could admire the scaly reptile with a long green tail sprawling languidly atop a stone wall, sunning itself. Passing the bins, a rather bedraggled feral cat smeared with what appeared to be custard, jumped directly in front of the pushchair, prompting Ana to tut, *"Vromiki gata,"* meaning 'dirty cat.'

By choosing to comment in Greek, I gathered my niece was addressing her remark directly to the feline rather than to me. Considering she lived under the same roof as Cynthia's vile cat, Kouneli, and was actually most fond of the mutant creature, I was surprised that Anastasia would express her disapproval of the stray. One would presume that she would have an affinity with grubby cats since she clearly shared her mother's adoration of Kouneli.

Hastening away from the vicinity of the less-than-fragrant bins, we continued on our way. Approaching Milton's house, I shushed Ana, not wishing to be waylaid by the local purveyor of porn. We almost managed a clean getaway, only foiled at the last moment when a plummy voice entreated, "I say, old chap, have you time to stop in for a coffee?"

Looking around, I saw no sign of Milton. Peering over the garden wall, I spotted my elderly neighbour attempting to haul himself up from the ground. Surrounded by cats, he appeared to have been engaged in a spot of weeding. Since Milton could hardly be described as nimble, a good half minute passed before he managed to assume an upright position. Still, it was commendable that he was tackling the weeding with his dodgy hip.

"So, what do you say, old chap? Coffee?"

Having suffered through numerous cups of Edna's diabolical watered-down instant, I firmly declined, saying that Anastasia and I had a lunch date to attend.

"Off anywhere nice, what?"

"We're having lunch with Hal…"

"That chap that's the spit of that old farmer with the tractor…"

"Hal is Panos' brother…"

"Edna had a bit of a queer turn when she ran into him in the shop. Thought she was seeing a ghost, what. The resemblance is quite uncanny…"

"Imagine how Spiros felt when he first encountered Hal in the graveyard…"

"I say, that would have likely finished Edna off."

I didn't believe a word of it. Although Edna liked to convey the image of being some fragile flower, I had seen her steely, snide side during her interactions with Violet Burke.

"Don't dash off just yet, what," Milton implored. "I've got something to show you. Just hang on half a mo' while I get it."

As Milton disappeared indoors, one of his adopted cats sprang into Anastasia's lap. Shooing it away, I warned my niece that the cat probably had fleas since Edna had adopted most of her clowder from the bins. "It could well be germy."

"Ooh, dirty cat," Ana said, her face scrunching up in visible disapproval. I was quite proud of Anastasia's early grasp of the inherent dangers of unhygienic things: she made an excellent pupil.

"Got it, old chap," Milton declared, emerging from the house with Edna in tow. Whilst his wife made a tremendous fuss of Anastasia, Milton thrust an envelope in my hands, encouraging me to, "Open it, old chap."

Duly following his instruction, I pulled a sheet of cheap cardboard from the envelope. Peering at it, I read, 'This certificate is awarded to Scarlett Bottom for submitting 'Delicious Desire' for participation in the Gold Star book awards.'

I couldn't help but wonder if Milton had failed to pick up on the blatant spelling errors inscribed on the certificate; to misspell not only the title of his book as Dilicious but also to miss one of the T's out his Bottom penname, was beyond embarrassing, serving to highlight the utter incompetence and disregard of those running the competition.

"Not quite first place what," Milton acknowledged with a crest- fallen expression. "I rather hoped it would pick up a pewter…"

"A pewter-coloured sticker?"

"Well, I was hoping it would catch the judges' eyes for workplace erotica," Milton moaned.

A tad confused by Milton's words, I asked him, "What's this about workplace erotica?"

"Well, as you may recall, old chap, the hero, Milo, held a managerial position at his step-brother's factory, Prick's Panties."

Naturally, having failed to read the book beyond the parts I had been forced to recite at the book club gathering when standing in for Milton, I was clueless about where the bulk of the action took place. If I'd been forced to guess, I would have said the smutty action predictably took place in the bedroom.

"You don't need to say it, old chap. I know I've been had. A fool and his money and all that…"

Recalling that Milton had shelled out a hundred quid for this meaningless certificate that simply acknowledged his participation, I did a quick mental calculation focusing on how much the scamming company must have made out of gullible authors eager to hand over their cash in their desperation for validation. It could potentially be a fortune if Milton's naivety was a common syndrome.

"I had my head turned at the thought of being able to stick a coveted gold star on my book cover," Milton admitted.

"Don't dwell on it, dear," Edna piped up. "You aren't the only fool. I encouraged you."

"But, think of all the cat food we could have bought with the money I wasted, old girl. I doubt I'm ever going to recoup the money I shelled out on publishing the book, what. And now I've thrown good money after bad for this useless certificate."

"You'll know better next time," I assured Milton, my words as fake as the certificate I was holding. I would put money on my elderly neighbour being just as cretinous the next time a scam designed to milk him of his money came along. He appeared to have made a lifelong habit of being taken for a fool. "And not everyone can boast about having a published book."

"True. Very true, old chap. But the idea was to make some money from it, what. I doubt I'll ever see a return on my investment."

He'd get no argument from me on that score.

"Well, we must get on," I said, using my foot to nudge yet another one of Edna's cats away from the pushchair.

Pushing the pram past what had been Kyria Sofia Kompogiannopoulou's house, I once again thought I spotted the curtain move in the empty abode. Perchance Sofia's daughter was inside, going through her late mother's possessions. I made a mental note to ask Spiros to check on the house on his return from Athens.

Before proceeding to Hal's, I needed to make a quick stop at the house to collect a jar of homemade tangy tomato chutney and a jar of last season's fig jam: it wouldn't do to turn up for lunch empty-handed. Although I had a glut of seasonal vegetables and fruit in the garden, taking such an offering to Yiota's farm would be akin to carrying coal to Newcastle. Hopefully, my jars of goodies should go down a treat.

Reaching the house, I was surprised to see Waffles the Goldendoodle tethered to my gate, the dog's presence sending Anastasia into a flurry of excitement. Throwing her arms around Waffles, my niece cuddled the curly-haired, designer dog with gay abandon. Looking around to see if I could spot Gordon Strange, I was puzzled to see Moira Strange descending our outdoor stairs; her presence unexpected since my mother had mentioned Moira had taken off for a modelling job in England.

After exchanging the usual pleasantries, Moira told me, "I should have telephoned first to check if Marigold was home. I just popped round on the spur of the moment to see if she was free for coffee."

"She's gone up to town with Athena…I thought you were in England."

"I would have been if disaster hadn't struck…"

"Disaster…that sounds ominous," I sympathised. "What happened?"

"I was halfway to Athens when I stopped for the loo and got bitten." The dramatic lilt in Moira's voice was enough for me to conjure up a horrific vision of a snake slithering up the inside of a toilet bowl. Dismissing the notion as ludicrous, I guessed a cat must have nipped her; Moira's morbid fear of felines could account for her overly dramatic tone.

"Bitten?"

"By a mosquito."

Clearly, I had allowed my imagination to run away with me.

"Look at the damage it did." Moira pointed to her left ear, the usually delicate shell-like lobe now a pulsating, angry red mess."

"That looks nasty," I acknowledged.

"It's infected. By the time I got to the airport, it was all red and blotchy. There was no point in flying to England as they needed both ears for the earrings shoot." Moira emitted a long-drawn-out sigh. "I really feel my modelling days could be over. It's simply not professional to cancel at the last moment, especially when my age is working against me."

"There's always ads for hearing aids." Realising my innocent comment could be perceived as a tad foot-in-mouth, I fully expected to earn a withering look. To Moira's credit, she just shrugged it off, turning her attention to Anastasia and Waffles, her face lighting up at the sight of the cute child and dog revelling in each other's company. Moreover, she was happy to keep an eye on Ana whilst I ran up the stairs to raid the chutney cupboard.

Continuing on our way to Yiota's farmhouse, my heart sank like a stone as we drew level with the taverna, the stone wall surrounding the outside seating area grotesquely defaced with bright red graffiti, the giant letters spelling out *kokkoras*, *malaka*, and *gamoto*. Pretty sure that *kokoras*, Greek for cockerel, had been misspelt by the graffiti artist, I recalled that it doubled up in meaning as coward. The other two expletives were far too repugnant to translate without risking ruffling readers' sensibilities.

Running the tip of a finger over a letter, I confirmed my suspicion that the paint was still wet, indicating the vandalism had taken place quite recently. Pointing at the wall, my niece declared it was dirty. Her observation made me reflect that the only upside to this shocking disfiguration of Nikos' wall was that Anastasia's lack of mastery of the Greek alphabet ensured she remained undefiled by the vile words, and that wet paint would be easier to remove than paint baked on by the heat of the sun.

Considering Nikos' anger over the graffiti he had encountered the previous evening and his ire this morning over the decapitated pigeon and deliberately dumped rubbish, I feared he might suffer a coronary if he happened upon this latest outrage. Moreover, the thought of the graffiti adding to Dina's anguish if she stepped outside, inspired me to take remedial action to spare her pain. Whipping out my mobile, I telephoned Vangelis and explained the situation. My friend immediately promised to round up a posse of willing helpers from the *kafenion* customers and be with me directly. In the meantime, I remained rooted to the spot, determined to do whatever was necessary to shield Dina from such filth if she happened to step outside. Nikos would expect nothing less of me.

As I waited on the street, the familiar figure of Litsa, clad all in black, hobbled across the road, leaning heavily on her stick. Drawing level with me, she swooped on Anastasia, smothering her with kisses. Litsa told me that Mathias had telephoned her and asked her to visit Dina; keeping Dina out of the way upstairs until the shocking graffiti was removed, would spare her feelings. I applauded Mathias' initiative. Since I confirmed Barry wouldn't be part of the cleaning party, Litsa had no cause to linger by my side, instead shuffling away to see her friend. Fortunately, the kitchen in the apartment over the taverna offered a sea view rather than a view of the street, thus shielding Dina from the activity that would shortly commence on the wall.

In no time at all, Vangelis arrived in the builder's van. In true village solidarity, Apostolos, Mathias, and Kyriakos, piled out of the back of the van, followed in close order by Papas Andreas. Thanking my fellow villagers profusely for leaping so readily into action, I asked Vangelis if the graffiti could be easily removed. As an aside, graffiti is one of those words that conveniently translates to graffiti in Greek, albeit with a different spelling, *nkrafiti*.

"I have the extra strong paint remover," Vangelis told me. "We will to apply to the stone and let it absorb. Then, we tackle it with wire brushes before the finish with the pressure washing."

"It sounds as though you have it all under control, Vangeli. I'd best be making tracks."

"You're leaving, Victor?" Papas Andreas questioned with a frosty look.

"Of course, he to leave. He have the baby," Vangelis snapped. "You think the Victor should to put the little Anastasia to work?"

As Vangelis organised his crew of volunteers, Andreas sidled up next to me. Running his hands through his straggly beard, he said, "Victor, that was quite the show you put on the other day. You certainly raised my mother's blood pressure."

"What show?" Even while I was clueless to the meaning of Andreas' words, I was impressed with how much his English had improved over the course of the last few years.

"When you stripped off in the garden."

"I wouldn't have done it if I'd known I had an audience."

Desperate to change the subject before the other volunteers got wind of my antics with Guzim's hosepipe, I openly praised Andreas' advancement in the English language.

Flushing a dramatic red, Andreas revealed, "I have been practising a little with Kyria Violet when she visits my mother."

"You'll be dropping ''appens' and 'daft 'apeths' before you know it," I said, thinking the Papas would never have any success wooing Geraldine if he adopted Violet Burke's somewhat coarse vernacular.

"Kyria Violet is too much busy to spare much time…"

"That's for sure," I concurred. "She has a remarkably busy work schedule for someone her age."

Continuing on my way, I sighed in relief that Anastasia's presence had spared me from joining the others in mucking in with the rigorous task of scrubbing in the heat. In a nod to the squad I'd left cleaning the wall, I burst into song, amusing Ana no end with my tone-deaf rendition of the chorus of the 70s Rose Royce hit, 'Car Wash'. I even threw in a couple of disco moves, winning a round of applause from my niece.

Chapter 10

Tulipa

Entering Hal's courtyard, Anastasia was giddy with excitement at the prospect of seeing the donkey which Hal had arranged as a gift for Yiota. There was no dissuading her from the notion that the donkey would be the spit of Eeyore, her favourite character in 'Winnie the Pooh.' Perchance once the new arrival had fitted in, Hal could attach a shiny pink bow to its tail to give it an Eeyore vibe.

Releasing Ana from her pushchair, I warned her to keep a safe distance from the ferocious guard dog, Apollo, explaining that the canine was not a cuddly pet but a working animal. Glancing over to where Apollo was chained, it struck me that my warning may have been unwarranted since the dog appeared to be more than a tad listless. In company with Christos' moustache, Apollo seemed to have mislaid its get-up-and-go: with barely enough energy to raise its head, the dog was a mere shadow of its former self. I would hazard that the formerly savage brute was practically on its last legs. It was hard to credit that the sluggish cur was the same beast that had savagely taken a piece out of Guzim's posterior.

A large wooden table set for an al-fresco luncheon was a new addition to the courtyard since my last visit, as was the makeshift canopy rigged above it to offer some shade. It looked as though Hal had been taking advice from Nikos since the canopy appeared to have been fashioned out of an old bed sheet. I smiled at the memory of Nikos promising canopies at Barry's wedding reception, said canopies turning out to be a canopy rather than the expected delicious morsels of finger food.

Hal emerged from the farmhouse. Once again decked out in a floral pinny, his hands were full of crockery and glassware. As Hal fired off a gregarious greeting, I handed over my goodies and introduced him to Anastasia. Alas, my darling niece was forced to temper her joyous anticipation when Hal told us he was still waiting on the delivery of the donkey, now en route and scheduled to arrive within the next hour.

"Apollo isn't looking too good," I remarked. "I can recommend an excellent vet up in town…"

"I took him to the vet yesterday," Hal responded, going on to tell me that he used the vet in the village where the *Dimarcheio* was sited. His words made me wonder if his rendezvous had been with Poppy's father, the veterinarian who had hosed me down on the occasion when, stuffed to the gills with bacon and meatballs, I had collapsed with heat exhaustion. Although he had been a perfectly pleasant chap, I still suffered from too much lingering embarrassment to consider dragging the cats along to visit him in his professional capacity. Marigold shared my reluctance, even more embarrassed than I to have her husband passed out on the bathroom floor, behind a locked door which needed breaking down to rescue me. "Yiota thought the dog was pining for Panos. The vet concurred that the dog is most likely depressed but also diagnosed Apollo with a Vitamin B12 deficiency and recommended fortnightly injections. He had his first jab yesterday and should soon regain some of his energy."

"So, he'll be back to terrorising the neighbourhood soon," I quipped.

"Take a seat, lunch won't be long. The minted pea puree is already prepared. I just need to pan-fry the fish cakes and cook the broccoli. I hope Anastasia isn't a fussy eater."

"Considering that Cynthia, my sister-in-law, is so unadventurous in the kitchen, Ana has quite the appetite for experimenting with new dishes. She loves fishcakes and broccoli. Minted pea puree could well be a first, but Ana is a great fan of my mother's mushy peas."

"Granny's peas," Ana interjected, clapping her hands in glee.

"I didn't realise Violet is a granny," Hal said, a puzzled look on his face.

"She is, but to my son, Benjamin. Anastasia takes liberties with the term granny."

"Does Violet make her peas from fresh or frozen?"

"From dried marrowfat peas."

"That's a new one on me. Perhaps I should ask Violet for her recipe."

I smiled at Hal's casual use of Violet, recalling my mother's constant reprimand when it came to Hal: *that's Mrs Burke to you*.

Hal suggested that whilst he was pan-frying the fishcakes, Ana and I could pick some of the summer violets growing wild to add a finishing touch to the table.

"After lunch, you can take them for your granny. Violets for Violet." I cringed inwardly at the suspiciously mushy expression on Hal's face as he spoke. I sincerely hoped he hadn't fallen into the role of a Violet Burke admirer: I was pretty certain my mother would make mincemeat of him in short-order. Moreover, after Panos' passing, Violet Burke had sworn off men, though she still enjoyed regular bouts of harmless flirtation with Captain Vasos. Saying that, I recalled that although my mother had also sworn off men after her disastrous marriage to the swindling serial bigamist Arthur Burke, it hadn't stopped her from carrying on with Panos or flashing his posthumous emerald engagement ring on her finger.

The lunch that Hal had prepared turned out to be a resounding success. I must admit that when he'd first mentioned broccoli, I had imagined the vegetable would be boiled for long enough to wash every last trace of green out of it. It is undeniable that whilst Greek food is generally delicious, Greeks do have a tendency when boiling vegetables, to boil them to death, a typical medley of veg including pulpy courgettes and squelchy carrots. I find the grey tinge decidedly off-putting. The theory I have developed regarding spongiform vegetables is that they are often left bubbling away in the pan for the same length of time it takes to transform a bunch of weeds into edible *horta*. Fortunately, Hal's broccoli was not only still green but it had a discernible bite to it, his minted peas speaking to a sophisticated palate. As for his fishcakes, they were quite sublime, crisp on the outside and perfectly fluffy inside.

Praising Hal's food, I risked Doreen's annoyance by insisting that Hal must join the expat dining club; Doreen having made it quite clear that it was not my place to extend invitations to our exclusive club was still miffed about the time Spiros and I had arrived with a guest lacking an invitation, the undertaker's aged uncle, Leo. Still, I reasoned that Doreen could sulk as much as she liked about my overstepping the mark. I simply wanted to increase the number of attendees who were capable of producing an edible meal, a surprisingly rare trait amongst our small band of English immigrants. Hal's finesse in the kitchen would be a welcome addition if we could persuade him to host.

Admittedly my motive was selfish but, eager to persuade Hal to join our expat gatherings, I decided to take a leaf out of Marigold's playbook and unashamedly dangle Violet Burke under his nose as a tempting morsel. However, before I had chance to dangle my mother, Hal pre-empted me, asking, "Does Violet attend these dinners?"

"Wild horses wouldn't keep her away," I exaggerated, quietly relieved that I hadn't been reduced to pimping out my mother.

"I think I will come along to these meetings. It will be good to expand my social circle," Hal declared.

Over lunch, Hal told me that he had been busy that morning, sectioning off a piece of the field next to the courtyard with a makeshift wire fence to house the donkey. Telling me he had plans to knock up a stable before winter to protect the animal from the elements, he asked if I fancied giving him a hand building the shelter.

Hastily dispelling the notion that I was in any way competent when it came to construction, I admitted, "You wouldn't ask if you knew my reputation when it comes to anything more taxing than securing a screw. My talents lie in other areas." I didn't mention that all my attempts to secure a screw had ended in dismal failure.

Raising his eyebrows quizzically, Hal's silent question was answered by Anastasia shouting, "Dirt." Hal looked around in alarm since he was obviously house-proud, even outdoors.

"Don't worry," I assured Hal. "Ana is referring to my expertise in dirt and germs rather than casting aspersions on your table."

"An expert in dirt?" Hal queried. "That's a new one on me."

"I was a public health inspector in my former life," I clarified.

"Well, you won't find anything amiss in my kitchen…"

BUCKET TO GREECE (VOL.17)

"Mucky sponges." Whilst Ana's contribution provoked laughter from Hal, I felt a surge of pride in my niece. She had her adults well trained, her constant repetition of the words 'mucky sponges' shaming Cynthia and Barry to never leave a soggy sponge in their wake.

We had just finished our lunch when the blast of a horn heralded the arrival of the donkey. I had to laugh at the sight of said donkey nimbly balancing on the open bed of the tatty old pickup that pulled in. Like the pickup, the elderly gent climbing down from the cab looked well past his best. Appearing wizened with age, he greeted us with a cheery grin, exposing gums as bereft of teeth as Guzim's as he introduced himself to me as Tasos. Despite Tasos's obvious decrepitude, his words boomed bold and clear in a manner akin to Captain Vasos, the sheer strength of his bone-breaking handshake taking me by surprise.

Speaking in Greek, Tasos lamented having to part with his adored donkey, Tulipa, the Greek word for tulip. As Hal reassured the doddery old gent that he would give a good home to the ageing donkey, Tasos explained to me that he had been reluctant to part with Tulipa until he ran into Hal, their meeting most fortuitous since he instantly knew that he had met a sympatico soul who would cherish his donkey and give her a loving home. Tasos told me that he had never expected to give Tulipa up but his wife was very ill and he couldn't tend to the donkey well whilst he was spending so much of his time at the hospital. Meeting Hal had been a stroke of good luck as no one else had been willing to give a home to the retired donkey, leaving Tasos with nightmares about being forced to sell it on to gypsies who would transport Tulipa to Bulgaria where, rumour had it, old donkeys were turned into dog food.

With Anastasia clamouring loudly to get close to the donkey, Tasos opened the back of the truck bed, carefully placing an old door to act as a ramp. Clambering up next to Tulipa, Tasos nuzzled her head and fed her a couple of carrots retrieved from his pockets before leading her down the makeshift ramp. Tulipa may well have been getting on in donkey years but she was still a very attractive specimen, her coat a glossy light chestnut, boasting a wide beige patch above her mouth. A dark stripe adorned the inside of each of her ears, and to my untrained eye, her plump belly indicated that she was well-fed.

Anastasia immediately called out, "Eeyore, Eeyore," only to be corrected by Tasos proclaiming the donkey's given name, *"To onoma tou gaidarou einai Toulipa."*

As Anastasis pouted, I explained to her, "Eeyore is a boy donkey. Tulipa is a jenny..."

"Jenny. Jenny," Ana cried out in excitement.

"No, Jenny is the term for a girl donkey. This donkey's name is Tulipa," I said, my words almost drowned out by the sound of Tulipa braying, the hee-haw sound instantly reminding me of Sherry's laugh.

"I originally thought to buy Yiota a working donkey that could help out on the farm," Hal told me. "But when I met Tulipa, I knew Yiota would love her and would want to save her from a premature end. Despite being retired, the donkey will serve as an excellent protector of the sheep and will keep the foxes away..."

"I had no idea that donkeys served as fox deterrents," I said, wondering if I should invest in one to protect my chickens.

"And Tulipa may be some help in the olive season," Hal continued. "We can also sell her droppings as nutrient-rich livestock manure."

"I'm sure that Sherry will snap the stuff up," I said. "She's very much into composting."

Announcing that he must leave and get back to his wife's hospital bed, Tasos's sorrow at leaving his donkey was somewhat abated by Hal's reassurance that Tasos was most welcome to visit any time. The elderly gent hurried away, no doubt embarrassed by the tears welling up in his eyes.

Gently guiding Tulipa, Hal steered her into the area he had sectioned off for the donkey behind the wire fence. Lifting Anastasia so she could pet Tulipa, Hal smiled wistfully. "I wish I had known Yiota when she was a child…I missed so much."

Ana was in her element making a huge fuss of the donkey. Within fifteen minutes, worn out by excitement and the hearty lunch, my niece fell asleep, her arms still wrapped around Tulipa. As I gently pried her away from the donkey and strapped her into her pushchair, Hal confessed that whilst he had enjoyed his life at sea, meeting Yiota so late in his life made him regret the family life he had missed out on.

Hal's words were drowned out by frantic honking announcing the unexpected arrival of Yiota's tractor. Parking up at the edge of the courtyard, Yiota shouted out in a fretful tone, "Help. Uncle Hal, I need your help."

Chapter 11

A Hard Landing

Hal and I hurried towards Yiota. As she jumped down from the tractor cab, I noticed her usually calm countenance had been replaced with a harrowed expression, her long brunette hair dishevelled as it came loose from her ponytail. I felt a pang of worry when I spotted tears streaking down her panicked face.

In a tremulous voice, Hal cried out, "What is it, *koritsi mou?*"

"It's Giannis…"

I took a step backwards. If Yiota's upset was caused by Giannis dumping her, Marigold or Violet Burke would be much better placed than I when it came to offering a shoulder to cry on. I thought it prudent to avoid sticking my oar in a romantic relationship; it was almost certain to come back to bite me in the proverbial.

"I was driving the tractor and didn't see him…" Yiota gasped. Bending over, she placed her hands on her knees, practically hyperventilating as she desperately tried to regulate her breathing. "He came out of nowhere…he was on a bicycle…"

"Try to calm down," Hal advised, taking his great-niece's hands in his own.

"I hit Giannis with the tractor and he flew off the bicycle…I thought I'd killed him…there was so much blood…"

Immediately understanding this was far more serious than a lovers' tiff, I was relieved when Yiota replied in the affirmative when Hal questioned if Giannis was still alive.

Not spotting any sign of a bleeding body in the tractor, I asked Yiota, "Where is Giannis now?"

Taking a couple of deep breaths to calm her nerves, Yiota said, "He's on the road just outside the gate. I need a hand to get him into the pickup to take him to the hospital urgently. He's covered in blood."

"But he's definitely not dead?" Hal persisted.

"He's alive…but he flew through the air and landed hard," Yiota wailed. "What have I done?"

Following Yiota's lead, both Hal and I took a couple of deep breaths; surviving an encounter with the hulking great tractor was no mean feat, though Yiota's mention of blood was a tad unnerving. Moreover, with talk of a hard landing, one couldn't rule out internal injuries.

Reassuring Yiota, Hal said, "You probably did the right thing not moving him. I'll call an ambulance."

"It will take too long, Uncle," Yiota protested. "I can get him up to the hospital much quicker in the pickup."

"That's true," I agreed. "With no local ambulance service, it could be an aeon before help arrives."

"We need to get him into the pickup," Yiota urged.

"You're in no state to drive, Yiota. You're too shaken up. I will drive Giannis up to the hospital," Hal decreed with authority. "Victor, go to Giannis and see how bad he is. Yiota, grab the first aid kit out of the kitchen and I'll get the pickup."

As Yiota dashed towards the farmhouse, she suddenly stopped dead in her tracks. "Where did that donkey come from?"

"Hal bought it for you. Her name is Tulipa." Whilst in normal circumstances, I wouldn't have considered it my place to steal Hals' thunder by announcing his gift, the circumstances were hardly normal with Giannis lying injured on the road with possible internal injuries. Since Giannis' need was greater than Tulipa's, I reminded Yiota to hurry and grab the first aid kit whilst I practically sprinted towards the road.

Sprawled out on the tarmac, Giannis' usual olive-hued complexion was now as white as a sheet, a stark background for the bright red blood dripping from his forehead onto his face. Fortunately, it appeared that Yiota had greatly exaggerated the amount of blood, her use of gross hyperbole understandable considering she was clearly in shock.

As I reached Giannis' side, I was relieved when he

attempted to sit up. Unfortunately, his efforts were thwarted when the weight he put on his wrist sent visible shockwaves of pain through his body.

"*Nomizo oti o karpos mou echei spasei.*" Wincing through the pain, Giannis told me he thought his wrist was broken, his words at least conveying that he was still compos mentis, incidentally another one of those phrases that is the same in Greek.

"*Tha chreiasteite mia aktinografia,*" I said, telling Giannis he would need an X-ray before going on to ask if anything else hurt. "*Ponaei otidipote allo?*"

"*O astragalos mou.*" As Yiannis replied that his ankle hurt, he gingerly prodded the said appendage, flinching in pain as he did so.

When I asked him about his head, Giannis assured me that he hadn't lost consciousness, seemingly unaware his face was a bloody mess. Helping him into a sitting position, I couldn't resist pointing out that he should have worn a cycling helmet, "*Tha eprepe na forate podilatiko kranos.*"

Whilst Giannis sheepishly acknowledged that he should have listened to me and worn a bicycle helmet, he nevertheless argued the point that a helmet wouldn't have protected his wrist or ankle. His sarcasm laden argument convinced me that Giannis was nowhere near death's door.

I was relieved when Yiota arrived with the first aid kit and a bottle of water, closely followed by Hal driving the pickup. As Yiota joined me at Giannis' side, the young man began to berate her for causing the accident, disparaging her ability behind the wheel of the tractor and vocally dismissing her as an inept woman driver. Even as Yiota wiped a wet cloth over his face to uncover the source of the bleeding, Yiannis continued to blast her for knocking him off the bicycle. Whilst admittedly, this wasn't an appropriate time for an exchange of whispered sweet nothings, there was no excuse for Giannis speaking to his girlfriend with such contempt. I could see Hal growing angrier by the moment: although having only recently discovered he had a great-niece, he was already fiercely protective of her and was having none of Giannis' furious remonstrations.

Interrupting Giannis' verbal onslaught, Yiota told him that the source of the bleeding was a nasty gash on the side of his forehead. Outraged by the volley of expletives Giannis was firing at Yiota, I reminded him again that his bloody gash could have been avoided by simply donning a cycling helmet. After sticking a plaster over the gash, Yiota tenderly wiped the rest of the blood away. Much as I was tempted to point out to Giannis that he could well end up with a rakish scar that may well enhance his god-like looks, I abstained, the Greek word for rakish eluding me.

With Giannis continuing to vent his anger, Hal and I helped the accident victim to his feet and hauled him into the pickup, admittedly none-to-gently since the pair of us were rather riled by the barrage of colourful language heading Yiota's way.

Gritting his teeth against the pain, Giannis finally put a sock in it. I have to say that the young man certainly went down in my estimation. To be frank, I found the petulance he'd directed at Yiota, quite appalling.

Granted, she had apparently been responsible for a couple of possibly broken limbs, but even so, there was no excuse for the disrespectful tongue-lashing he directed her way. The damage inflicted on Giannis by the tractor was purely accidental yet with the way he was carrying on, one would suppose it was intentional on Yiota's part, even though she was clearly distraught about the accident. I considered Giannis partly responsible: it was sheer recklessness on his part to cycle along a pot-holed road, clad in nothing more than shorts and a tee shirt offering zero protection, and lacking a helmet despite the warning I had given when he fixed the Punto's air conditioning. I certainly wouldn't put it past him to have been breaking the speed limit as he frequently did when he raced through the village on his motorcycle.

As Hal and Yiota joined Giannis in the pickup, Hal promised to phone me from the hospital to keep me updated. Before driving off, he asked me to fill Tulipa's water barrel from the outside hosepipe and make sure the donkey was settled comfortably before I left.

Fortunately, Anastasia had slept through the commotion, thus sparing her tender ears from Giannis' expletive laden language. Whilst she continued to snooze, I cleared the table and washed our dishes, sparing Hal the burden of clearing up once he returned from the hospital.

Ana continued to doze whilst I took care of the donkey, directing the hosepipe into the barrel. With the water slowly trickling into the receptacle, I woke Anastasia, knowing she would want to say goodbye to Tulipa before we left. Holding my niece aloft, Ana wrapped her arms around the donkey's head, planting a huge sloppy kiss on its nose. Since I knew that it was extremely rare for donkeys to pass diseases to humans, Ana was able to enjoy the contact with Tulipa without receiving one of my lectures about germs.

Strolling home from the farmhouse, I was relieved to see that the wall outside the taverna has been scrubbed clean of the obscene graffiti, Vangelis and his team of geriatric helpers having done a wonderful job.

As we continued on our way, Barry's van came to a screeching stop beside me. Jumping out, the doting father made a beeline for Ana. Clearly intending to plant a smacker on his daughter, he stopped in his tracks when Ana scrunched up her face and pointed out he was dirty. No doubt she didn't fancy being enveloped in a cloud of builder's dust.

"We're just off to finish a few bits on a snagging list. We won't be more than a couple of hours and then we're knocking off for the day," Barry revealed. "Can you drop Ana off at mine in two hours?"

"Rightio," I agreed.

"Hello, Mr Bucket," a familiar voice piped up from inside the van.

"Tonibler. What are you up to?"

The child prodigy, sitting in the cab next to his father, flashed me a grin, revealing the gap where he had recently lost his milk teeth. I didn't think it appropriate to comment on Tonibler's tooth exfoliation in case the boy was self-conscious. Instead, I engaged in an exchange of greetings with Blat, pretending to look surprised when he revealed that he still hadn't received a personal invitation from the great Tony Blair to up-sticks to the great Great Britain. Despite the lack of contact from the British prime minister, Blat remained the eternal optimist.

"We need to take Tonibler along to the job...unless you want to take him for the next couple of hours," Barry suggested. "I'm sure he'll have more fun with you and Anastasia than sitting around while we work.

"It would be my pleasure, if it's okay with Blat," I assured Barry.

"If it's no trouble for you, Mr Bucket," Blat said.

"No trouble at all," I assured Blat, giving the child a hand as he clambered down from the van.

Now that the interminable thirteen-weeks' school holidays had begun and Tonibler was too young to be left home alone, he would likely be dragged along with Blerta or Blat to their workplaces on the days when they couldn't find a babysitter. It was a relief to see that Tonibler wasn't having to spend the school holidays still kitted out in his bizarre, oversized school uniform. Hopefully, by the time school resumed in September, he might have finally grown into the ginormous grey blazer with flapping cuffs.

For now, at least, the only thing that made Tonibler stand out as an oddity was his green tee-shirt emblazoned with Tony Blair's smarmy face. I could have sworn I'd seen Blat wearing an identical tee: perchance Blat's had shrunk in the wash and he'd passed it down to his son. There again, it struck me as equally likely that Blat had purchased matching tops for father and son, rather in the manner of those nauseating cringe couples announcing their loved-up connection to the world through the medium of matching pullovers.

I am forever grateful that never once in our decades of marriage has Marigold tried to kit the two of us out in anything matchy. I recalled a Christmas back in Manchester when Benjamin and Adam had exchanged identical shirts as festive gifts. Clearly horrified, the two of them made a pact to ensure they never wore them at the same time, matchy-matchy really not their thing, Benjamin even remarking that matching outfits, in his opinion, were more than a tad camp.

Tonibler entertained Anastasia with a constant stream of chatter as we made our way home. Casting my mind back to my trip to England with Violet Burke for Kevin's wedding, I couldn't help but reflect on the difference between Tonibler and Tyrone, Chardonnay's young son. Whilst Tonibler was articulate and well-mannered, an absolute pleasure to be around, Chardonnay's spawn was a young ruffian, well on his way to becoming a delinquent.

Delighted to see how Ana hung on Tonibler's every word, it crossed my mind that the pair of them could become a likely match in the future. Coming to an abrupt standstill, I had a word with myself: *what on earth was I thinking?* Marigold's meddling matchmaking must be contagious.

Chapter 12

Jammie Dodgers

Arriving home with the two children, I was happy to have Tonibler along: as always, he proved to be excellent company, his genuine enthusiasm for soaking up knowledge quite exceptional. If I had the chance, I would give Tonibler a quick lesson on English homophones: it would be vital to his mastery of vocabulary if he could differentiate between words that sounded the same such as peace and a piece, and pale and a pail. Perchance a pail wasn't the best example to use since it would inevitably lead to talk of buckets.

When Anastasia gabbled away to her young friend all about Tulipa, I promised that the next time I visited Hal, I would bring Tonibler along to meet the donkey.

Opening the balcony doors to offer a through breeze, I spotted the Albanian shed dweller heading off on his moped.

"There goes Guzim," I said over the sound of his exhaust backfiring.

"Guzim is as thick as mince," Tonibler proclaimed.

Barely able to suppress my snort of laughter, I duly reprimanded Tonibler for his inappropriate language. It didn't take a genius to work out where he'd picked that little gem up since it undoubtedly had a ring of my mother about it.

"You can't say that, Tonibler. It's not polite to poke fun at your elders."

"Mrs Burke says it." Tonibler's assertion proved I was spot on about Violet Burke's influence.

"Mrs Burke should learn to hold her tongue around impressionable children."

Anastasia immediately stuck her tongue out and grabbed it with her hand, her words indecipherable as she tried to tell me she was holding her tongue.

"Should Mrs Burke wash out her mouth with soap?" Tonibler asked.

"Most definitely," I agreed, prompting both children to dissolve in giggles.

Thinking up ways to entertain my young charges, I decided they would find it fun if we engaged in a spot of baking and made some homemade biscuits for afternoon tea. I had all the ingredients on hand to make ginger biscuits though I would need to ration the Lyle's golden syrup as the tin was perilously close to being empty. Next time any of the local expats went back to

England, I would ask them to sneak a tin back in their luggage.

After supervising both Ana and Tonibler as they thoroughly scoured their hands, I took the precaution of checking that neither child had any plasters that might fall in the dough and present a choking hazard. I had no wish to repeat the incident when Tonibler's plaster fell off his spectacles. Landing in a vat of curry, the missing plaster inadvertently set off a ludicrous chain of events, eventually ending in broken ribs. Also, tempted though I was to shake the pair of them down for ticks, I resisted.

I was totally gob-smacked when Tonibler requested, "Can we make Jammie Dodgers, Mr Bucket?"

"How on earth have you heard about Jammie Dodgers?" I asked, genuinely flummoxed since I had never once spotted a packet of the shortcake biscuits with a jammy centre for sale in Greece. Maybe Blat had discovered they were Tony Blair's favourite biscuits, thus extolling them to his son.

"Mr Barry told me about them. He said they are his favourite biscuits. He said they were named after Roger the Dodger."

"That's right," I said, recalling that Tonibler had practically devoured a couple of Beano Annuals which Moira Strange had picked up for the child on one of her visits back to England to model her ears.

"Did you like Jammie Dodgers when you were little, Mr Bucket?"

"I don't think they were around when I was a child, but my son, Benjamin, loved them. When I was a nipper, I was very fond of custard creams."

"What is a nipper, Mr Bucket?"

"It's an informal term for child."

"Like kid?"

"The term kid ought to be reserved for baby goats," I schooled my young charge.

"What's a nipper in Greek, Mr Bucket?"

"Just stick with *paidi*," I advised.

"Child," Tonibler confirmed.

"Can we make the great Jammie Dodgers, please?" Tonibler persisted.

"Well, they are packet biscuits but we could try to knock up a decent copy," I agreed, my cupboards home to a glut of homemade strawberry jam from my home-grown strawberries. Amazingly, my ready acquiescence was enough to stop Tonibler badgering me.

I appointed Tonibler the task of weighing out the ingredients. Watching her friend, Anastasia appeared enraptured. There was a look of intense concentration on Tonibler's face as he studied the dial on the kitchen scales, measuring everything with pin-point precision. With the flour and butter measured out, I encouraged the pair of them to get their hands stuck in the bowl for a spot of rubbing whilst I paid a quick visit to the bathroom.

Although gone for less than two minutes, it was long enough for Ana to unleash her naughty side. I returned to hear Tonibler acting like both a big brother and a public health inspector.

"Ana, don't do that, it's dirty. It's been on the floor. It could have picked up germs."

"Dirt," Ana trilled.

BUCKET TO GREECE (VOL.17)

Rushing over to see what had prompted Tonibler to rebuke Ana, I saw my niece kneeling on the kitchen floor, feeding a reluctant Catastrophe with a great wodge of the raw biscuit mixture.

"Don't do that, Ana. You don't want to make the cat sick," I chided. "I'm pretty sure that flour and butter are on the list of items your Aunty Marigold says are banned foods for cats.

The feline gave credence to my words by promptly throwing up. Anastasia managed to look the picture of innocence as she apologised. After scouring Ana's hands again, I supervised the children as they added sugar to the bowl. When the telephone rang, I charged Tonibler with keeping an eye on Anastasia whilst I took the call. It was Cynthia, checking that everything was fine with her daughter.

As I assured Cynthia that Ana was having a whale of a time and keeping out of mischief, Clawsome sauntered over in my direction. Spotting the cat covered in bright red blood, my heart sank and I cut the telephone call short, a tad annoyed when the feline reached me and rubbed her body against my leg, transferring blood to my slacks.

"Clawsome, there's a time and a place for such shenanigans," I reproached, hoping the blood would come out of my slacks if Marigold gave them a good scrubbing with cold salty water before bunging them in the washing machine.

Picking the cat up and holding her at arm's length to examine for injuries, I realised I had mistaken jam for blood. I hurriedly slung the cat onto the balcony before it could leave jammy paw prints all over the sofa: it would give Marigold the perfect excuse to demand we splash out on a new one and I was in no mood for splashing. I returned to the children, only to be confronted with the jaw-dropping sight of my niece seemingly wearing the entire contents of a full pot of strawberry jam. Having perfected the art of looking cute and innocent, Ana beamed at me, seemingly unaware that the evidence of her raid on the jam jar was all over her face in the form of a jammy moustache and beard, fat globs of the sticky sweet stuff adorning her glossy curls, her pretty dress splattered with the luscious fruity preserve.

I really should have known better than to turn my back on my niece for even a moment. The last time Cynthia had left the Buckets in charge of the toddler, Ana had raided my supply of shoe polish, adding a generous coat of the gloop to her eyelashes. Cynthia, less than pleased to arrive back to a child sporting a couple of shiners, had read me the riot act about keeping tins of shoe polish out of Ana's reach. My sister-in-law only calmed down and admitted such mishaps could happen to anyone when Marigold confessed that she was the one responsible for not keeping a keen enough eye on our niece, absolving me of responsibility. Fortunately, Barry had seen the funny side. He'd reported that even a week later, streaks of black shoe polish ran down Ana's cheeks every night at bath time.

Ana continued to grin mischievously whilst running a finger over her jam smeared frock and popping it in her mouth as though she'd never heard of using a teaspoon. Her usual obsession with anything being dirty apparently didn't stretch to edible treats.

"I think the best way to clean you up, Ana, is to give you a good hosing down outside, clothes and all." I would never hear the end of it if Marigold returned to find jam all over the bathroom. "We'll be back in a jiffy, Tonibler. You can get on with rubbing all the ingredients together."

When I'd finished hosing Anastasia down, I gave her a quick rub down with a towel before the two of us returned to the kitchen, confident she would soon dry off in the heat. The last thing I expected to see was my kitchen floor awash with soapy bubbles. My immediate thought was that the washing machine must be on the blink to be spewing such a flood, my assumption dispelled when I recalled the washing machine lived in the bathroom.

The culprit soon became clear when I spotted Tonibler balancing on a chair in front of the kitchen sink. The boy was attempting to control a squirming Clawsome as a veritable river of water brimming with soap suds poured from the sink to the floor.

"Tonibler, what on earth are you doing to the cat? I left Clawsome on the balcony."

"I thought I'd help out by giving her a bath. She was covered in jam. All her fur was sticky."

"You appear to have more bubbles than water," I observed. "It doesn't look as though the cat is enjoying a bubble bath."

"I think I used too much washing up liquid," Tonibler confessed, struggling to keep hold of the writhing feline.

V.D. BUCKET

With a squeal of joy, Anastasia cried "Bubbles," plonking herself down in the flood and scooping handfuls of soapsuds over her head.

Slithering out of Tonibler's grasp, Clawsome streaked past me in a froth of foam, making a beeline for the door, one of the few times I had ever seen the feline voluntarily venturing outside. Sighing in dismay at the state of my kitchen, I wondered if a small bribe might convince Violet Burke and her mop to come to my rescue.

Chapter 13

Turquoise Lettuces

Dropping a still damp Anastasia back at Barry's place, Cynthia's absence spared me a lecture about her daughter arriving home in a soggy, jam-stained frock, my brother-in-law immediately seeing the funny side of Ana's mischievous antics.

Heading home, I realised Marigold was back when I saw the Punto parked up outside. My heart quickened and I bounded up the outdoor stairs with a spring in my step, eager to see my wife. Despite all our years together, the thought of seeing Marigold never fails to set my heart aflutter.

To my annoyance, I was suddenly drenched by a deluge of water spraying everywhere. It appeared to be coming from just outside the front door at the top of the stairs. Spotting the source of my soaking, I cried out, "Marigold. What on earth is that in my salad spinner?" I was pretty certain that turquoise lettuces most definitely weren't a thing.

"It's just my swimming cossie," Marigold blithely replied, as though contaminating my essential kitchen tool with intimate items of clothing was a matter of no consequence. Considering Marigold's sacrilegious action to be on a par with Violet Burke's repulsive habit of soaking her swollen feet in my washing-up bowl, I mentally consigned my salad spinner to the dustbin even though I was very attached to it.

Giving her one-piece another spin and subjecting me to a second soaking, Marigold trilled, "It's not as though I'm wetting the house, Victor. I am spinning my cossie outdoors."

"But why?" Rather than voicing the thought that my wife must have taken leave of her senses, I bit my tongue.

"This is my favourite bathing suit. Your mother recommended hand washing my cossie and giving it a good spin in this thing to extend its life. Vi swears blind that it's not good to bung one's swimming costumes in the washing machine, she says it reduces their elasticity and leads to sagging." Perish the thought that Marigold could end up with a saggy bottom. "You know that Vi has had that skirted swimsuit of hers since just after the war and it still looks as good as new."

I might have known Violet Burke had some part in this irresponsible usage of my salad spinner. "Do stop waving it around," I pleaded. "You're wetting me…"

"Athena and I stopped off for a swim on our way home. It was so refreshing." Marigold gave the spinner a final enthusiastic jiggle before retrieving her costume and heading inside. As I followed behind her, she changed the subject, asking, "Did you have a lovely day with Anastasia, darling? I'm just exhausted after all that driving. I hope you're planning to cook up something nice for dinner."

"Anastasia kept me so busy that I haven't had a free moment to think of cooking," I said.

"How was darling Ana?"

"She was as good as gold." As I replied, I cast my eyes around the kitchen to ensure that I had scrubbed away every last trace of strawberry jam: it would be a magnet for ants. Spotting a telltale glob of the sticky red stuff on Catastrophe's ear, I nudged the cat onto the balcony with my foot until I had the opportunity to give it a discreet buffing.

"I had young Tonibler over for a couple of hours too. I gave him a quick lesson in homophones…"

"Really, Victor, it's the school holidays. Couldn't you have given the boy a break?"

"It was his idea. Tonibler has an insatiable knowledge for learning," I said in my own defence before changing the subject. "You'll have to fend for yourself in the food department. I promised Nikos I'd give Dina a hand again this evening…"

"Again?"

"Dina's still very upset about Eleni leaving and taking the children…"

Clasping her hands in front of her chest, Marigold's

voice oozed empathy. Surprising me, she responded by saying, "Oh, I feel for her, I really do. Imagine if Cynthia left Barry and took Anastasia...it doesn't bear thinking about."

"Fortunately, Cynthia and Barry appear to have a good marriage," I said.

"But one never really knows what goes on behind closed doors." Chewing on her bottom lip, Marigold's eyes darkened with worry. "I think you ought to have a quiet word with Barry, Victor...make sure there are no ripples in their marriage."

"He's your brother," I pointed out.

"But he's more likely to confide in you...he thinks of you as a brother..."

"Well, he thinks of you as a sister..."

"I am his sister. Must you be so vexatious, Victor? Anyway, I think any discreet probing would be better coming from you. I'd hate him to think I was interfering. I know Barry is my flesh and blood, but sometimes he can be a bit thoughtless. Take yesterday evening as an example; Barry left Cynthia at home while he went gadding off to the taverna..."

"But you are the one who strong-armed Barry into going with you to make up the numbers with Toby and Felicity." As Marigold faced me down with a set jaw and a look of steely determination, I crumbled. "You want me to discreetly probe into the state of Barry's marriage?"

"It's for the greater good, darling. Now, are you planning to work in the taverna all evening?"

"Yes, but don't worry, I'm not going to make a habit

of it. I just want to be there for Dina until she regains her composure. You don't mind, do you?"

Peering at me through narrowed eyes, Marigold took me by surprise by changing her tune. "I think it's marvellous that you'll be there this evening, darling, perfectly splendid. You'll be in the ideal position to report back to me…"

"Report back to you?" Clearly, my wife had some hidden agenda up her sleeve, making me wonder what fresh hell awaited me.

"Yes, report back on how Sherry's first date with Vasos goes. They're meeting up in the village taverna this evening."

Dropping this little bombshell on me as though it was common knowledge, Marigold avoided my eye. To put it mildly, I was not amused. The last thing I wanted to do with my evening was to get roped into playing the role of unwilling translator for two soppy lovebirds: it had been taxing enough trying to avoid them on Pegasus. I cringed at the prospect of spying on the pair, imagining Sherry braying endlessly whilst Vasos bellowed his choice selection of limited English words, clueless to their actual meaning.

Deftly changing the subject before I could even think of protesting, Marigold asked, "Now, have you got any plans for tomorrow, darling?"

"I'm going to have to go into town. Pelham mentioned he intends to pay for the apartment in cash. I don't like to think of so much money lying around so I'll bob up to the bank and deposit it in the business account."

"Don't forget to wear those underpants with the

special compartment I sewed in for carrying cash. Even if some opportunistic thief mugs you, they won't get their hands on your money in there."

"Yes, dear," I meekly agreed. Having purchased a secure money belt, I had no intention of taking Marigold's advice but there was no reason for my wife to know that. After all, she had spent a lot of time sewing a secure pocket in my Y-fronts, a quite unnecessary precaution in my mind since I had never heard of a single case of anyone being mugged in town.

"I'll give Doreen a call in a minute and let her know that you'll be able to give her a lift to the main police station in the morning."

"What?" Was there no end to my wife's determination to insert me slap-bang into the middle of her friends' lives? "The police station. Has Doreen gone and got herself embroiled in something illegal?"

"Of course not. Doreen's almost as much a stickler for the law as you are. Surely you haven't forgotten that she has her moped test tomorrow."

"Why can't she go to town on her moped?"

"Duh. She hasn't passed her test yet…"

"I'm never going to get a moped into the back of the Punto," I objected.

"Nor will you need to. There's a bike available at the testing place."

Realising I had left myself wide open to being lumbered with Doreen, it seemed pointless to object. At least Doreen had mellowed somewhat since taking up with Manolis: she certainly didn't irritate me half as much as Sherry did.

BUCKET TO GREECE (VOL.17)

"Do you want to come along too, Marigold?"

"I think I'll give it a miss since I already went up today. Or perhaps I should come along as I could do with popping into Marks and Sparks for a refund," Marigold prevaricated. "I bought a dress today that I'm having second thoughts about. It's not terribly flattering. I think it makes me look a bit on the fat side."

Marigold's words left me speechless. It was practically unheard of for my wife to admit to purchasing a new frock rather than just happening upon some old thing in the back of the wardrobe.

"Perhaps I'll hang on to it for now. I'll see how it looks after a couple of sessions in Doreen's new Weight Loss Club. You never know, I might lose that problem kilo."

"Your figure is perfect," I said in all honesty.

"Oh, you're just biased," Marigold cooed, her smile indicating my compliment had hit the mark. "We're having our first meeting of the Slimming Club in a couple of days. I do find it off-putting though, the way that Sherry insists on referring to it as the Fat Club. She says calling it that will encourage us to take it seriously. I suppose I ought to bake a cake to take along; perhaps one of my *portokalopitas*." Amazingly, the irony of taking a cake to a slimming club get-together appeared to go completely over Marigold's head.

"Since you're not cooking this evening, I suppose I could get in the slimming mood by just having a salad for dinner. Even though Athena and I only had a light lunch in town, I'm not that peckish."

"Did you have something nice?"

"It was lovely. We ate in a nice *taverna* opposite the beach; the young waiter was very easy on the eye. Athena and I shared some *xtapodi ksidat* and *a horiatiki,*" Marigold said, referencing octopus in vinegar and a traditional Greek salad.

"That certainly sounds like diet food," I commented, thinking the two of them had been remarkably restrained.

"Well, we were still a bit stuffed from the *bougatsa* and *galaktoboureko* we enjoyed with our morning coffee. Athena appreciates a custardy pastry as much as I do."

Conjuring an image of ginormous pastries groaning under the weight of a liberal dousing of icing sugar, I could well imagine that the pair of them had been full to bursting by the time they ordered lunch.

"By the way," I said. "I met Spiros' rich doctor today. With Spiros racing off to Athens to meet Sampaguita's plane, he asked me to step in and show that big house on the square."

"Ooh, what's he like?" Marigold's interest was clearly piqued.

"He is a she," I responded.

"No."

"Oh, yes. Doctor Fotoula Papadima."

"A female doctor, how wonderful. I always feel more comfortable seeing a woman medic. What's she like, Victor?"

"To be honest, I haven't got a clue. It was like conversing with a robot. She batted all my questions away with one-syllable answers and made it blatantly obvious that she had no intention of discussing her business."

"You should have made more of an effort to get to know her..."

Our conversation was interrupted by my mother barging into the kitchen without so much as a by-your-leave and barking, "Who's that the pair of you are on about, then?"

"We were just talking about the new doctor," Marigold said. "Victor showed her the house she's interested in on the square but apparently, he didn't manage to find out anything about her."

"To be honest, I found her very standoffish," I said. "In fact, her attitude bordered on the downright rude. I mulled the notion that she took against me because I'm a foreigner. But then, Vangelis stopped by to discuss some modifications to the house and she treated him with equal disdain. I'm sure her nostrils gained some extra width from the way she looked down at us."

"'Appen she's not too keen on fellas," Vi suggested before blowing me down with a feather. "Personally, I thought she was right nice, a lovely woman. Fancy you passing yourself off as one of them estate agents, Victor. I'd no idea Fotoula was talking about you when she said that the chap who showed her around had been right pushy, not to mention a bit full of himself."

"Pushy? What a completely baseless accusation. I was the very antithesis of pushy." Bristling at the very notion I had been full of myself, I snapped. "That's slander..."

Brushing my comment off, Marigold interrupted, saying to Vi in an incredulous tone, "You've met the doctor?"

"Aye, lass. We got to chatting in the shop and then

we sat down outside and had a right good natter over a couple of coffees. It's going to be a right bonus having a doctor on hand in the village. Not that I'm one for seeing a doctor over the slightest little thing. I've never been one of them hypochondriacs..."

"You certainly have a very robust constitution, Mother."

"Well, all that bottoming and bicycling keeps me fit, lad."

"Did you at least manage to find out more about her than Victor did?" Marigold asked hopefully.

"Hold your horses, lass. If you stick the kettle on for a cuppa, I'll fill you in."

"Victor, put the kettle on," Marigold said. "I need to make a start on that trifle for Giannis."

Telling my mother to take the weight off whilst I brewed a pot of tea, I found myself as eager as Marigold to learn more about the doctor.

"Right, so Fotoula's a doctor..." my mother began.

"I think that's already been established, Vi," Marigold interrupted.

"Will you ever let me finish a sentence, lass? She told me she got right fed up of the grind and fancied moving somewhere quieter and less frantic..."

"That certainly describes Meli," I observed.

"Aye, it does that, lad. It can take a fair bit of getting used to the quiet of Meli after the bustle of Warrington...at first, I found it a bit strange that there were no drunks staggering home when the pubs chuck out."

"Well, there aren't any pubs in Meli, Vi," Marigold pointed out.

"Course, Meli comes with its own kind of noise that can take a bit of adjusting to," Vi continued. "Half the time there's too much silence to contend with and then the din of them chihuahua things doesn't half take some getting used to…"

"What on earth, Mother? There isn't a single chihuahua in Meli."

"There are swarms of the things, you daft 'apeth. You must have heard them…"

"Swarms of chihuahuas?" Realising my mother had likely committed a malapropism, I asked, "Are you by any chance referring to cicadas, Mother?"

"Aye, 'appen I am. What did I say?"

"You said chihuahuas which are a breed of dog."

"Those tiny toy dogs," Marigold clarified.

"Well, I wasn't that far off the mark then. You must have heard the way that Panos' old guard dog carries on some nights, barking enough to raise the dead…mind you, it's more of a pathetic yowl these days."

"Apollo is missing his master."

"He's not the only one." Violet Burke rubbed the emerald engagement ring adorning her finger, her double chin visibly sagging.

"You were telling us about the doctor, Vi," Marigold reminded her mother-in-law as she poured a generous measure of sherry over the trifle's sponge base.

"Well, I reckon it will be a big improvement to have a doctor up here, especially with her being a woman. I telling me to drop my drawers."

"You were going to tell us more about the doctor," Marigold pressed.

"'Appen I could fill the two of you in if you didn't keep sticking your oars in. She's decided to buy that big house on the square. Fotoula has ideas to have some of the downstairs converted so she can open a private practice and see patients in the village; she reckons she could be up and running before the end of the year."

"Where was she working before?" I asked.

"She was one of them military doctors, same as her father and grandfather before her..."

"How fascinating," I said.

"'Ere, Marigold. Pour me a nip of that sherry," Vi demanded. "It's been a right trying day."

"Is the doctor married?" Marigold hadn't even met the woman yet and her thoughts were already heading towards a spot of matchmaking. She just can't help herself.

"She's a widow," Vi replied. Marigold and I both cringed as my mother added a tot of sherry to her cup of tea. "She told me her husband had been right wealthy and left her a bundle."

"That house is awfully big for one person," I remarked. "Will she be living there alone?"

"'Appen she will, lad. This cuppa's right good. I was fair parched." It was obvious from Vi's reply that she had no clue if the doctor would be rattling around on her lonesome in the largest house in the village. "'Ere, Marigold, top my cuppa up, lass. You've no idea what a day I've had."

Stashing the bottle of sherry back in the cupboard, Marigold topped Vi's cup up with tea, refusing to rise to Violet Burke's bait and ask what in particular had been so trying.

"I was really surprised when you jacked your job in at the *kafenion*," I said. "I was under the impression that you quite enjoyed working there."

"Really, Vi. You've given up your job at the kafenion?" Marigold was clearly taken by surprise.

"Well, I wouldn't say I've quit it for good. I'm expecting Christos will come to what little senses he's got and see the error of his ways…"

"What's he done now?" Marigold asked, all agog for the latest gossip.

"That slapper he's been knocking around with was getting under my feet in the *kafenion* again today…"

"Maria?" Marigold queried.

"You know her?" It was my turn to be surprised; Marigold had never mentioned meeting Christos' lady friend to me.

"No, I haven't met her. I only know of her from Doreen…she's had plenty to say about her…"

"Ah…"

"And none of it good. Doreen hasn't taken to her at all…"

"From my brief encounter with Maria, I'd say she and Doreen are like chalk and cheese," I ventured.

"That Maria's nowt but a slovenly sket. You should hear the gob on her. Common as muck," Violet Burke pronounced, oblivious that the way she spat 'sket' and 'gob' whilst gurning grotesquely made her sound as common as muck herself.

"The first time I met her, I was cleaning the apartment over the *kafenion*. Maria was sprawled out practically starkers on Christos' bed, no shame at all. She was smoking away like a chimney and dropping her dog ends in a coffee cup. I chucked a sheet at the brazen hussy but 'appen I'd have been better off stuffing it in her gob."

"Even so, it seems a bit drastic to walk out of your job," Marigold said.

"Well, I reckon that Christos will have the nouse to know what side his bread is buttered. Slappers like that Maria are ten a penny but right good chars are like gold dust."

I reflected that whilst slappers might possibly be in rich supply, I hadn't exactly spotted a queue of them lining up to take up with Christos.

"You really think Christos will dump Maria to win you back, Vi?" Marigold's tone dripped with scepticism.

"He's already dumped her," I told them. "Christos said she was too moody and none of the customers liked her."

"We'd best keep our ears peeled then. 'Appen he'll be showing up at mine ready to do a bit of grovelling."

"Perchance that's him now," I said as the sound of someone knocking on the *apothiki* door filtered upstairs.

Chapter 14

Butter the Parsnips

Leaning over the balcony, I called down to a discernibly nervous-looking Christos, the Greek man anxiously pacing on the street below. "If you're looking for my mother, she's up here. Come on up."

Upon hearing my words, Christos exhaled audibly, no doubt relieved that he didn't have to deal with Violet Burke in full harridan mode, on his lonesome. Whilst I would normally prefer Christos to keep his distance from the Bucket residence and more particularly from Marigold, since he can never resist fawning all over my wife, I was keen to see if he could charm Violet Burke back to work. Charm wasn't a word one usually associated with the oily Greek.

Christos looked particularly greasy, his forehead dripping with sweat, both the hair on his head and the hair on his moustache looking as if they'd been dunked in a barrel of mucky fat. His subdued appearance was at noticeable odds with his typical swaggering nature. I could only imagine that it must have been no walk in the park to be stuck in a car with the ghastly Maria after dumping her. If I was more gullibly inclined, I might almost have felt sorry for him: having to contend with two bolshie women in one day must have been very emasculating.

Inviting Christos through to the kitchen, I was relieved to see that he only had eyes for one woman, and for once it wasn't my wife. Simpering in a manner that made me speculate if he'd been taking lessons in obsequiousness from Guzim, Christos stuttered, "Violet…"

"You can stick with Mrs Burke. I'm not keen on fellas getting overly familiar," my mother barked.

"Of course, Violet…I mean, Mrs Burke…we need you. I want you to come back…"

"Well, lad, I want slender ankles and a gold-plated mop, but wanting won't get…"

"I bought you a bottle of brandy." Whipping a bottle of *Metaxa* out of his carrier bag, Christos presented it to my mother.

"I see you went for the cheap three-star *Metaxa*…it's hardly what I'd call pushing the boat out," Vi grumbled, staring at the proffered bottle with derision.

Catching Marigold's eye, the two of us could barely suppress our involuntary laughter, both of us acutely aware that Violet Burke happened to favour the three-star brandy she was now pretending wasn't upmarket enough for her.

"This bottle's been opened," Vi complained.

Christos avoided her eye. No doubt he'd been tempted to take a swig from the bottle on his way over, for Dutch courage.

"I bought you this huge box of chocolates..." Christos simpered.

"I hope they've not got them hard centres. I can't be doing with toffee getting stuck in my teeth..."

Visibly blanching at the notion he may have messed up his peace offering, Christos scanned the box, sighing in relief before announcing, "They are the soft centres, Mrs Burke. Please say you'll come back to work tomorrow. We can't manage without you. I gave up Maria for you...you said I must choose between the two of you and I chose you..."

"You've got another thing coming if you expect me to take that Maria's place in your bedroom, you mucky bugger. I can't be working for you if you can't control your urges..."

Christos' mouth gaped open in horror, seemingly oblivious that my mother was intentionally winding him up.

Marigold, unable to keep her laughter under control for another second, unleashed a most unladylike snort which she attempted to cover with a contrived coughing fit.

"Mrs Burke, the only thing I want you to do in my bedroom is clean it. Please say you'll come back to work," Christos implored.

"I think a pay rise might convince my mother to return," I suggested, beginning to feel a tad sorry for the grovelling Greek. Violet Burke clearly had no intention of making things easy for him, determined to wring every last drop of contrition from Christos.

Shooting a look of irritation in my direction, Christos delved once more into his carrier bag, producing a bunch of plastic flowers and presenting them to my mother with as much chivalry as he could muster. Although not a betting man, I would wager that one of the graves in the churchyard was missing its floral embellishment. Vi surprised me by accepting the plastic floral offering with grace, telling Christos, "I'm quite partial to a nice artificial bloom indoors. Real flowers are full of mites that might migrate to Petey's fur."

"So, you'll come back?"

"You must think I was born yesterday," Vi snorted. "It'll take more than a bribe of brandy, chocs and flowers..."

The look of panic on Christos' face indicated he was at his wit's end. It wouldn't surprise me if his next move was to get down on bended knees and offer a diamond ring. Obviously, my imagination was running away with me as Christos' next words were decidedly down-to-earth.

"I will buy you a new mop," Christos ventured hesitantly, perchance wondering if he ought to offer it gold-plated. "Mrs Burke, did I mention how beautiful you look today."

"That goes without saying but you needn't lay it on so thick. Fancy words won't get your parsnips buttered."

Clearly aware Christos was engaging in false flattery, nevertheless Violet Burke fluffed up her unnaturally red hair.

"Parsnips?"

"*Pastinakia*," I ventured, offering parsnips in Greek.

"They're a vegetable," Vi said. "If you mash them up, they go right well with a roast chicken."

"What's that got to do with buttering?" Christos appeared more confused than ever.

"Never mind about the parsnips. I'm going to need to hear some proper talk of hard cash if you want me back." The death stare accompanying Vi's words left no doubt that she was all business.

"I'm willing to pay you an extra twenty cents an hour…" Christos suggested.

"Make it a euro," Vi countered.

"Forty cents…"

"Eighty…"

"Fifty…"

"I'll shake on seventy-five and that's my last word," Vi declared, staring Christos down with a steely look.

"Done," Christos agreed, holding his hand out.

"I'll give the actual shake a miss. You're looking even oilier than usual, lad."

"Let me show you out," I said to Christos, steering him towards the door before he could turn his attention from my mother to Marigold. Now he was footloose and fancy-free again, I didn't want him littering my kitchen for a minute longer than necessary. Fortunately, Christos appeared just as keen to leave as I was to see the back of him.

"I'll see you in the morning, Mrs Burke," Christos called out.

"That you will, lad."

Returning to the kitchen after seeing Christos out, I saw that Vi was beaming widely. "That Christos is such a sucker. I'd have settled for fifty cents an hour," she chortled. "Now, who's for a nip of this brandy?"

"Not for me. I'm in charge of the deep fat fryer again this evening," I said as Vi and Marigold triumphantly raised a toast to getting one over on Christos. It warmed my cockles to see the two of them getting along so famously.

"So, you're helping Dina out again, lad?" Vi asked.

"Yes, she's still dreadfully upset about Eleni leaving and taking the children."

"I know. Poor Dina was blubbing again while I was peeling the spuds earlier. I'm surprised that wife of yours hasn't put her foot down about you gadding about again this evening…"

"I am right here, Vi. Not to mention that it was you who volunteered Victor's services in the first place," Marigold pointed out, refusing to be affronted by her mother-in-law's dig.

"Well, the money's not to be sniffed at," Vi remarked, even though I suspected she coined in a better hourly rate at the taverna than I did. On reflection, it occurred to me that I was probably working in the taverna for free as a favour.

"Actually, it's turned out quite well," Marigold said. "I've tasked Victor with reporting back to me on Sherry's date with Vasos."

BUCKET TO GREECE (VOL.17)

"Sherry's going on a date with my old mucker, Vasos? I'm not sure what to make of that," Vi said, her face screwed up in what could be either disapproval or indigestion. "'Appen he could do better for himself. That Sherry can bore the hind leg off a donkey."

"Well, since Vasos won't be able to understand anything that Sherry witters on about, she's unlikely to bore him," I pointed out.

"And I do think it's a bit harsh to say Vasos could do better," Marigold added. "Whilst I've always liked him, I've never thought of him as anything remotely like a catch. He strikes me as a bit of a disaster when it comes to women."

"Not a catch? You must want your head examining. You're way off the mark there, lass. There ain't many fellas that have their own yachts to boast about. Still, I reckon on reflection that Sherry deserves a decent fella to put a smile on her face after what she put up with from that freeloading German hippie. So, where are the two of them off to on this here date?"

"Obviously, to the taverna or Victor wouldn't be able to spy on them."

"'Appen I'll mosey along there myself later..."

"I'm sure they won't welcome a gooseberry," Marigold objected. I was surprised that Marigold hadn't come up with some excuse for stepping into the role of a fly on the taverna wall herself.

"Who said owt about playing a third wheel? It just so 'appens I'm in the mood for a plate of chips."

"Is there something amiss with your frying pan, Mother?"

"Less of your sarcasm, lad."

"I don't think Sherry will appreciate you crashing her date. It could make her very self-conscious," Marigold said. Her eyes took on a glint as she added, "But I suppose you could report back to me, Vi. I expect that Victor will be about as much use as a chocolate teapot in relaying how the date goes. He probably won't notice if there are any romantic sparks flying."

"Not unless they land in the deep fat fryer. 'Appen I can keep Dina company in the kitchen and spy from there," Vi mulled. "Hang on a sec, something's vibrating in my pinny."

Whipping out her mobile phone, Violet Burke greeted Yiota loudly. After listening to Yiota with bated breath, Vi immediately adopted a concerned grandmotherly tone, telling the young woman to calm herself down and reassuring her it wasn't her fault. As Vi moved over to the balcony for a better reception, Marigold asked me if I knew why Yiota needed to calm down.

"Yiota was out in the tractor earlier and knocked Giannis off his push bike..."

"Oh, no!" Marigold exclaimed, the colour draining from her face. "Was Giannis injured?"

"He may have possibly broken his wrist and his ankle," I replied. "Hal drove the three of them up to the hospital. They'll need to X-ray Giannis to determine exactly what is broken."

"You might have mentioned this earlier, Victor. You can see that I'm knee-deep in making a trifle for Giannis..."

"Well, I very much doubt that his injuries will have affected his appetite," I pointed out as Vi returned to the kitchen.

"That was Yiota," Vi said as though the two of us were in the dark despite her mentioning Yiota's name endless times during her call. "That poor lass. She was calling me from the hospital. She's only gone and knocked Giannis off his bicycle with that bloomin' great tractor…"

"Yes, I was just telling Marigold."

"You knew about it and said nowt?"

"I was over at Yiota's when it happened. I helped to scrape Giannis off the road and into the pickup."

"Well, Yiota's feeling that guilty that she's insisting Giannis must move in with her till he's better. She reckons he'll find it too difficult to fend for himself with a broken wrist, what with his mother being away. Course, I can always pop round and give the lad a hand in the shower," my mother said with a lewd wink.

"Really, Vi." The shocked tone Marigold affected was anything but sincere. No doubt most of the women in the village would be willing to pop round to Yiota's to help the dishy honey man out with his ablutions.

"Did Yiota say anything about Giannis' ankle?" I asked.

"Nowt but a sprain…"

"To be honest, I'm surprised Yiota wants to have anything to do with Giannis after the way he was carrying on earlier," I observed. "She must have a very forgiving nature."

"What on earth do you mean?" Marigold asked. "You

do realise he's Yiota's boyfriend or did that salient fact go over your head? Naturally, she'll want to extend a helping hand to her partner and look after him."

"Giannis was in the vilest of tempers after coming off the bike. He said some terrible things to Yiota...he was downright nasty. She was already feeling dismally guilty even though it was an accident. Giannis' words were very cutting."

"She didn't say nowt about that to me," Vi said, a look of concern on her face. "I'll have his guts if he's been upsetting the lass."

"He certainly went down in my estimation over the way he spoke to Yiota. At the very least, he owes her a grovelling apology," I said. I couldn't help wondering if by chance Giannis had inherited the unpleasant side of his grandfather Haralambos' character. If he had, he had hidden it well until today, always presenting as a personable and amiable young man who would go out of his way to extend a helping hand when one was needed.

"I expect that whatever Giannis said was in the heat of the moment," Marigold opined. "Perhaps his life flashed before him in the face of that great big tractor."

"Aye, 'appen." My mother certainly didn't look convinced. No doubt she intended to get to the bottom of things rather than letting Giannis off the hook as quickly as Marigold had. "Yiota's a strong woman who won't take any bollocks, but when it comes to that Giannis, she's got a blind spot."

"She's most definitely a strong woman," I concurred. "Look at the way she took over the farm with no experience, determined to make a success of it."

"Aye, she's making a right go of it and she doesn't let that Guzim twist her round his little finger like some folk I could mention."

"Are you having a dig at me, Mother?"

"Well, lad, if the cap fits."

"Right, I'd best be getting off," Vi declared, adjusting her tweed. "I promised Yiota I'd pop round to her place and make up the bed in the spare room for Giannis..."

"Surely that's not necessary, Vi?" Marigold posited. "Not with Yiota and Giannis being an item..."

"Aye, it is. Yiota doesn't want her uncle knowing she's sharing her bed with Giannis."

"That's rather reminiscent of the days when Barry used to pretend that he was sleeping on our sofa when he was courting Cynthia," I said.

"And the daft lad fooled no one," Vi quipped, grabbing the bottle of *Metaxa* and the bunch of plastic flowers. "You might as well have these chocs, Marigold. I'm watching my diet."

"You're very welcome to join us at the new Slimming Club, Vi. We have our first meeting this week."

"Are you implying I'm fat?" Vi scoffed. "Anyway, I doubt any dieting will get done with you lot. It sounds like another excuse for you ladies of leisure to sit around drinking coffee and guzzle cakes." My mother's observation was nothing if not astute.

"Don't forget to report back on Sherry's date with Vasos," Marigold reminded my mother as Vi left. "Pass me the custard powder, Victor. I might as well finish this trifle for Giannis. He's lucky to only have suffered a broken wrist."

"Well, he may well be left with a scar on his forehead."

"He's lucky he's a man, then. A scar can be very sexy on a man, it can add such a distinguished air. Just look at that Robin Ellis fellow in 'Poldark.'"

"But his scar was just makeup for the telly," I pointed out without teasing my wife that I knew all about the crush she used to have on the 'Poldark' actor.

Whilst Marigold whipped up the custard, I took a telephone call from Hal telling me the three of them were still in the hospital. After waiting for several hours, Giannis had been duly X-rayed and was now waiting for the doctor to manipulate the fractured wrist back into place.

"It has been bedlam here," Hal told me. "A school football team was here to get their TB injections…"

"TB?" I queried.

"They cannot play without them," Hal said. "I have never seen so much acne in one place."

"It's probably down to teenage testosterone," I quipped.

"Ah, the doctor has finally come to fix Giannis' wrist. Giannis is lucky it was a nice clean break."

"Has he apologised to Yiota for the way he spoke to her?"

"Well, he's stopped his griping but hasn't come out with anything I'd call a proper apology. He'll be getting his comeuppance any minute, though. The doctor is positioning his elbow and wrist as we speak, ready to yank it back into place…"

The rest of Hal's sentence was drowned out by the

sound of someone screaming like a banshee. As the scream echoed around my kitchen, it was followed by a string of Greek expletives.

"The doctor is just telling Giannis that when he told him manipulating the wrist back into place wouldn't hurt, he was lying," Hal said in a satisfied tone. "Did you hear the way he screamed like a big girl's blouse?"

Clearly, Hal had been spending more time with Violet Burke than I realised, her northern vernacular evident in his words.

"Indeed, I heard him screaming," I confirmed, thinking Giannis' agony might serve as a decent payback for the way he'd spoken to Yiota.

"Right, they just need to put the plaster on and then we are out of here," Hal told me.

"My mother has just popped round to yours to make up a bed for Giannis."

Hal snorted. "Yiota won't want to offend Violet's sensibilities by letting on that she'll be sharing a bed with Giannis."

"Indeed, my mother can be a bit of a prude," I fibbed, greatly amused by the way that the youngsters thought they had pulled the wool over the eyes of their elders.

Chapter 15

A Stroll Down Memory Lane

Abandoning the trifle and leaving the custard bereft of its whipped cream topping, Marigold decided to accompany me to meet Pelham and Bill. Motivated by her conviction that there was something decidedly dodgy about Pelham holidaying with a chap, Marigold wanted to investigate first-hand, rather than, as she put it, getting a half-baked tale from me. My ex-co-worker had telephoned to say they were almost at the village, having taken a public bus from Athens to town and another bus down to the coast, before winging the final leg to Meli in a taxi. The two of us jumped in the Punto, eager to settle our second lot of paying guests into the Sofia Apartments.

BUCKET TO GREECE (VOL.17)

It was lucky that I was driving slowly when, without warning, something splattered against the windscreen with a resounding thwack. Slamming the brakes on hard, I winced before warning Marigold, "Don't look, darling. It's positively gross."

Staring intently ahead and seemingly taking the flying object in her stride, Marigold didn't even cringe as she said, "I know it goes against the grain to say I hope it's not dead, but Cynthia will have a fit if you've killed it."

"The screaming habdabs at the very least," I agreed. "Technically it would count as death by suicide but can you imagine? We'd never hear the end of it."

"Not only is it still alive, it doesn't even appear to be stunned. What on earth has the vile creature got in its mouth?" Marigold asked without even wincing as she peered through the blood-smeared windscreen.

"The revolting mutant," I began, referencing Cynthia's vile cat, Kouneli, "appears to have sunk its fangs into a headless pigeon."

I could have kicked myself for not taking a closer look at the pigeon Nikos had shoved into a bin bag that morning. It was impossible for me to discern if the headless corpse that Kouneli was now mauling on my bonnet was the same one from earlier. It would be beyond bizarre if the village was suffering a glut of decapitated pigeons. If indeed it was a different bird, I would have to conclude there was an insane bird executioner on the loose in Meli.

Firing a venomous look in my direction, Kouneli leapt from the bonnet with the pigeon still clamped between its teeth, darting away into the undergrowth. Aware that we needed to get a move on to greet Pelham, I settled for using the windscreen wipers to remove the bloody evidence of Kouneli's crime.

"Do you think Kouneli bit the pigeon's head off?" Marigold wondered aloud.

"I suspect there's more to it than that," I replied, giving Marigold the low-down on the dirty tricks that someone was playing on Nikos.

"I wonder if Kostis is behind it?" Admittedly, Marigold was a tad biased, having never forgiven Kostis for taking a potshot at Catastrophe, resulting in the pampered cat requiring a caudectomy. Even now, Catastrophe's balance was still out of kilter.

"Nikos doesn't believe that Kostis has anything to do with it. Kostis hasn't been seen in the village since Nikos threw him out."

"Well, if you ask me, it's a bit of a coincidence," Marigold mulled as I pulled in beside the taxi parked opposite the taverna, indicating to the driver that he should follow me.

Leading the way up the hill towards Sofia's, I felt a surge of pride at the sight of the apartments, transformed from a run-down abandoned house into luxurious holiday accommodation. Naturally, Barry and I couldn't take all the credit: we had benefited enormously from the help that Vangelis and Blat had given, not to mention additional assistance from Marigold, Cynthia and Doreen. Even Guzim had played his part, and Spiros may or may not have bunged a few officials the odd brown envelope of my hard-earned cash to speed up the permissions. I preferred to know nothing about the latter, thus rendering myself free from guilt by association.

Alighting from the Punto, we watched as Pelham handed some cash to the taxi driver.

"Are you sure that Pelham said he was arriving with a man called Bill?" Marigold queried as a woman stepped out of the taxi. "That's not another man..."

"And it's definitely not his wife, Lydia," I added, noting the woman was pleasantly plump compared to Pelham's scrawny wife. Taking in her face full of freckles and a shortish blonde bob glossy enough to rival Cynthia's locks, my immediate impression was that the stranger was the outdoor type.

"Perhaps Pelham is a bit of a dark horse," Marigold speculated. "Do you suppose that's his piece on the side?"

"You sound just like my mother. Let's wait and see."

As Pelham joined the woman, I noticed he hadn't changed much since I'd last seen him. About ten years younger than me, the stuffy way he carried himself added an extra ten years to his image. He seemed as pasty as ever, the only marked difference being that his receding hairline had receded quite a bit further, his bald patch glowing shiny red with the tell-tale sign of painful sunburn.

The taxi driver called out a cheery, "Auf Wiedersehen," before driving off.

"Perhaps she's German," Marigold hissed.

Certainly, the woman's hearing was sharp enough to catch Marigold's comment.

"Hello, there. I'm English, not German," she breezily declared with a wide grin. "I've no idea why that cabbie kept trying to talk to me in German. I couldn't understand a word that he said. Mind you, if he'd talked in Greek, it would have gone way over my head too."

As the woman turned to help Pelham with their luggage, Marigold whispered in my ear, "He probably assumed she was German because she cultivates her armpit hair."

"Oh." Swivelling around, I caught Marigold's drift. Having once seen it, it was a sight I couldn't un-see.

"Victor. Good to see you again," Pelham greeted me with a limp, damp handshake. "You're a lifesaver having a place in the countryside. After clocking the most important sites, neither of us could get on with Athens. Too hot and crowded."

"You should see it in August," I replied, thinking his long, beige belted Macintosh, was hardly appropriate attire for a Greek summer. If he'd paired the unsuitable coat with a fedora, at least he would have protected his head from sunburn.

"But the Acropolis and the Parthenon were quite magnificent," the woman gushed with a genuinely warm smile, sticking her arms through the straps of an enormous rucksack, a couple of pairs of hiking boots dangling from the lumpy-looking travel bag.

"This is my sister, Bill," Pelham said by way of introduction.

"Bill is your sister," I parroted.

"It's short for Wilhelmina," Bill said, rolling her eyes. "I can't stand it. It's such a stupid name, not to mention a mouthful. Our parents had the most outlandish taste in names.

Poor Pelham got the worst of it as father was going through his P.G. Wodehouse phase, hence my brother got saddled with Pelham Grenville.

"There was a Wilhelmina in 'Malory Towers,'" Marigold commented.

"So absurd that anyone wants to ban Enid Blyton," Bill piped up.

"Well, it's good to see you again, Pel..."

"It's Pelham," Pelham corrected me.

"And lovely to meet you, Wilhelmena."

"It's Bill," she corrected me. "And likewise, lovely to meet you too, Vic and Marigold. "I've heard so much about you."

"It's Victor," I corrected her.

Unfortunately, I couldn't reciprocate Bill's sentiments since I'd been clueless to the existence of Pelham's sister until this very moment. Indeed, they struck me as an odd pair of siblings. Right off the bat, I could tell that Bill was charming and confident, whilst Pelham tended to hold back. Moreover, he was an absolute stickler for rules and noticeably self-effacing, his general timidity often fooling restaurant and takeaway owners into presuming he was a bit of a walkover: he was anything but when it came to handing out star ratings.

"Let me show you the apartment," Marigold offered. "Everything is brand spanking new. You'll be the first people to stay in it."

"What an honour," Bill declared with no trace of sarcasm.

"I should have asked on the phone..." Pelham began as we followed Marigold.

"Asked what?"

"If the apartment has an adequate kitchen for self-catering."

"It does indeed," I confirmed.

"Pelham, we'll most definitely be eating out some of the time," Bill said authoritatively. "I'm not spending all my time cooking. This is my holiday too and you know how much I enjoy trying out new restaurants. You'll just have to get over your phobia of dining out."

"But how am I supposed to know if these foreign kitchens are up to scratch?" Pelham asked. "They could get up to anything."

"Victor was like that too when we first moved abroad..." Marigold said as we entered the apartment, immediately leading the way through to the kitchen in a bid to quell Pelham's visible anxiety.

"I've been trying to persuade Pelham to try hypnosis to allay his fears," Bill said.

The siblings gushed with praise as they explored the apartment, Pelham ecstatic with the kitchen. Nevertheless, even though the pair appeared to be more than satisfied with their accommodation, I worried that we may well lose the booking. Bill's insistence that she wanted the two of them to try out new restaurants dinged an alarm bell, since there was only the one taverna in the village and they didn't have a hire car. Bill may well expect our local to be a bit more up-market and Pelham may not be as easily won over by Nikos' place as I had been. Pelham had form for being a tad over the top when it came to germaphobia, an excellent trait in his profession but a definite impediment when it came to the personal. My anxiety was assuaged when Pelham announced that a car hire company was dropping off a vehicle the next morning.

"I'll be happy to compile a list of tavernas further afield that I can recommend…" I offered.

"You just know they'll be hygienic if Victor has given them his seal of approval," Marigold said before getting down to the nitty-gritty of why Pelham was holidaying without his wife. "So, no Lydia. Is she poorly?"

"Lydia and Pelham went their separate ways three years ago," Bill revealed sotto voce whilst Pelham continued to explore the kitchen. "I'm afraid that Pelham's obsession with hygiene got too much for her. She was practically afraid to breathe in case she inhaled bacteria-laden air. She's doing so much better since the divorce and at least it was amicable. I ran into her in the Arndale Centre a month or so ago and we had coffee together. She'd never have done that before. With a bit of meat on her bones, she didn't look half as spindly as she used to."

"Victor used to be a real worrywart when it came to eating out due to his hygiene concerns but he's mellowed so much since he hung up his hair net," Marigold said, beaming with pride as though I was an obstinate child that had grown out of a bad habit. "Now, who's for a cuppa? I'll put the kettle on. Victor, show Pelham the garden and I'll bring the tea out." Knowing my wife as I do, I realised she was trying to get rid of Pelham so she could interrogate Bill and glean some more insight into the divorce.

V.D. BUCKET

Sinking into our seats at the patio table, Pelham visibly relaxed as he breathed in the wonderful scent of herbs which Marigold had planted, and drank in the blissful peace only disturbed by the lilting tinkle of goats' bells in the distance and the cicadas singing in the olive trees. Naturally, I was keen to catch up and find out what I'd been missing in the fascinating world of inspecting grubby kitchens.

Recounting his latest adventures in the exciting domain of public health inspecting, I was just a tad jealous that Pelham had recently discovered a thick layer of mould inside a cooling fan, blowing contaminated air all over the food preparation area. I had always considered the restaurant a tad dodgy, but never been able to pin anything down other than minor infractions. The mould, combined with the crumbling grout parting ways with the tiled area and falling into the pans on the hob, was enough for Pelham to have grounds to close the restaurant down. There was always a certain satisfaction in closing a place down, even if it was only on a temporary basis until the hygiene violations could be rectified.

Since Pelham tended to veer towards the timid, I had often wondered how he had the nerve to stand up to some of the more bolshie restaurant and takeaway owners. I was touched beyond measure when Pelham told me that I was sorely missed at work.

"You know, Victor, when I first joined the team, I learnt a lot from watching you in action. As I grew more confident in the role, I tried to replicate my approach to the job on you. You were an excellent role model, a consummate professional at all times."

Swallowing the lump in my throat, I accepted his compliment. "Most kind of you to say."

"Have you had the chance to connect with any Greek public health inspectors?" Pelham enquired.

"I've met the one who inspected the *kafenion* and *taverna* in this village…"

"And did he pass them?"

"He passed the *taverna* right off the bat but there were some toilet issues which had to be sorted before the *kafenion* got the all clear." I was relieved to assure Pelham that there was no question regarding their current status. If I'd reported an issue, I was certain that Pelham would spend the rest of his Greek foray self-catering, refusing to leave the apartment kitchen.

Pelham was greatly amused as I recounted almost exceeding my non-existent authority that morning when I'd mistakenly identified one of Maria's false eyelashes as a fat brown bug that had no place in the *kafenion kouzina*. "Sometimes, it is easy to forget that I have no right to barge into kitchens over here, and no actual authority to close places down."

"I'll need to bear that in mind myself if Bill succeeds in dragging me into strange places," Pelham said.

"Thanasis, the Greek public health inspector, is an amiable youngster. Whilst still a bit wet behind the ears, he demonstrated his honourable character by turning down the brown envelope Manolis tried to bribe him with, thus putting the job before money."

"That's the ticket," Pelham said. "I suppose there are corrupt individuals in most countries, expecting to pay their way out of a necessary closure. I'm particularly proud that our office has never had so much as a single inspector accepting a bribe, at least that we know about."

"There's certainly no place in our industry for anyone who would be prepared to put their personal fortunes above the public good," I concurred. "I hold the view that public health inspectors tend to be in it for the calling, rather like doctors."

"Spot on, Vic," Pelham agreed.

"It's Victor," I reminded him.

Work chatter ceased momentarily when Marigold arrived and put the tea on the table before offering to show Bill the various floral blooms in the garden. Presumably, my wife hadn't finished interrogating Bill yet.

I felt a buzz of excitement when Pelham confided, "I had an appalling case of mop sink chicken about a month ago."

"A nasty business indeed. And of course it's not just limited to chicken. There's also mop sink prawns."

For those not familiar with the technical jargon associated with public health inspecting, mop sink chicken is a term referring to the nasty habit of defrosting chickens in the sink designated solely for filling and emptying mop buckets. This deplorable practice usually results in a strict dressing down for the owner and the summary dismissal of the guilty employee.

Recalling my own encounter with mop sink chicken, I told Pelham about the time an Indian restaurant employed a shifty individual from Bangladesh as a cleaner. Said fellow neither spoke nor understood a word of English and was totally clueless when it came to hygiene standards.

"Can you believe he mopped the kitchen floor with the same mop he used to clean the toilets?" I said. "I kid you not, after mopping the toilets, he swiped the same mop over the food preparation surface. If I hadn't caught him in the act, he could have wiped out half the population of Manchester. Naturally, I insisted he was fired on the spot. The owner tried to defend him because the cleaner was his wife's nephew but I made it clear that someone with a demonstrably ignorant understanding of hygiene had no place working within even a whiff of food. He reminded me of a Bangladeshi Manuel from 'Fawlty Towers.'

"I've run into many Manuel types over the years, representing a variety of nationalities, though oddly enough, I've never run into a Spanish Manuel," Pelham said.

"Me neither."

"Did you know that mop sink chicken is big in the States too? I had an interesting email chat with Walt, a public health inspector based in Arkansas. Did you know there's a small town in that state called Greasy Corner?"

"I wonder if there's a greasy spoon in Greasy Corner?" I quipped. "It sounds like the sort of place my mother would enjoy. She's big on mucky fat and chips."

"Walt was telling me all about a restaurant owner in Arkansas and how, apparently, it's legal there to eat roadkill. Anyway, this one restaurant owner encouraged the locals to slip any roadkill his way and in return, he'd bung them some easy cash. When anyone turned up at his back door with some fresh roadkill, he'd feed it through the sausage machine and turn it into bangers. It turned out that some of the roadkill wasn't the result of an accidental encounter, some drivers going out of their way to hit anything which may result in a cash payment. Walt told me it was the height of hilarity to hear a bunch of rednecks singing the praise of roadkill by extolling the virtue of meat that was free of additives and antibiotics."

"You can rest assured that if you eat in the local taverna, the meat that Nikos rears is totally organic," I told Pelham as the ladies joined us to drink tea.

"I might have guessed the two of you would be talking shop," Marigold said. Turning to Bill, Marigold added, "Even though Victor is retired, he still insists on keeping up to date by reading about all the most recent developments in food safety hygiene."

"It's enough to bore the hind legs off a donkey," Bill said bluntly.

"Well, I happen to retain an interest," I said. "After all, it's a fascinating subject..."

"Only to the two of you," Marigold remarked.

"You wouldn't be so dismissive if you were laid up with a nasty bout of Salmonella," I said.

"Or Shigella," Pelham added. "Victor, did you read the latest research on the dangers of blowing out birthday cake candles?"

"The dangers of blowing out birthday cake candles," Bill repeated, making no attempt to hide her eye-roll. "Whatever next?"

"It's just common sense," I said.

"I don't get it..." Bill replied.

"The saliva of the person blowing out the candles

becomes aerosolised and lands on the icing..." I explained.

"And if the person blowing the candles out is particularly snotty or has something infectious, their bacteria-laden spit adds that something extra," Pelham added. "One really might as well just spit all over the cake and have done."

"It's at times like this that I can understand why Lydia became terrified of food," Bill said. "You can't go through life seeing health hazards at every turn."

"It pays to be precautious," I argued.

"The birthday candle thing is nothing new," Marigold said. "Victor's been harping on about it for years. He used to try and confiscate any birthday cake that Benjamin brought home from a party in case the birthday boy had been particularly snotty."

"Now, that's what I call a very wise precaution," Pelham backed me up. "Victor, do you remember that time when most of the children who attended a birthday party at a pizza place came down with a bad case of gastro?"

"Oh goodness. That brings back some memories," I said. "And we couldn't find a single health violation when we investigated. The kitchen was spotless and all the food was stored in exact compliance with safety laws."

"I recall at the time that you suspected the birthday cake..."

"But there was no way to test it since the children had devoured the whole thing."

"You were ahead of the times in your thinking, Vic," Pelham praised.

V.D. BUCKET

"I think the two of you have gone too far in your stroll down the memory lane of the Food Standards Agency," Bill bluntly declared. "Now, do tell us how you discovered this wonderful village and made the move to Greece."

Chapter 16

A Blithering Idiot

Strolling towards the taverna for my evening shift, I ran into Nikos, once again sifting through a pile of stinking rubbish that had been summarily dumped in one of his roadside fields. The foul mix of rancid food and the contents of bathroom bins desecrated the lush greenery.

As Nikos shoved the rotting mess into a bin bag, his constant string of colourful expletives was rather muffled behind his improvised face mask: fashioned out of a bandana, the mask was an absolute necessity to counteract the grossly rank smell. Without similar protection, I felt a twinge of nausea as the revolting stench drifted my way on the slightest of breezes, leading me to believe whoever had dumped the rubbish, had left it to stew and fester for a while.

Even though Nikos was Marigolded up in bright yellow rubber gloves, I made a mental note to ensure that the taverna owner had more than a quick rinse before going anywhere near the outdoor grill with the chosen meat of the day. Despite the rubber gloves, it would probably be wise for Nikos to give his hands a thorough sterilising with some of his homemade *raki*, in addition to soap and water.

"Victor, I am at the end of my tethered," Nikos greeted me. Wiping the back of his hand across his forehead, he left a trail of green slime in its wake. "He is the fourth bag today of the, how to say in the English, *skoupidia?*"

"Rubbish," I translated. "Have you still no idea who's behind it?"

"Yes..."

"Who is it?"

"I don't know..."

"But, you just said yes when I asked if you knew who is responsible..."

"I said yes to agree I had no idea."

"It's all semantics anyway." Seeing the confusion on Nikos' face, I added, "Oh, never mind. Do you really think it is someone with a vendetta against you? Think hard. Do you have any known enemies?"

"I cannot to think of any the enemy. I get along with everyone."

"That's true. You even muddle along with my mother."

"The Violet is a woman to admire." Furrowing his

now green brow, Nikos appeared deep in contemplation before announcing, "Wait, I did come to the blow with the Sotiris…"

"Ah, now we're getting somewhere…"

"But that was back in the 70s…"

"It seems a long time to hold a grudge…"

"And the Sotiris move to the Australia…I think I hear he is dead." It appeared the only possible culprit that Nikos could rustle up, could be ruled out as a suspect. "Victor, you want to help me clean this mess?"

"Do you have a spare pair of Marigolds?"

"What has your wife to do with it?"

"No, not Marigold…Marigolds. The yellow gloves you are wearing. Do you have another pair on you?"

"No."

"Then I really can't help you out since I'm on my way to handling food in your kitchen. I couldn't possibly risk transferring bacteria onto your customers' food. Perhaps you could bung Guzim a couple of euros to clean up your fields and scrub your graffitied walls if this mindless vandalism continues…he's used to sticking his hands in chicken manure. A bit of muck never bothers him."

"You think he could to be the discreet and not tell the Dina? I cannot to see her more upset."

"I'm sure you can pay him for his silence," I assured Nikos before continuing on to the taverna with a cheery wave, relieved beyond measure that whoever was so openly taunting Nikos, apparently had no beef with me. I believed it was no random attack: all the evidence thus far led me to conclude that it could hardly be a coincidence that every targeted field and wall belonged to the taverna owner.

Reaching my destination, I found the place deserted bar Dina, busy slicing thin rounds of green peppers for the Greek salad. Mustering a weak smile, Dina told me she was delighted to see me whilst insisting she felt strong enough to manage the kitchen duties on her own. However, when I asked if she had heard from Eleni, Dina's tears started flowing again as she lamented how much she was missing her daughter-in-law and her grandchildren. It particularly upset Dina that she was missing any important milestones with the new baby, Dina, named in her honour. At least Dina had no clue about the nasty campaign targeting Nikos. She had quite enough on her mind to worry about as it was, without piling more tribulations on her. It struck me that Nikos really was an exemplary and protective husband, going out of his way to shield his wife from any further angst.

The arrival of Barry took me by surprise and brought a genuine smile to Dina's face. After asking Barry to fill her in on all the news about Anastasia, she appeared much calmer when Barry said he needed to speak to me urgently.

"*Pigaine. Pigaine,*" Dina ordered, practically shooing the pair of us out of her kitchen as she told me to go. I gathered that even though Dina didn't have enough English to eavesdrop, she respected our right to privacy. I should add that Dina's English language skills comprised nothing more than the odd word she had picked up from my mother, but unlike Vasos, she actually understood the English words she uttered.

BUCKET TO GREECE (VOL.17)

Stepping out of the kitchen with my brother-in-law, I was a tad puzzled when he asked me what was so urgent that I'd insisted on dragging him out of his home.

"You've lost me, Barry. I've no idea what you're talking about," I said as the two of us hovered in the taverna doorway.

"Marigold phoned and told me you needed to see me urgently and that I'd find you here."

"Perhaps you've got builders' grime in your ears, Barry. I never said any such thing."

"But Marigold was most insistent. She made it sound like a matter of life or death..."

"Let me give her a quick call and see if I can get to the bottom of this," I said. "Darn, it's engaged. I'll try again in a minute."

As the two of us waited for Marigold to stop gabbing and free up the line, Barry revealed, "Kouneli arrived home earlier with a headless pigeon corpse jammed in its mouth..."

"Hmm." I considered it best to keep my own counsel about my earlier encounter with Cynthia's detestable cat. I'd never hear the end of it if the mutant feline had given itself a nasty case of concussion by flinging itself on my windscreen.

"I was worried that it might scare Anastasia, but my daughter has spirit." Barry practically swelled with pride as he spoke. "She found it quite hilarious to watch Kouneli desperately shake its head from side to side in an effort to eject the bird. When I finally intervened and managed to prise the pigeon free, Kouneli looked like something out of a horror movie."

"So, nothing new there then," I quipped.

"Vivid red blood was dried on all around Kouneli's mouth, mangled feathers sticking to it as though the blood was glue."

"I wonder if the pigeon had sticky blood syndrome which can make blood gluelike. I really don't know if it's a condition found in birds." Since Barry appeared clueless about Kouneli's encounter with the Punto, I felt it safe to proffer some advice. "It might be a good idea to get the cat checked out by a veterinarian. The pigeon could well have been diseased. If it was sickly, it may have transmitted something nasty to Cynthia's cat. I'd hate to think of Ana catching anything."

Staring at me as though I'd lost the plot, Barry said, "I doubt there's some peculiar disease going around that results in pigeons losing their heads."

"Well, either Kouneli bit the pigeon's head off or the bird was a victim of the mindless moron who has been lobbing decapitated pigeons in Nikos' fields."

"It seems whoever has targeted Nikos, has upped his game. A nasty business."

After discussing the abominable vendetta against poor Nikos with Barry some more, I finally managed to get hold of Marigold on the phone. Stepping outside, I said, "Marigold, why on earth did you tell Barry that I needed to see him urgently?"

"Because you do, Victor. Honestly, you have a mind like a sieve. Surely, you've not forgotten about our chat earlier when you agreed to probe into the state of Barry and Cynthia's marriage?"

"Seriously? You consider that urgent? I told you if

there's any probing to be done, you should do it. You are his sister after all."

"But Barry thinks of you as a brother. I really think man-to-man is the best way to go, Victor. Just think how awful it would be if Cynthia left Barry and took Anastasia away from her father."

"This is going to be so embarrassing," I snapped. "And there's no point fluttering your eyelashes down the phone line, Marigold."

"I'm not."

"You most certainly are. After so many years together, I'm well up on all your little tricks."

"So, you'll do it," Marigold pressed, no doubt still batting her eyelashes down the telephone line. In her defence, Marigold's eyelashes were genuinely her own, unlike the fake ones which Maria had been planning to glue into place in the *kafenion* kitchen.

"I'll give it a go if it will stop you worrying needlessly," I reluctantly agreed. Stepping back into the taverna, I girded myself to interrogate my brother-in-law, despite my discomfort. Deliberately avoiding Barry's eye, I adopted a nonchalant tone to ask him, "How are things between you and Cynthia?"

"What do you mean?"

"Just wondering if everything is fine with your marriage...any problems to speak of?"

"Why on earth would you ask me that? Has Cynthia said something?" Barry's tone expressed his annoyance at the surprising turn of our conversation. "I don't believe this. If Cynthia is unhappy, why would she confide in you instead of talking to me directly?"

"I've never discussed your marriage with Cynthia. As far as I know, she's still head over heels for you."

"Then why are you bringing it up?"

"Blame your sister. Marigold insisted I ask you."

"So, you're saying that Cynthia has been confiding in Marigold?" Barry's jaw clenched in annoyance as he spoke.

"Absolutely not. Look, I'll come clean. Marigold has got some ridiculous bee in her bonnet." I inwardly cringed at my unfortunate choice of vocabulary, any mention of bonnets reminding me of the frilly pink monstrosity I'd been wearing when I was discovered abandoned in a bucket. "Eleni leaving Kostis and going back to her parents' house with the babies, hit a nerve with your sister. She's worried about Cynthia leaving and taking Ana away. You know how Marigold dotes on Ana...she just couldn't bear to lose her."

"So, you're certain that Cynthia really hasn't been talking to you or Marigold about our marriage."

"Most definitely not. As I said, Marigold just worked herself up into a bit of state. You know what she's like."

"If Marigold is so worried, why didn't she ask me herself instead of having you do her dirty work?"

"She thought you'd prefer to confide in me."

"That's for sure. You know I think of you as a brother," Barry declared. "So, you're positive there was nothing more to it than Marigold working herself into a tizzy?"

"Absolutely nothing," I assured Barry.

"I will be having strong words with my sister. And

as for you, Victor, you shouldn't let Marigold walk all over you."

"Happy wife, happy life. Just because something is an obvious cliché doesn't make it any less true," I said. "Anyway, you're a fine one to talk, Barry. You know how difficult it is to resist Marigold's bidding. She's like a dog with a bone when she's focused on some stuff and nonsense."

"Or like a cat with a pigeon," Barry snorted, his earlier annoyance quelled.

"Remember the time you shredded my manuscript on Marigold's instructions?" I reminded him.

"Yes. But I did you a favour. You said yourself that your second attempt at the book was much better. Right, I'm going home now to my loving wife and my adorable daughter."

"Or you could hang around here...it promises to be quite entertaining later..."

"How so?"

"Sherry is due to have a romantic liaison with Captain Vasos."

"I think I'll give it a miss. Cynthia will be pleased that Sherry is having a date..."

"I thought Cynthia disliked Sherry..."

"That's old news, Victor. Do keep up. The pair of them have bonded over their mutual loathing of chemical weedkillers and their mutual love of composting."

"Indeed. Sherry has become quite fanatical about composting."

"I'm leaving now, Victor."

"Enjoy the rest of your evening."

"I'm sure I will. I plan to go home and romance my wife. Perhaps Marigold's interference has done me a favour after all, by reminding me that I should show my appreciation for Cynthia more often; I'd hate for her to think I take her for granted. When I think about it, I owe Marigold a thank you."

"It was me that did her dirty work by broaching the subject." Despite my protest, no thank you was forthcoming.

"I'll buy a bottle of Nikos' finest *spitiko* from you to take with me."

"I think a shop-bought bottle of wine might be a more romantic gesture," I advised.

"You're right. Cynthia does loathe the use of unnecessary plastic."

As Barry took off in Cynthia's old banger, I spotted Hal approaching. Dressed in slacks with a razor-sharp crease, paired with a short-sleeved button-down, he would have looked exceedingly smart were it not for the excessively muddy wellies ruining the look. Much as I was enjoying getting to know Hal, I rather hoped he wasn't on his way to the taverna: Violet Burke would have a fit if he left a trail of wet mud all over the newly mopped floor.

Stepping back onto the street, I greeted Hal, asking him how the patient was.

"I've left Giannis lounging around on the sofa with Yiota waiting on him hand and foot. I thought I'd give the pair of them some time alone," Hal said with a grimace. "Something in my water tells me that Giannis is going to be lounging around for as long as Yiota is willing to put up with it. It will put extra work on Yiota's shoulders. I don't mind catering for Giannis if it eases Yiota's burden, but if he speaks down to Yiota again, he'll feel more than the sharp end of my tongue."

Hal was such an amiable chap that it was hard to imagine his tongue having a sharp side. Personality-wise, Hal was remarkably easy-going, very much like his brother, Panos. In response to my raised eyebrows, Hal explained, "If he puts a step out of line, he'll feel the weight of my welly up his backside."

"Giannis may not be as much work as you imagine," I said. "Once word gets around about Giannis' accident, I'm sure that all the ladies in the village will be turning up to do the Greek version of meals on wheels, delivering home-cooked food."

"I don't think they will," Hal said glumly. "I'm sure they would have done if Giannis had gone back to his own place. Once word gets around that he's staying with Yiota, they may well consider it an intrusion and keep away."

"In my experience, the village ladies are all in favour of intruding. I know that Marigold plans to pop round with one of her trifles for Giannis." Distracted by the excessive amount of wet mud on Hal's wellies, an odd sight when we hadn't had any rain for weeks, I asked him if he had been helping Yiota out on the farm.

"No, farm work isn't for me. I'm more than happy to play the role of fisherman and housekeeper."

"So, what's with all the mud, Hal?"

"When we got back from the hospital, I took Yiota across to meet Tulipa…"

"Was she happy with the new arrival?"

"It was love at first sight. Yiota is totally smitten with the donkey."

"That is good news. So, what's with the mud?"

"The field I put Tulipa in was awash with mud when I got back from the hospital, practically flooded…"

"But we haven't had any rain."

"The hose leading into Tulipa's water barrel had been left on full and the water had been running all afternoon. The barrel overflowed."

Casting my mind back to earlier, I recalled directing the hosepipe into the barrel but I had no actual recollection of turning the water off before I left.

"Yiota asked me what blithering idiot left the water running." Hal chortled as he said, "I told her, that would be Victor."

Realising I may as well man up and take the barb of blithering idiot on the chin, I confessed. "Guilty as charged. Please accept my sincere apology."

"It's fine, Victor. We're due a summer storm later which will add even more water to the muddy mess in Tulipa's new home. Well, I'd best get on. I promised to pick up Giannis' prescription for painkillers from the pharmacy."

As Hal continued on his way, I reflected that if word of the storm got out, it would likely make for a quiet evening in the taverna. I had a feeling that most of the regulars might not fancy a good soaking.

Chapter 17

Henry the Hoglet

The taverna was still empty of customers when Sherry arrived for her date with Vasos. Epitomising the image of the old idiom, mutton dressed as lamb, Sherry was done up like the dog's dinner in a clingy, sparkling sapphire, sequin number, rather than one of her usual billowing kaftans. Her appearance reminded me of the time when Marigold advised Geraldine to go for the tarty look to repel the marriage proposal of her nylon-haired suitor, Ashley, the chap who was enamoured of examining samples of sexually transmitted diseases under a microscope.

I considered Sherry's outfit more suited to a dark and smoky nightclub than a spit and sawdust taverna, musing that the low-cut neckline could well pose a cardiac threat to the old-timers, unused to having bosoms thrust in their faces. Hoping to avert any medical emergencies, I steered Sherry across to a seat that would ensure only her back was visible to the locals. Admittedly, I was rather tactless when I blurted, "Does Marigold know what you're wearing this evening?"

Ignoring my question, Sherry volleyed a question of her own.

"Is it too much, Victor? I think it could be too much. I've got a cardie with me. Do you think I should tone it down with the cardie?"

"Breathe, Sherry, breathe," I instructed. Since it appeared I was destined to be stuck with hyperventilating women that day, I thanked my lucky stars that Marigold is always nothing if not level-headed, rarely panicking, except understandably, if she spots some type of vermin in the house. "Although I can't claim to be an expert in women's fashion, I do think donning the cardigan will make you feel less conspicuous. You don't want Captain Vasos staring at your cleavage all evening."

The fleeting look of bewilderment crossing Sherry's face made me think that was exactly what she wanted.

"Vasos hasn't arrived yet," I told Sherry.

"I'm terribly early. I wanted to arrive before the place gets packed." In a tremulous tone, Sherry added, "I tend to feel jolly self-conscious walking into a strange place on my lonesome."

Her worry about feeling self-conscious hardly aligned with her choice of venturing out in a totally unsuitable frock that screamed 'look at me.' In an effort to calm her down, I kept my thoughts to myself, assuring Sherry, "Well, you aren't alone. I'll be working here all evening and Vasos will be here soon."

Confident my reassuring words had done the trick, I decided a shot of alcohol wouldn't go amiss: as an aside, since I was in charge of the deep fat fryer, I had no intention of joining Sherry in knocking a drink back. "Let me get you a glass of *spitiko*."

With bread, cheese and olives to soak up the wine, Sherry announced between gulps of *spitiko*, "I had my third Greek lesson this morning."

"How are you finding learning the language?"

"I fully intend to persevere even though it's jolly difficult. I'd really like to be able to chat to Vasos more; his English is only marginally better than my Greek." Sherry's last couple of words were muffled as she tucked heartily into the bread. At the rate she was going, the bread basket would likely be empty before Vasos arrived. I assumed that once Sherry joined my wife and Doreen in the much-exalted new Fat Club, the bread basket may well become a banned item. The number of times the word carbohydrate had recently passed Marigold's lips had been quite excessive.

"Actually, Vasos has no English beyond a few random words he's memorised and uses totally out of context. He generally has no idea what he's saying when he throws out an English word."

"Could that be why he threw a suet dumpling at me? I mean…"

"I know what you mean," I said, thinking that Violet Burke had a lot to answer for. "He does it all the time, it's perfectly harmless. If the two of you really want to strike up a romance, you will each need to work on the other's language."

Holding a fat purple olive at eye level as though giving it the third degree, Sherry mused, "It will be worth it. I really do like Vasos. He's such a kind soul. Even though I can't understand him, he makes me laugh."

Or bray, I silently said to myself, watching as Sherry clamped down on the olive, threatening to dislodge a prominent denture on the pit.

"Luckily Vasos talks a lot with his hands," Sherry cooed. "I know he's not particularly tall, dark and handsome..."

"Well, he's dark. That's one out of three..." I joshed, wondering if Sherry had noticed that Vasos only came up to her shoulder.

"But he has the type of energy I admire. Vasos is such a positive person, definitely a glass half-full..."

Staring at her half-full glass of wine, Sherry swigged the contents in one.

"He certainly exudes positive energy," I agreed. Perhaps I had misjudged Sherry as desperate to date anyone she could label her boyfriend. It seemed evident from her words that it was Vasos' amiable personality which she found attractive. "And as my mother never tires of saying, he comes with his own yacht."

The ensuing bray led me to believe that Sherry was now more comfortable than she had been when she arrived. Marigold would be delighted to hear that I had played a small part in putting her friend at ease.

"I have something for you, Sherry."

"For me? How exciting. What is it?"

"It's an old phrase book I found very useful when we first moved to Greece." Handing the well-thumbed book over, I told Sherry, "I relied on it a lot. I found it very helpful to memorise some of the phrases and try then out on the locals."

"What a good idea. Do you have any phrases you would recommend?"

"I've highlighted some of them with a yellow marker pen." Pointing at a highlighted phrase, I told Sherry, "I got a lot of mileage out of this one: *O prothypourgos sas einai omorfos.*"

"That sounds jolly important. What does it mean?"

"It means 'Your prime minister is very handsome.'"

"I can see how that may come in useful. That young man, Blat, is quite obsessed with Tony Blair."

"Let me find another useful phrase for you. Ah, I don't suppose 'My wife is a vegetarian but plays the piano very well' will be much use to you."

"I could change wife to husband but Vasos isn't a vegetarian. Do you know if he plays the piano, Victor?"

"I think you're getting a bit ahead of yourself. You haven't even had a first date yet and you're already seeing Vasos as your hubby."

"I'm just a bit eager," Sherry confessed.

Pointing to a phrase in the book, I said, "I found this one very useful. *Ena provato echei faei ta santouits mas.*"

"What does it mean?"

"It means, 'A sheep has eaten our sandwiches.'"

"Oh, I can definitely see how that would be jolly handy to know."

"I'd best go and give Dina a hand in the kitchen," I said. Deliberately avoiding Sherry's eye, I suggested, "You might want to button your cardigan up." Fortunately, Sherry's cardie of choice could best be described as frumpy, grey in colour with numerous bobbles. Perchance she had never heard of removing matted-up bobbles with a piece of sticky tape.

I was able to keep an eye on Sherry from my vantage point in the kitchen. Not only was she a massive fidgeter, she was also a dedicated clock-watcher, checking the time on her watch every few minutes. When a couple of tables of regular Greek old-timers turned up, they were naturally curious about the presence of a woman with her back turned. Sherry had never been what you'd call a regular taverna goer or part of the Greek community.

As I served Mathias and his cronies with bread and oregano-speckled feta cheese swimming in olive oil, they resumed the heated argument pertaining to the number of lives a cat enjoyed. I could well imagine the subject would crop up endlessly in the ensuing weeks. I refused to engage yet again: I had found it exasperating enough to spend one evening arguing the toss.

I was taken aback when Spiros arrived with Sampaguita, since the undertaker had earlier shared his intention to whisk his wife off to a romantic setting for a candlelit dinner. Naturally, I was delighted to see Sampaguita again and buoyed up to see Spiros practically glowing in her company. Enveloped in aftershave and with his loving wife on his arm, Spiros stood taller.

"What happened to your plans for a romantic dinner down on the coast?" I asked Spiros.

"The Sampaguita has the enough travel today. We make the romantic evening tomorrow," Spiros replied, waiting patiently as his wife exchanged greetings with everyone. There was no doubt that Sampaguita had by now won most of the locals over, blending into the community rather than sticking out like a sequinned thumb as Sherry was doing. Since marrying Spiros, Sampaguita was afforded a level of respect, as the wife of the undertaker, that had been missing in her early days in Meli when she had often been, as a single female foreigner, the subject of unwarranted gossip.

Spiros used his head to gesticulate towards Sherry, prompting me to mouth, "She's waiting for *Kapetanios* Vasos. They have a date."

"*Bravo*," Spiros said. "We must to celebrate this evening. The Doctor Papadima make the firm offer on the house. The nephew in the *Athina* will to shake on the deal. I am the confident it will all go through quickly. The nephew have all the papers right and the doctor pay in cash. There will be the little something in it for you, Victor, for saving my chop this morning."

"Saving your chop?"

"Your the *brezola*."

"It's bacon, Spiro. I saved your bacon." Quite how Spiros could confuse his *brezola* with his bacon eluded me since the Greek word for bacon was *beikon*. "Anyway, there's no need to split your commission, Spiro. I was happy to help you out."

"It is only the right to give you the cut. The doctor was much the impressed with how you were the professional." That was news to me since Doctor Papadima had definitely conveyed the impression that she considered me a bungling idiot. Moreover, Spiros' words contradicted Violet Burke's second-hand claim that I was pushy and too full of myself. "Maybe I should to pay the Violet Burke some the commission too."

"Don't say you had my mother showing her the house as well?"

"No. But the Violet really sell the doctor on the village as the much good place to live. She talk up how welcome Meli is to the foreign."

"Foreign as in anyone not born in the village," I queried.

"*Akrivos*," Spiros confirmed by saying exactly.

"I'm impressed that my mother has such hidden talents." Certainly, as a foreigner, a foreigner with a bolshie personality to boot, Violet Burke had been accepted as part of the village community at a much quicker pace than the other immigrants, something I attributed to her down-to-earth, no-nonsense, attitude, coupled with her total lack of airs and graces.

As Sampaguita joined us, I noticed she appeared less bashful, addressing me as Victor rather than Mr Bucket, right off the bat. Asking Sampaguita if she had enjoyed the visit to her homeland, she told me, "I have no escape from the heat. It's the hot and sweaty season there too."

As she filled me in on her trip, it didn't escape my attention that Sherry was doing a passable imitation of a gulping goldfish. Realising that Vasos still hadn't arrived, I excused myself to find out why Sherry appeared so antsy.

"Oh, Victor. Vasos just telephoned but I couldn't understand anything he was saying and then the line suddenly went dead. Do you think he was standing me up?"

"I'm not really up on current trends on the dating scene but I think if someone stands you up, they just blank you, rather than telephone. Actually, I think ghosting is the new blanking. Dating these days seems very complicated." Seeing Sherry's crestfallen expression, I added, "I expect Vasos was just calling to let you know that he's on his way."

Fidgeting nervously with the buttons on her cardigan, Sherry said, "I do hope you're right...but he could have had an emergency that prevents him from coming. Perhaps you could translate if he calls back?"

"It depends how busy it gets," I responded, desperately hoping that I could avoid getting involved. Looking around the taverna, it was surprising to see only half of the tables occupied. Perchance the villagers were staying away, having heeded the dismal weather forecast that Hal had warned me about. If the taverna didn't reach peak capacity, I might have the opportunity to leg it home before the predicted downpour started.

In general, the Greeks in Meli paid close attention to the weather forecast, accepting the predictions as though they were gospel. I realised that unlike the villagers who had come prepared with waterproof jackets and umbrellas, I had nothing to protect me from getting thoroughly soaked if the weather turned. It could well be my wake-up call to glue myself to future forecasts.

Finally arriving at the taverna ready to man the grill,

Nikos declared that after handling the rubbish dumped in his field, he needed a shower before tackling the meat. After telling me to give the customers a glass of *spitiko* on the house for making them wait, he hurried upstairs.

As I toured the room, filling up glasses from Nikos' five-litre plastic bottle of homemade wine, Sherry once again demanded my attention.

"Vasos just called again but I couldn't see you to translate," Sherry pouted, her cheeks flushed.

"I was just outside with Nikos..."

"I couldn't understand most of what Vasos was saying, but, Victor, you'll never guess..."

Adopting a stoic look, I refused to rise to the bait and enter into a guessing game.

Pressing her hands to her heart, Sherry practically squealed with giddiness. "Vasos declared that he loves me..."

"Well, I wouldn't read too much into that," I advised. "Last week on the boat, Vasos declared his love for a fifty-year-old meat packer from Gloucester who was holidaying with his wife. Vasos very nearly ended up with a black eye."

Sherry's face visibly fell. "So, if Vasos says 'I love you,' it's just another suet dumpling."

"Well, he does scatter the words around rather indiscriminately. I can't tell you the number of times I've been on the receiving end of one of Vasos' declarations of love." I could only hope that Sherry wasn't the jealous type. If she and Vasos started courting for real, it wouldn't do for Sherry to have a green-eyed fit whenever Vasos dropped 'I love you,' on every female he encountered, from random boat passengers, to Cynthia and Violet Burke.

"I should have realised it meant nothing. He also said something which sounded as though he was calling me saggy..."

"I very much doubt that...he's hardly likely to have picked up saggy," I said. "Could he by any chance have been saying '*se agapo?*'"

"Possibly..."

"Well, *se agapo* means I love you in Greek."

With Sherry now grinning maniacally, I was about to head back to the kitchen when I was distracted by the evening bag which she'd left on the table: it appeared to be moving on its own steam. Thinking the events of the day must have tired me more than I'd realised, I rubbed my eyes. Removing my hands from my eyes, I realised I wasn't delusional: something pushing against the fabric indicated there was definitely some kind of activity inside Sherry's bag.

"Sherry, why is your handbag moving?"

"It's just Henry..."

"Henry?"

"My hoglet."

"What on earth is a hoglet?"

"A baby hedgehog. I discovered a hedgehog nest next to my compost heap last week. There was a mother and four hoglets. I looked in on them every day but yesterday the mother and three of the babies had gone. This little darling had been abandoned so I took him in."

"Into your handbag..."

"Silly. That's just for now. I didn't want to leave him

home alone, he might have been frightened. Cynthia gave me some jolly good advice on caring for a baby hedgehog. She advised me to keep him warm indoors until he's old enough to cope in the wild." Somehow, I couldn't imagine Cynthia advising Sherry to stick Henry in her handbag and bring him out for dinner. "I've made him a comfy bed in a shoebox at home. It's best to keep him indoors until he's bigger as he's too small to protect himself from predatory foxes. Once he's bigger, he'll be able to roll into a ball to protect himself."

"It's a pity my chickens don't have a built-in fox deterrent."

"Would you like to see Henry?"

Clueless if hedgehogs posed a sanitary threat in a setting where food was served, I mulled Sherry's question. Before I had reached a decision, she took Henry out of her handbag, the hoglet wrapped in a small face cloth. Henry was so tiny that he easily fitted on Sherry's outstretched palm. There was no denying he was incredibly appealing, his big black eyes alert and curious, his button nose incredibly cute, the quills on his back not extending to its face or belly.

"Isn't it prickly?" I asked, trying to recall if Nikos kept a first aid box handy in case Henry went on the attack and bloodied Sherry's hand.

"Not really, his spikes are still quite soft. I use the face cloth to avoid any sudden pricks. He does so love to be hugged and held."

Henry confirmed Sherry's words by purring in contentment on her hand. Surprisingly, I really could see the appeal though I doubted Henry would be quite so appealing when he morphed from hoglet to full-blown hedgehog, in all his spiky glory.

"Would you like me to bring Henry a saucer of milk?"

"Only if you want to kill him. I'm sure he'd welcome a saucer of water though. Cynthia said that once Henry is a bit bigger, he'll be a wonderful help in the garden..."

"What? You fancy tasking him with a bit of weeding," I quipped.

"Really, Victor, do you ever take anything seriously? Hedgehogs protect the garden by eating all the pesky bugs that make a beeline for the plants."

"That's handy."

"What's the Greek word for hedgehog, Victor?"

"I can't say I know. Let me look it up." Grabbing my pocket English to Greek dictionary, I looked up the word, inwardly groaning when I saw it was comprised of four practically unpronounceable syllables. "It's *skatzochoiros.*"

"Gosh, that's a bit of a jolly mouthful. Can you say it again?"

"*Skatzochoiros.*" Reluctantly repeating the word, my tongue tripped anything but smoothly until I became distracted by a couple of unwelcome intruders. "What on earth? Sherry, keep a tight hold on Henry."

Bold as brass, Cynthia's vile mutant cat, Kouneli, strode into the taverna, another miscreant feline hot on its heels. Grabbing the sweeping brush to rid the taverna of the cats, I speculated that the usually solitary Kouneli could be resorting to strength in numbers by forming a gang. The last thing the streets of Meli needed was a gang of delinquent tomcats reaping havoc.

After I'd shooed the cats out of the taverna with a little help from the sweeping brush, Spiros called me over.

"It is the on," he declared. "The doctor make the phone. Later this week, I go to the notary with the Doctor Papadima to set the sale in flow..."

"In motion," I corrected. "Has word got around yet that the village is set to have a doctor?"

"I wait until the paper is sign... I not want to jingle it..."

"Jinx it..."

"*Milas gia ton neo giatro?*" Mathias interrupted, asking if we were speaking about the new doctor. It appeared that Barry was right in his assessment that some of the local Greeks knew a smattering of English but never let on.

"So much for keeping it quiet until the papers are signed," I lamented.

When Apostolis the barber said he had heard the new doctor was a woman, his words triggered a raucous argument between the customers, half of them livid at the very notion of a woman practising medicine, the other half just thankful that Meli would be acquiring a professional medic, regardless of said medic's sex.

At least half of the gathered company were excited at the prospect of having a doctor on hand, sparing them from travelling for examinations and repeat prescriptions.

It didn't take me long to conclude that the objectors were outraged at the thought of being examined by a woman since it would likely involve stripping off.

"*Den einai sosto*," Mathias shouted, declaring it wasn't right.

Those firmly against a female doctor quieted somewhat when Spiros pointed out that no one was forcing them to see the new medic if they preferred to only undress in front of men. Some of the customers were just so set in their traditional ways that they held firm to outdated beliefs that women should spend their time at home, cooking, knitting, and catering to every whim of their menfolk. I had it on good authority, well, according to Vangelis, that men in remote villages such as Meli tended to hold less enlightened views than men in the cities.

Considering that Greece is the birthplace of democracy, women didn't obtain the right to vote until 1952, way behind other European countries, excepting Portugal. In 1953, Eleni Skoura became the very first woman to be sworn in to the all-male Greek Parliament. I considered myself fortunate in having enlightened friends like Spiros and Vangelis, neither of them stuck in the dark ages. Saying that, if I ever develop prostate problems, I think I could well be embarrassed if a woman doctor conducts the examination.

"Victor. I'm going to call it a night, Vasos has obviously stood me up," Sherry sniffed. "How much do I owe?"

Sherry had managed to scoff her way through the entire contents of the bread basket and polished off all the olives and cheese, even though I had served enough for two.

"It's on the house," I told her. Feeling a twinge of pity

that her much anticipated date with Vasos had gone nowhere, I was more than happy to slip a couple of euros into the cash box. "I'll walk you out."

Waiting whilst Sherry returned the now sleeping Henry to her handbag, the sound of a car backfiring, preceding the squealing of brakes, drew me to the door. An involuntary smile crossed my face: it turned out that Vasos hadn't stood Sherry up, after all. Unbelievably, Vasos stepped out of his vehicle barefoot before rummaging around in his car as though on a search for buried treasure.

"Ta vrike." Holding aloft a pair of tatty flip flops, Vasos shouted 'found them' before slipping them onto his feet and bounding inside.

Chapter 18

A Language Minefield

"Vasos has just arrived," I hastened to tell Sherry. Admittedly, rather selfishly, I was somewhat relieved that the good *Kapetanios* hadn't left Sherry hanging, thus sparing me from Marigold's inevitable endless dissection of the disastrous details of her friend's love life. "He didn't stand you up, after all."

"Oh." The single long-drawn-out syllable was all that Sherry could manage, though her face flushed as red as the fruit on my strawberry plants. Breaking into a grin, her false teeth appeared more prominent than ever. Having convinced herself that Vasos was a no-show, his sudden arrival left her speechless, a most unusual occurrence where Sherry was concerned.

V.D. BUCKET

Stepping inside, in his typical gregarious fashion, Vasos greeted each of the customers with a hearty slap on the back. Making his way across the room to Sherry, he stopped to envelop me in a bear-hug, thankfully sparing me an enthusiastic thwack. Squirming in an effort to free myself from Vasos' iron grip, I was pleasantly surprised to breathe in the minty fresh aroma of toothpaste and soap, rather than his more familiar scent of *ouzo* and sweat. Unable to free myself from Vasos' smothering embrace, there was no denying his superior strength even though he was so much shorter than me.

Amazingly, Vasos appeared to have showered rather than resorting to his usual trick of squirting his own body weight in aftershave to disguise his often-fetid smell. Moreover, the good *Kapetanios* had obviously made an effort with his appearance, boasting what appeared to be a brand-new tee shirt free of food stains, paired with actual trousers rather than shorts. Only his feet let him down as he flapped across the room in a pair of disintegrating flip flops, held together with nothing more than a strip of foil tape, more usually associated with sealing dodgy joints on *somba* pipes. With footwear on my mind, I admonished Vasos for driving his old banger barefoot, telling my friend that I was pretty sure it was illegal to drive without shoes. I was surprised when Vasos confidently asserted that barefoot driving was actually legal, though there was talk about the government passing a law to prohibit folks from driving in flip flops.

Reaching Sherry, Vasos bent over her, depositing a smacker of a kiss on her cheek and mussing her hair.

Since Sherry was sitting down, for once Vasos had the height advantage. Fawning over his date, he declared she was beautiful and noted her dentures dazzled him with their brightness, before launching into an extended apology for his tardiness. Although likely clueless to anything Vasos was saying, Sherry beamed like a Cheshire cat.

"Victor, *parakalo metafraste*," Vasos called out, asking me to please translate.

Thinking Sherry may well handbag me if I translated Vasos' clumsy comment about her false teeth, I determined to remain uninvolved.

Shrugging, I told Vasos I was working, "*Doulevo*." If I hadn't had any work to be getting on with, I don't mind admitting I would have invented some busy work to avoid being drawn in.

"*Mono gia ena lepto*," Vasos wheedled, saying just for one minute, adding he had a gift for Sherry. "*Echo ena doro gia tin Sherry.*"

Unable to resist Vasos' persuasive plea, I reluctantly capitulated. Hovering by the side of their table, I expected Vasos to present Sherry with a bunch of flowers he'd nicked from the graveyard. Instead, I was almost lost for words when he unveiled a totally practical gift, producing two dictionaries, an English to Greek one for Sherry, and a Greek to English one for himself.

Sherry was stunned, asking me to tell Vasos that she was touched by his considerate and generous gift, promising to use it to better communicate with him.

Since Sherry's sentiment was a bit of a mouthful in Greek, I simply told Vasos that she liked it, "*Tis aresei*." Sherry would need to start flicking through the pages of her gift if she wanted anything more elaborate than the bare basics when it came to expecting me to translate.

"*Thes ouzo?*" Asking Vasos if he wanted his usual tipple of *ouzo*, I was surprised when he asked for a lemon Sprite, saying he was driving. "*Ochi. Apla ena lemoni Sprite. Odigo.*" It was practically unheard of for Vasos to eschew an offer of alcohol. I considered it boded well: if Vasos was determined to remain sober for his date, perchance he was taking it seriously.

After bringing Vasos' drink, a plate of cheese and olives, and another basket brimming with Dina's fabulous homemade bread, I topped up Sherry's glass of wine before making my way over to Spiros.

"Spiro, it may be nothing but I'm sure I saw the curtains twitching in Kyria Kompogiannopoulou's house."

"Twitching?" Biting into a plump black olive, Spiros furrowed his brow. "You mean there are the bird in the house?"

"Birds? No...why would the curtains twitching make you think of birds?"

Pausing to mop a dribble of olive oil from his chin, Spiros said, "The Gordon Strange tell me he twitches..."

Spiros' words began to make sense when I recalled that Gordon was becoming something of an avid bird watcher.

"I've never seen Mr Strange having jerking movements," Sampaguita interjected, a look of genuine concern on her face. "Maybe I should recommend he visits a doctor."

Momentarily feeling as though I was in the twilight zone, it belatedly occurred to me that for once

Sampaguita's usually impeccable English comprehension had let her down, the happy couple both attributing different meanings to my reference to twitching. Without further ado, I corrected my choice of words, telling them that I thought I had seen the curtains move in Sophia's empty house.

"Victor, the curtain he is most likely the nothing," Spiros declared. "What is it the Marigold says? You are too much the worry-weed."

"It's worry-wart," I corrected.

"Wart. What is the wart?" Spiros asked.

"Well, a wart is that unsightly thing Despina has on her face…"

"But what has the wart to do with the worry?" Spiros was nothing if not persistent.

"To be honest, I'm clueless. I have no idea how the phrase originated," I admitted.

"Probably the Sofia's daughter go in the house to check everything is the okay," Spiros suggested. His practical response was a tad unexpected since Spiros loves nothing more than getting his teeth stuck into a good conspiracy theory.

"I expect you're right," I agreed, by now desperate to drop the subject, reflecting that the most innocuous remarks could lead to a perplexing minefield of language confusion.

Making my way back and forth to the kitchen, I caught snippets of Vasos and Sherry's attempts at conversation. It struck me that Sherry was making a real effort to try a few Greek words out, even though her accent was pretty atrocious: still, it was very early days and mastering the complexities of the Greek alphabet was no easy task. I made a mental note to encourage her to keep up with her studies.

When Vasos rather bluntly asked his date how old she was, *"Poson chronon eiste?"* I was surprised that Sherry appeared excited by his question, most women of my acquaintance reluctant to admit to their age.

"I know this one," Sherry brayed. "I practised it in my first Greek lesson. You are asking me my age."

Vasos shook his head in the Greek sign of agreement, even though he was baffled by Sherry's English words. Without further ado, Sherry announced in faltering Greek that she was forty, *"Eimae saranta,"* thereby knocking at least a good decade or two from her age. I considered she had either botched up her Greek numbers or she was trying to pull the wool over Vasos' eyes. I could barely contain my amusement when Vasos gleefully told Sherry he was the same, proclaiming he too was forty. *"To idio. Eimai saranta."* Whilst I gave Sherry the benefit of the doubt due to her limited Greek, Vasos was clearly pulling the other one.

Taking a break whilst Nikos chucked the evening's choice of chicken wings on the outdoor grill, I stepped out onto the street. Spotting Pelham and Bill strolling by, I greeted them, asking if they were coming inside to eat.

"No, we're just taking an evening constitutional," Pelham replied.

"I couldn't persuade my brother to try out this place tonight, so we dined on crusty bread with olives, tomatoes and cheese. The quality of food in the village is exceptional."

"The tomatoes were so flavoursome," Pelham raved.

"Straight from the vine. You won't catch Meli tomatoes hanging around on supermarket shelves," I boasted.

"Your village shop is fascinating," Bill said. "It's a veritable treasure trove of fascinating finds. I particularly loved those barrels of loose olives marinating in oil. Pelham was a bit wary in case someone had sneezed over the barrel but as soon as he tasted one, he overcame his reluctance."

"There's hope for him yet," I said with a wink. The way that Bill stared at me, made me wonder if my wink had come over as more of a twitch, or maybe I just had twitches on my mind.

"Those nectarines from your garden were just spiffing," Pelham added.

"You must stop by one morning and collect some freshly laid eggs from my chickens," I invited.

"Fancy that. It would never have crossed my mind back in the days when we worked together, that Vic Bucket would end up keeping chickens in a foreign country."

Brushing over his annoying diminution of my name, I replied, "Well, Pel, retiring in Greece opened many doors I'd never anticipated…"

"It's Pelham…"

"And it's Victor."

"Oh, don't start a petty squabbling match over your names. Just be grateful that neither of you are stuck with Wilhelmina," Bill chided.

"Neither of us are likely to be stuck with a girl's name," Pelham argued.

"Actually, it's all the rage," I said. "My godson is named Victor Mabel."

"Mabel?"

"The family are Albanian," I said as though that explained everything.

Raising his eyebrows, Pelham adroitly changed the subject, enthusing, "There appears to be some fabulous walks around the village. We're planning to make a day of exploring the area on foot tomorrow."

"You really should check out the caves on the way to Nektar," I advised, giving the pair directions. Unlike Marigold, Bill didn't strike me as the squeamish type: I doubted a cauldron of bats would put the wind up her. "Are you sure you won't come in for a glass of wine? Nikos makes his own and it's amazingly good."

"Another time," Bill promised as the colour faded from Pelham's face. "Neither of us are dressed for an evening out."

Realising that it was Pelham's fear of the taverna failing to live up to his exacting hygiene standards rather than any unsuitable fashion choices, I didn't press the matter. I knew from personal experience that Pelham's hesitation was a natural side-effect of our mutual occupation.

The sun had set and the last of the light was rapidly beginning to fade when Marigold and Violet Burke approached the taverna, deep in conversation. Arm-in-arm, it was difficult to discern if my wife was bearing the brunt of her mother-in-law's weight, or if Marigold was clinging onto Vi to prevent herself from toppling off her high heels. Either way, it warmed the cockles of my heart to see my two favourite women acting so chummy.

"Marigold, you're looking exceptionally chic," I flattered my wife. "What are the two of you doing out?"

"We've been over to Yiota's," Vi declared.

"I wanted to drop off my trifle for Giannis." That would account for Marigold making an extra effort with her appearance. She certainly wasn't alone in dolling herself up for the local Greek god: Meli was fast turning into a village of glamourous grannies since Ioanna had left her son to fend for himself. I didn't recall the same attention to appearance coupled with best bib and tucker, when I had been the one on the receiving end of the ladies' largesse, back when Marigold had been in England.

Earlier, I had run into Litsa. Instead of sporting her usual black widow's weeds, she had been done up in a rather fetching green outfit. Struggling with an enormous casserole dish, she had visibly blushed when she told me she'd cooked up a big pan of *youvarlakia*, meatball soup, for Giannis. It appeared age was no barrier when it came to appreciating the toned physique and striking good looks of a much younger man. It seemed that Violet Burke was alone in not fussing about her appearance before dropping in on Giannis. Unlike Marigold, who had changed her frock and opted for a pair of impractical shoes simply because they better displayed her ankles to advantage, Violet Burke was decked out in a pair of unflattering denim bell bottoms which sagged around her backside, and a pair of neon-orange Crocs that I suspected might well glow in the dark.

"I took the lad some mucky fat sarnies," Vi huffed, the walk perhaps a bit much for her after a long day charring.

"Which were spurned by Giannis," Marigold said.

"Aye, but that Hal fella polished them off."

"I think he did that to get in your good books, Vi," Marigold opined. Turning to me, my wife rolled her eyes. "I do believe Hal is rather taken with your mother."

"You don't half spout some nonsense, lass. Anyhow, the reason I went over there with Marigold was to make sure that Yiota was not taking any nonsense from the lad. I didn't like what I heard before. It was a bit of a shocker to hear Giannis had got all shouty with Yiota. Much as I hate to drag someone's name through the mud, there's no denying that Giannis comes from bad stock. 'Appen he might take after that, what was his name, that depraved grandfather of his?"

"Haralambos," I volunteered.

"You forget that it could be said that Victor came from bad stock too, yet he turned out just fine; he's law-abiding to a fault. After all, Victor's biological father was a convicted criminal who served time in Strangways," Marigold pointed out.

"Aye, but Vic knocked me up before he went all bent. And in Vic's defence, he was locked up for one of them white collar crimes..."

"Whilst Haralambos committed his crimes while employed as an agricultural policeman," I was saying when Mathias cut me off by shouting for more wine.

"Victor. Ferte perissotero krasi."

"*Ena lepto.*" I called out 'one minute' to Mathias before turning my attention back to the ladies.

"Can I persuade you both to come in for a glass of wine?"

"Is Sherry in there with Vasos?" Marigold asked.

"She is indeed," I confirmed.

"Then I'd better give it a miss. Sherry will get herself all flustered if she thinks I'm spying on her date. And I promised Doreen I'd stop by to help her deworm Tickles. It's not easy getting Tickles to swallow a pill and Norman's about as useful as a block of lard."

"'Appen I'll come in and take the weight off, lad, if you can run to a plate of chips."

"I think I can manage that...I'll see you later, Marigold."

"I won't wait up. I want to be up with the lark to start on some potting whilst you go gadding to town with Doreen."

"You needn't have any worries on that score, lass. That Doreen won't go turning Victor's head. He's only got eyes for you."

"Oh, for goodness' sake, Vi..." Marigold said before planting a kiss on my lips.

"Come on, Mother. Let's get you some chips," I invited, lending my arm.

As soon as we stepped inside, Vi proclaimed, "Well, if it ain't my old mucker, Vasos." Acting as though his presence was a total shock, my mother's performance deserved an Oscar.

Spotting my mother, Vasos practically hurled himself into her arms, shouting "Violet, I love you. *Ela, katse mazi mas.*" Making a total fuss of Vi, Vasos invited her to sit with them. Although the actual meaning of Vasos' words eluded Sherry, his action of holding a chair out for my mother was self-explanatory, eliciting a look of green-eyed jealousy from Vasos' date.

"Really, Mother, you could show a little discretion," I hissed in her ear. "Sherry isn't going to appreciate you playing gooseberry."

"Don't go getting your knickers in a twist, Victor..."

"*Ti einai knickers?*" Vasos boomed as Vi sank into the proffered chair.

Noticing the rest of the customers unashamedly gawping, I simply fibbed, saying, "*Den metafrazetai,*" meaning, 'it doesn't translate.'

"Victor, pop in the kitchen and ask Dina if she fancies sharing a plate of chips with me," Vi demanded.

After consulting with Dina, I told my mother, "Dina's frying chips for the two of you, now." My words did nothing to temper the obvious irritation written all over Sherry's face. Having mastered the art of being tactless, Violet Burke stared Sherry down.

Excusing himself, Vasos made a beeline for the toilet. Alone with Violet Burke, Sherry had the opportunity to tell the older woman to sling her hook. Since Sherry found my mother a tad intimidating, she wasn't so blunt, instead suggesting that Vi should find somewhere else to sit as she wanted to enjoy some alone time with Vasos.

"Hold your horses, lass. I'll be shifting soon enough when the chips are done. I just want a bit of a catch-up with Vasos."

"But we're on a romantic date." Sherry emphasised her point by directing a shooing gesture towards my mother, Vi simply ignoring it.

Returning to the table, Vasos grinned from ear to ear, proclaiming, *"Oi dyo agapimenes mou gynaikes mazi,"* meaning, 'My two favourite women together.'

"I bet you say that to all the girls," Vi quipped, impressing me with her grasp of Greek comprehension.

"Mrs Burke, what did Vasos say?" Sherry asked.

"You ain't half got some nerve, you cheeky mare. You just told me to bugger off and now you want a favour." My mother's words left Sherry lost for words for the second time that evening.

"Victor, *ti einai* bugger off?" Vasos shouted.

"Den metafrazetai." Playing it safe, I resorted to fibbing again, once again saying 'it doesn't translate.' Desperate to avoid being dragged in further, I escaped to the kitchen.

Dishing out a couple of plates of chips, Dina set them down on the small table in the kitchen, asking me to tell my mother that the food was served.

Keeping a safe distance, I called over to my mother. "Grub's up. Dina has set a place for you in the kitchen."

"Ti eipe o Victor?" Vasos boomed, asking my mother what I had said.

Flicking through her new dictionary, Sherry loudly blurted in hesitant Greek, *"Kampia mesa kouzina."* I inwardly cringed as Sherry told Vasos there was a grub, in the maggot rather than slang for food sense, in the kitchen.

Vasos immediately responded by asking if I wanted

him to come in the kitchen to kill it. A tad piqued that Vasos imagined I would need assistance in killing grubs, I declined his offer, recollecting there had been nothing unmanly in the way I had taken care of the fat brown grub in the *kafenion*, even if it had turned out to be nothing more threatening than a false eyelash.

Chapter 19

A Fried Bucket

Hovering in the taverna doorway, the enormous clap of thunder that followed the vibrant flash of lightning almost drowned out Nikos sniggering, "Victor, you are the big girl blouse."

"I gather you've been picking up Violet Burke's Lancashire vernacular again," I fired back.

"It is just the drop of rain."

"It's an absolute deluge," I retorted, reluctant to step outside where I would undoubtedly assume the mantle of a drowned rat.

"I get you the *omprela*," Nikos offered before ferreting around in the dark corner of the taverna that served as the home for lost property. I churlishly accepted the decrepit old brolly Nikos handed to me, the metal ribs only loosely connected to the dangerously dangling canopy, threatening to do some lethal damage. Without further ado, Nikos gave me an encouraging shove onto the street, clearly eager to lock up for the night and see the back of me.

Normally, I would have taken offence at Nikos' perfunctory dismissal of me, but I knew he had an awful lot on his mind with the crazy pigeon beheader and demented graffiti artist still on the loose. At least the rain ought to keep the vindictive vandal indoors and thwart any plans he had to splatter more paint about. Of course, although it was only a presumption that the delinquent was male, it seemed unlikely that a woman would resort to such measures as deliberately decapitating pigeons.

Squelching my way home in soggy shoes, I was struck by the utter blackness of the night, the only illumination coming from the irregular flashes of lightning providing quite a dramatic sight, purplish tentacles stretching down from the horizon and touching the sea. As the rain continued to pour, I grappled with the less-than-useless umbrella: if it wasn't for my loathing of littering, I would have tossed it onto the street. Thoroughly soaked, I reflected that one shouldn't expect to need wellies in June.

For once the street was a cat-free zone; I assumed every last stray had run for cover and taken shelter from the storm, many of them dive-bombing the rubbish bins for cover. A couple of lights in the distance reassured me that the electric was still on; at least I wouldn't need to grope around in the dark when I reached home.

BUCKET TO GREECE (VOL.17)

I felt grateful that Spiros and Sampaguita had walked my mother home an hour earlier, thus sparing her from ending up sopping wet. Reflecting on the events of the evening, it seemed that the romantic date between Vasos and Sherry had been a success once Violet Burke had been banished to the kitchen with her chips. Even when Vasos had spilt olive oil down his brand-new tee shirt and ended up with some chicken skin in his hair, Sherry hadn't flinched, gazing at Vasos adoringly, the picture of a doting girlfriend.

Henry the hoglet, venturing out from Sherry's handbag for a second time, had been well received by Vasos, his reaction earning him extra brownie points from his date. Having retrieved the chicken skin from his hair, the captain had duly tried to feed a sliver of the stuff to Henry. Shaking her head, Sherry prised the skin free of Henry's mouth, telling Vasos, "I'm not sure chicken skin is good for Henry. He'd probably prefer a nice snack of mealworms."

"Ti?"

Flicking through her new dictionary with lightning speed, Sherry grimaced, before calling out to me.

"Victor, there's no way I can pronounce mealworms in Greek. It has about twenty letters. Can you please tell Vasos that Henry prefers mealworms?"

"I've no idea what the Greek for mealworms is," I admitted.

"It's here, in the dictionary," Sherry insisted, thrusting the book under my nose. Scanning the word, I had to agree with Sherry that the word appeared unpronounceable. Nevertheless, I gave it my best effort.

"*Vaso, o Henry protima ta alevroskoulika.*"

"*Pes stin Sherry tha fero liga tin epomeni fora.*" As Vasos asked me to tell Sherry he'd bring some next time, I could only hope that he would choose a different venue for their date. Just the thought of mealworms loose in the taverna was the very stuff of a public health inspector's nightmares.

Relaying Vasos' words to Sherry, I realised mealworms were the last thing on her mind. All she had heard was the promise of next time, meaning another date was on the cards. At least I would be able to report some good news to my wife.

Reaching the house, I noted Marigold had thoughtfully left the outdoor light on for me. Nevertheless, I almost jumped out of my skin when I heard a plaintive meow coming from the region of my feet. Bending down, I discovered poor Pickles practically wedged between two large terracotta plant pots: clearly, its bedraggled state indicated the cat hadn't managed to take shelter indoors before the rain started teeming down. As I scooped the cat into my arms and headed inside, it nuzzled its wet fur against me in a show of gratitude. In turn, I was forever grateful that Pickles hadn't taken after his mutant father, Kouneli.

Grabbing a towel, I gave Pickles a good rubbing down before treating it to a tin of sardines. Discarding my drenched clothing, I hopped in a hot shower. As I tiptoed silently into the bedroom in search of pyjamas, the sound of snoring indicated Marigold was dead to the world. A flash of lightning momentarily lit up the bedroom, revealing Catastrophe and Clawsome snuggled up next to Marigold on my pillow. It appeared I had unjustly maligned my wife by assuming she was the snorer, the rattling din actually coming from Clawsome. How something smaller than a sausage dog could produce such a racket, amazed me.

A flash of lightning preceded a large bang coming from my office, the crash of thunder that followed taking out the electricity. Fortunately, the power outage lasted only a moment. With the light restored, I crept through to my office to investigate the bang, ruling the cats out as the culprits.

The source of the bang immediately became apparent when I spotted the laptop. As was my habit, I had left the computer turned on earlier, ignorant that a sudden storm was on its way. Instead of my usual screensaver, a lovely picture of Marigold in the garden collecting a basket of lemons with a dreamy smile, the screen was black. My frantic attempts to turn the laptop back on were futile, the machine as dead as the proverbial doornail. I could have kicked myself but decided to leave that job for Marigold: after all, my wife was forever nagging me to turn the laptop off whenever I wasn't using it, acting as though the few cents it cost to run rivalled her costly long-distance telephone calls to Geraldine, back in England. The two of them could happily gab for hours at my expense.

My frustration turned to gloom when I realised that my book about moving to Greece was lost inside the fried machine. A beacon of hope beckoned when I recalled that at least I had a hard copy. I had printed the pages and sent them off to James Scraper, my former boss at the Foods Standard Agency. In turn, he had returned them, the pristine pages defiled with copious amounts of purple jottings. Although I had been tempted to sling them, I'd hung onto them.

Once I had overcome my outrage at Scraper's opinion that my literary masterpiece was both pompous and pretentious, I had meticulously edited the book in line with his numerous suggestions. Moreover, I had spent many hours painstakingly retyping the whole thing to incorporate the edits. Since I still had the printed purple-defiled pages shoved in a drawer, I realised not all was lost: I could purchase a new laptop in town the next day and then retype the manuscript yet again. In the meantime, I had to accept that my Bucket was fried.

The only silver lining in the dark cloud was my recent self-taught ability to touch type, thus sparing me from knocking another copy out at a snail's pace using only two fingers. Alas, there was no silver lining to cling to when it dawned on me that the half-written sequel was lost forever in the deep bowels of the destroyed machine. Thank goodness most of my notes pertaining to our day-to-day adventures in Greece were handwritten: I should be able to cobble something together.

Moving through to the kitchen, I made myself a mug of rich hot chocolate, adding just a dash of *Metaxa* to the hot drink. Glancing outside, it appeared the storm was over; it never ceased to amaze me how Greek storms could come and go so quickly. Stepping out onto the balcony, I inhaled the intoxicating scent of newly watered herbs, thinking my neighbours would be happy that their olive groves had received a good watering to plump up their product. Sensing the almost immediate evaporation of the water dumped by the storm in the warm night air, I felt relieved that I wouldn't need to drive through rapids to get to town the next day.

The silence was broken by the sound of a speeding car coming to a stop just metres before our house. Stepping back into the shadows, I watched as a figure staggered out of the passenger side, the engine still running. The car then reversed at speed before doing a nifty three-point turn and heading out of the village. Eyeing the figure below, it soon became apparent that whoever it was, he was three sheets to the wind and barely capable of remaining upright. The mystery of his identity soon became clear when I noticed he was smooching up to a traffic cone; it had to be Norman. I remained clueless to the identity of the driver who had unceremoniously dumped him outside my house.

As he waltzed past the *apothiki* as though the cone was his dancing partner, I briefly considered going down to offer my assistance to the bumbling idiot. My mind was torn as I pondered the dilemma: on one hand, it was the neighbourly thing to do; on the other, I had already changed into my pyjamas and Norman was only a five-minute walk, or stagger, from home. The dilemma resolved itself in short order when Norman reached my gate and, to my disgust, decided to use it as a urinal. Tutting at his boorish and uncouth behaviour, I decided to let him stew in whatever he'd been imbibing, only hoping that Norman's stream would serve as a fox deterrent.

Chapter 20

Drop the Mou

"I've brought you a coffee," Marigold snapped, pointedly slamming the steaming mug down on my bedside table. The sheer force of the slam caused the glass jar containing a slew of ticks that had met their intoxicating end by drowning in a lethal reservoir of clear rubbing alcohol, to rattle. If my wife thought that the juxtaposition of floating tick corpses with my coffee cup would force me to mend my ways, she was sorely mistaken.

The convenience of keeping the liquid grave handy outweighed Marigold's continual gripes about it. Since I was the one that was expected to dispose of any ticks hanging about on the cats, my wife would simply have to put up with my chosen, and swift, method of extermination, at least until the end of the tick season: thankfully, I had it on good authority that the end of blood sucking season was almost nigh. Marigold was quite happy to condone my murderous ways as long as I didn't thrust them in her face.

"You're up awfully early," I commented, smoothing my button-down and knotting my tie.

"I've so much to do in the garden. I need an early start transplanting some cuttings and potting the plants I bought yesterday. I won't be able to water them once the sun gets too hot."

Staring meaningfully at the glass jar next to my coffee, Marigold once again pleaded with me to get rid of it. Using her feminine wiles, she batted her eyelashes at me; sensing I wasn't in the mood to be won over by her charms, she flounced down to the garden, at least having the good grace to spare me a pout. Sipping my coffee, I savoured the rich brew, appreciating that even though Marigold was annoyed with me, she had gone to the effort of grinding my beans rather than slinging a mug of unspeakably vile instant my way. Eyeing the jar and its kicked-the-bucket contents, I could vaguely understand why my wife might find it unsettling. Without further ado, I duly shoved it out of sight in the back of my underwear drawer.

Discarding the Y-fronts that Marigold had adapted with a secret compartment to hide money, I stashed Pelham's cash for his stay at Sofia's inside my new money belt, securing it beneath my slacks. It was a relief not to have a wad of cash burning a hole in my underwear.

Feeling revitalised after my coffee, I headed into my office in the hope that a miracle may have occurred overnight to restore life to my now defunct laptop. Alas, it was still kaput so I slung it into a bin bag to chuck in the communal bins.

Headed outside to let Marigold know I was ready for the off, I hoped that Doreen would manage to turn up on time; it wouldn't do for her to be late for her rendezvous at the police station. Surprisingly, there was no trace of last night's summer storm that had ended as quickly as it began, beyond the lingering scent of herbs, the aroma magnified by the treat of a thorough watering.

Finding Marigold on her hands and knees in the herb garden, I schmoozed, "There you are, darling. Your hair looks particularly lovely this morning."

"You must have X-ray vision, Victor. In case it's escaped your notice, I'm wearing a sunhat." Sarcasm fairly dripped from Marigold's tone. Leaning back on her haunches, she raised a hand to shield her eyes against the bright sunlight, leaving a smudge of soil across her forehead.

"Adding pots of herbs to that old ladder was inspired. It looks quite fabulous," I praised.

Taking a leaf out of Doreen's book, Marigold had reclaimed a decrepit-looking old wooden step ladder from the bins. For the sake of accuracy, I should amend that to read Marigold had instructed me to drag said ladder home from the bins. Marigold had persuaded me that it wouldn't do her reputation any good to be spotted scavenging, whilst my reputation, apparently, was already a lost cause.

Duly sanded and painted, the rungs now served as additional housing for Marigold's many pots of herbs, their green foliage glistening in the glorious morning light.

"And to think you scoffed when I persuaded you to drag it back from the bins," Marigold reminded me, snipping away at the lemon grass with a sharp set of pruners. "You should start including this lemongrass in your salads, Victor. As it's supposed to be good for digestive issues, it might help with your heartburn."

"I'll try that," I promised. "It certainly tastes better than chalky Gaviscon."

"Cooee. Are we ready for the off?" Doreen called out, dabbing her forehead with a hankie as she tripped across the garden to join us. Kissing Marigold in greeting resulted in some of the soil from Marigold's face leaving an unsightly moustache beneath Doreen's nose. "I just hope I manage to pass this test first time and get my moped diploma. This broken toe makes it hard going, walking from mine to yours."

If Doreen was angling for the sympathy vote, she could forget it. Her grossly hyperbolic description of her slightly bruised little toe as broken only existed in her imagination.

"All good to go," I confirmed, eager to get an early start.

Since neither Marigold nor I had risen to Doreen's toe bait, she harped on about it a bit more for good measure.

"I think I'll be able to ride the new moped as soon as I pass the test. It will be much cooler riding through the village, rather than walking. And of course, it will be much less strain on my broken toe."

"Are you never going to let it drop?" I churlishly complained, Doreen having prodded the bear once too often. After a tad too much wine at baby Dina's recent christening, Doreen had insisted I dance with her, even though she is fully aware that I have two left feet. "I didn't mean to stand on your toe, but yet again, I apologise."

"Stamped, more like..." Doreen grizzled before Marigold interrupted her by chiding me, "Victor, you could attempt to sound sincere." Turning to Doreen, she reassured her friend, "You're sure to pass the test with flying colours. You've been swotting for days."

Curious on one point, I asked Doreen, "Why *did* Manolis splash out on a brand-new moped for you?"

"Guilt," Doreen and Marigold replied in unison.

"What did the poor chap have to feel guilty about?"

"My Manolis *mou* can occasionally be insensitive." Doreen surprised me; I thought Manolis could do no wrong in her eyes. Perchance the flush of new love was wearing off.

"He can be totally clueless," Marigold ventured. Obviously, Doreen had been confiding in my wife who was no doubt well up to speed with any and all of Manolis' perceived shortcomings. It rather unnerved me to think such confidences probably went both ways; Doreen may well be up on what Marigold considered all my perceived flaws.

"My Manolis *mou* sometimes comes out with thoughtless opinions that he really ought to keep to himself…" Doreen said rather tentatively, seemingly reluctant to criticise the love of her life.

"He should most definitely keep them to himself," Marigold backed up her friend, whilst batting a persistent wasp away.

"It's because my Manolis *mou* is Greek…" Doreen pondered. No matter how many times I explained to her that my and *mou* had the same meaning, she insisted on lumping them together whenever she uttered her boyfriend's name.

"Most definitely. No well-brought-up British gentleman would come out with some of the things Manolis spouts." Marigold had certainly climbed on her high horse in defence of her friend, the pair of them yet to clue me in regarding the nature of Manolis' supposed transgression. "Victor just wouldn't…"

"But you've got Victor well-trained…"

"I'm not a dog," I objected.

"Well, I got him early when he was still malleable…" Marigold continued as though I wasn't there.

"My Manolis *mou* is beyond guidance at this point, his opinions are set in stone," Doreen complained. "He's adamant that not only is he right, but that every woman would value his opinions…"

"His opinions on what?" I blurted, heartily sick of the pair of them skirting around the subject. "And for goodness' sake, can you just drop all the *mous*."

"Really, Victor. Must you be so rude to Doreen?"

"You've said yourself that you're sick to death of my *mou*…" I muttered under my breath.

"Manolis likes to comment on what I wear," Doreen

said, pointedly dropping the unnecessary *mou* and adopting a vinegarish expression.

"But sometimes he goes too far..." Marigold added.

"How so?" I prompted. I knew from bitter experience that commenting on my wife's choice of clothes in anything other than the most flattering manner, was a foolish endeavour that wouldn't end well for me. If ever my opinion was sought, the correct answer was always *you look perfectly lovely in that* and *no, your bum doesn't look big in it.*

"Well, take the other evening," Doreen said. "We were going down to the coast for a romantic dinner and Manolis said to me, 'Doreen, your clothes fit you just right this evening.'"

"Not quite the smoothest of compliments but hardly a hanging matter," I stated.

"Let Doreen finish..."

Appearing a tad flustered, Doreen's voice rose a couple of octaves as she continued. "Manolis said, 'Your clothes suit you this evening, they fit you well. The top is loose and does not cling...sometimes you wear terrible clothes...'"

"He didn't?" I was genuinely shocked. Knowing how much Manolis adored Doreen, it seemed a very odd thing for him to come out with.

"He did," Marigold confirmed as Doreen swung her arms around like a windmill in an effort to deter the persistent wasp that had switched its attention from my wife to her friend.

"Manolis told Doreen that she should always wear loosely fitting clothes, rather than clothes with a more fitted form that do nothing for her."

BUCKET TO GREECE (VOL.17)

Having been married for close to four decades, I realised that Manolis was skating on dodgy ground. Marigold would have a fit if she'd gone to the trouble of dressing for dinner and I tactlessly went and burst her bubble by telling her that her chosen frock did nothing for her figure. Fortunately, Marigold has developed an excellent sense of style, knowing which outfits look good on her. On the other hand, Doreen had rather let herself go during the twilight years of her marriage to Norman, her new found romance with Manolis tempting her to experiment in both the hair and wardrobe department. It could be said she hadn't quite settled on a suitable style as yet.

"So, one evening last week, Manolis told Doreen that her dress did nothing for her and that she should stick to something similar to Sherry's kaftans," Marigold said.

"Needless to say, Manolis' harsh words put a damper on my evening. I thought that I looked rather nice but his words made me feel fat and frumpy. It was most upsetting," Doreen said. "A few days later, I raised the matter, telling Manolis how he'd made me feel. He just brushed it off, telling me that every woman should be grateful to hear if something didn't suit her…"

"Quite ridiculous," Marigold chimed in. "Who on earth made Manolis the arbiter of good taste?"

"I told Manolis it was tactless and that he'd hurt my feelings," Doreen continued. "But Manolis just doubled down, saying how strange it was that I didn't want him to critique my clothes choice. Then, he went and dragged Christos into it. The pair of them never agree on anything but Christos backed Manolis all the way on this, insisting that every woman should be grateful for a man telling them when they don't look their best."

"I can't imagine anyone valuing slimy Christos' opinion, especially considering the state of some of the things he wears," I said. Last time I'd been in the *kafenion*, Christos' outfit of shiny leisure trousers sporting an elasticated waistband and paired with a grubby tee-shirt and accessorised with tacky bling, reminded me of the way the chavs had dressed at young Kevin's wedding back in Warrington.

"Not to mention that dreadful pornstache under his nose," Marigold added. "Even though Manolis refused to back down on his opinions and insistence on how grateful the female population of Meli ought to be to receive them, he did feel terrible for upsetting Doreen, hence the shiny new moped."

"Well, Doreen, I think you look perfectly lovely this morning in that fetching frock," I fibbed. It wouldn't surprise me to hear that Manolis would agree with me that horizontal stripes were not a good look, having a tendency to pile the kilos onto the wearer. But, unlike Manolis, it was an opinion I would never voice in Doreen's hearing, having indeed been well-trained by Marigold. "We really should get going, Doreen. After dropping you off for your test, I need to get over to the National Bank."

"Good luck, Doreen," Marigold said, once again batting the wasp in her friend's direction. "I'm sure you'll pass with flying colours."

"Ouch," Doreen screeched, clutching her nose. "That dratted wasp just stung me."

Chapter 21

Help with the Answers

After slinging the bag containing the now defunct laptop in the village bins, we set off for town. Even though Doreen was well doped up on antihistamines, she proved to be quite chipper on the drive. Pressing a vinegar-soaked hankie against the tip of her now glaringly red nose, she shared snippets of local gossip she'd picked up from spending so much time in the *kafenion* with Manolis. She also shared her worries that Norman was increasingly sozzled these days, the booze even taking precedence over his obsession with traffic cones.

As Doreen spoke, an unwelcome image of Norman treating one of his precious witches' hats to an unseemly public display the prior evening, infiltrated my mind. Although I didn't want to raise the subject, I was a tad curious if he'd made it home. Fortunately, Doreen was the one to raise the subject.

"He came home in a terrible state last night, falling over the furniture. The racket he made was enough to raise the dead. I didn't appreciate being woken up..."

"I thought you stayed over with Manolis these days?"

"I did until Christos dumped that ghastly woman, Maria. Before that, my Manolis *mou* and I had the place to ourselves when Christos slept at her place. Now that Christos is back on the shelf, he doesn't like it when I stay over with Manolis, and Norman objects to Manolis staying over with me."

Changing the subject, Doreen told me Norman's passion for creating patisserie goods showed no sign of waning but the results were less than stellar because he was often half-cut when he weighed out the ingredients. Doreen confided she was particularly worried the house could go up in flames if, in the midst of one of his drunken bouts, Norman forgot all about a pan left on the hob or did something unthinkable with his blowtorch.

Doreen's suggestion that we could perhaps stage an intervention and confront Norman about his drinking, held little appeal to me: I didn't fancy being dragged into a potentially messy situation. With that in mind, I decided to make no mention of Norman's drunken antics the previous evening until I had talked it through with Marigold. I could always count on my wife giving sage advice.

At least Doreen was able to confirm that the vile Smug Bessie had dropped Norman like a hot potato following the Hungarian themed expat dinner party. In one sense, it was a blow to hear: a liaison between the two of them would have been a convenient excuse to exclude Norman from future gatherings since no one could tolerate the ghastly woman. I guessed we were stuck with Norman for the foreseeable.

As we reached the outskirts of town, Doreen put a sock in her chatter, instead mumbling under her breath as she tried to remember the pertinent facts she would need for the written portion of the moped test. Realising we were almost there, just a soupcon of fear roiled my insides. Despite being a law-abiding and tax-paying Greek resident, the thought of entering a police station sends iced blood flowing through my veins, imbuing me with a sense of gratuitous guilt. Taking a deep breath, I told myself to remain calm, reminding myself that the test for Doreen's diploma was being held at a different police station to the one I'd been escorted to after inadvertently flouting the law against Sunday trading. My horrific experience of being held there until the cavalry from Meli arrived to rescue me, was one that I was in no hurry to repeat.

Parking up at the police station, I hastily gave the car a good once-over to ensure there was nothing to attract the attention of an overzealous police officer. All four tyres had been filled with air to their requisite level and I had polished the Punto to within an inch of its life, ensuring the flash of the indicator lights was in no way impeded by a layer of grime.

One might consider my precautions a tad excessive since I only intended to park up for long enough to drop Doreen off: however, Doreen implored me to at least walk her inside the police station since she was a visible bag of nerves, her hands shaking like the leaves on an olive tree on a breezy day. I had already been forced to lob a perfectly decent *spanakopita*, spinach pie, out of the car window so that Doreen could make use of the paper bag as an antidote to her hyperventilating en route to town. Rather than risk Doreen having a full-blown nervous breakdown, I agreed to accompany her inside for a bit of moral support. After all, it was the gentlemanly thing to do: Marigold would expect nothing less of me.

A bevy of police officers cluttered the entranceway to the police station, looking ever so important in their smartly pressed, dark blue uniforms, impressive weapons visibly displayed on their hips.

Fortunately, they appeared more interested in chatting amongst themselves than in pulling Doreen aside for a strip search, even though the way she was quivering would have immediately put her on my radar as someone up to no good.

A policewoman wearing mirrored sunglasses that hid her eyes, stepped forward to assist us, asking if she could help, "*Boro na se voithiso?*"

The holstered handgun prominently displayed on the officer's hip did nothing to dispel Doreen's nervousness, so I stepped up, telling her that Doreen was there to take the moped test.

"*Gia to diploma?*" The officer clarified if it was for the diploma and I confirmed it was.

"*Ela apo do.*" Staring at the unsightly red blotch adorning the end of Doreen's nose, the officer told us to come this way.

As we fell into step beside the officer and began to ascend a flight of stairs, Doreen piped up, asking me what the officer had said. The young woman immediately switched to English, saying to Doreen, "You don't speak Greek?"

"No, I don't, sorry. But my Manolis *mou* is Greek."

"Really?" Managing to draw her attention away from Doreen's pulsating nose, the police officer stared me down before saying, "You don't look Greek." She had obviously jumped to the conclusion that I was Manolis.

"No, I'm not Greek, nor am I Manolis," I hastily added. "This lady is a friend of my wife."

"I rather hoped that after all this time, you would consider me a friend too, Victor," Doreen griped.

"I drove you to town, didn't I?"

As the officer once again fixated on Doreen's red and blotchy nose, I felt uncomfortable on Doreen's behalf. Hoping to satisfy the officer's curiosity and dispel any notion that Doreen had been recklessly overdoing the sun in the manner of a naïve tourist, I explained that she had been stung by a wasp, "*Tin tsimpise mia sfika.*"

"*Ti?*"

"*Mia sfika.*"

"*Ti?* Tell me in English."

"A wasp."

"*Ti?*"

"A wasp." As the officer continued to look confused, I added, "Like a bee. Black and yellow."

"Ah. *Mia sfika.*"

"That's what I said."

The officer's voice oozed sympathy as she said, "The foreign have much the difficult with the pronounce of the Greek '*sf*'."

"It's very difficult," I agreed. Some of the most essential words in the Greek language suffered from being almost unpronounceable to a foreign tongue by beginning with the combination of '*sf*'. It had taken me months to get to grips with the word for a mop, *mia sfoungaristra*, and a sponge, *ena sfoungari*, despite them being two of the most important and necessary words in any language.

After sympathising over Doreen's sting, the police officer realised Doreen was a bag of nerves and took pity on her. Putting a reassuring hand on Doreen's arm, the officer told her, "Don't worry. The test, he is simple, the multiple choice. I can to give you the question in English."

"Oh, that's such a relief," Doreen said. Her response surprised me: surely, she hadn't been panicking that the test would be in Greek. Since Doreen neither spoke nor read the language, she would have been up the proverbial creek without an English option.

"The multiple choice is only the two answer so you to have the fifty-fifty chance to guess the right," the officer continued. "And please not to worry. I can to tell you the correct answer so you can to pass."

Doreen broke out in a hesitant smile, somewhat reassured by the young officer's offer to help. Although my natural inclination was to presume the police officer was winding Doreen up as it must surely breach the law to tell the answers to someone taking the test, said police officer appeared totally genuine. It was some comfort to me to think that at least the officer wouldn't be able to take the practical part of the test for Doreen: Doreen would have to demonstrate her competence in riding a moped before she would be let loose on the roads.

"Doreen, as you appear to be in capable hands, I'll take off," I said.

"Yes, yes, you can to go," the officer told me. "You could not to come in the test room anyway. It would not the do for you to help with the answer." Offering help with the answers apparently counted as cheating unless the answers came from the mouth of a police officer.

Promising to come back to collect Doreen once my business in town was completed, I made my way back outside, pleasantly surprised to be feeling relatively unscathed by the whole business even though a police station had been involved.

Chapter 22

A Sweet Granny

My heart sank when I clocked the sheer mass of people clutching their numbered tickets and clogging the waiting area of the bank, every seat already occupied. Cautiously stepping over outstretched legs whilst muttering *sygnomi* under my breath, I made my way to the ticket machine, aware that many eyes were focusing on me as the newcomer. With the prospect of an interminable wait to endure, there was little else to do other than study the cluster of people stuck in bank purgatory, no one making any effort to hide the fact they were openly gawping. Leaning my frame against a conveniently empty bit of wall, I joined the ranks of my fellow people watchers, my eyes swivelling towards the door as another newcomer took my place as the latest arrival.

Three tellers were working away at their windows, their pace as typically slow as ever. The gentleman being attended to at the teller's window nearest to me struggled with the chained-up ballpoint pen before signing a couple of papers with a flourish. As he gathered his things together, the waiting customers shifted, checking the numbers on their tickets against the electronically displayed number on the wall, several of them positioning themselves to make a run for the cashier's desk as soon as the gentleman concluded his business. This posturing, position-wise, proved to be a complete waste of time, the teller exiting his window as soon as the customer he was attending to departed. Hoping the teller wasn't off on an extended coffee break, I resigned myself to a long wait.

A sudden flurry of activity revitalised my interest. Returning to his window, the bank teller pressed the buzzer, changing the number. When no one approached the window, he pressed the buzzer again, then again. There was a collective gasp of hope from the audience and plenty of repositioning, everyone hoping the person holding the ticket with the next-up number had grown tired of waiting around and legged it.

A middle-aged woman practically pounced on the teller's window as a final electronic clack announced her turn, prompting plenty of mouths to downturn in weary resignation. With all the attention focused on the nearest window, the audience had neglected to keep their beady eyes on the teller's window at the far side of the room.

V.D. BUCKET

As a young woman concluded her business, there was a new scramble, everyone mimicking the position of a swimmer poised on the starting platform, ready to dive into the race, shuffling forward expectantly in the hope that anyone holding the next number had taken themselves off for coffee.

Knowing my ticket number wasn't even close to being called, I had nothing to get excited about, discreetly surveying the other customers and stifling a chortle at the sight of one old fella done up in thick woollen pullover, seemingly immune to the high temperature.

"Victor." My attention was claimed by the young woman who had just concluded her business at the far window throwing her arms around me and kissing me on both cheeks. "Victor, it's so good to see you again."

Taken completely by surprise, I could feel myself flushing, aware that every eye in the bank was now riveted on this unexpected exchange between myself and this radiant beauty. It took a moment for me to place her since her presence was so unexpected; observing her flowing raven hair, her high cheekbones and her distinctively striking black eyebrows, recognition dawned. "Poppy."

Although I hadn't seen Poppy since she and Giannis had ended their romance and gone their separate ways, I surmised it may not be tactful to bring up her ex's name nor mention he was now involved with Yiota. Instead, I asked her how her studies in Streptococci were going and if she was still enjoying her time at the Laboratory for Bacterial Evolution and Pathogenesis in Edinburgh. Poppy said that she must hurry as she'd left her grandmother in the coffee bar opposite the bank, insisting I join the two of them there when my business in the bank was concluded. Pointing out that by the time I was finished, she and her grandmother would have most likely moved on from morning coffee to afternoon tea due to the bank moving at a snail's pace, I was beyond delighted when Poppy slipped me a ticket bearing a number only ten buzzes away from being seen to. Many patrons sneaked an additional ticket on the way in to assist any friends who may happen to turn up, a widely accepted practice. I was immensely grateful for Poppy's foresight.

Promising to join Poppy as soon as I had finished, I waved her off and settled in for a shorter than anticipated wait. Glancing around, I couldn't help but notice the incredulous, even jealous looks, on the faces of some of the older gents. It wasn't every day that I was singled out for attention by a young woman with the stunning looks of a supermodel.

After lightening the load in my money belt and duly depositing Pelham's cash in the Sofia Apartment's business account, I headed across the road to join Poppy for coffee. It was a pleasure to see Poppy's grandmother, Kalliope, again, though I was somewhat embarrassed as I recalled our previous meeting.

Marigold and I had accepted Poppy's invitation to join her family for lunch, Kalliope piling my plate high with servings of tasty homemade dishes. Alas, our luncheon was abruptly curtailed when, suffering from heat stroke, I passed out on the bathroom floor. The ignominy of the events that followed should be a lesson to everyone about the danger of overdoing the sun: after the bathroom door had been broken down to facilitate my rescue, I had been summarily dragged outside and hosed down to lower my temperature by Poppy's father, a veterinarian. Even though he was more accustomed to dealing with animals, he managed his human patient well, only his style lacking finesse.

Enjoying a coffee in the company of two beautiful ladies offered me an opportunity to use my Greek as I duly made enquiries about the health of the veterinarian and all the other family members gathered at that fateful lunch, in turn answering questions about the health of Marigold and other Meli villagers. Poppy revealed she was only back in Greece for a short holiday, visiting her family during a break from her studies.

The conversation switched to English as Poppy and I engaged in a fascinating discussion about her PhD studies in bacteria, Poppy excited about the direction her research was going. Although Kalliope couldn't understand our words, she smiled sweetly, nodding sagely. Although it felt rude to exclude Kalliope from the conversation, my skills in the Greek language certainly didn't stretch to PhD level.

Pulling a twenty euro note from her purse, Kalliope sent Poppy inside to settle the bill, overriding my protestations that coffee was on me. No sooner had Poppy disappeared inside than Kalliope put her hand firmly on my arm. Leaning in close towards me, I could feel her breath on my face as she adopted a wheedling tone.

"*I engoni mou einai toso kalo koritsi, alla tha itan kalytera na pantretei ton Gianni kai na spoudazei anoita vaktiria se mia xenic hora."* I did a double-take at her words. I had not expected her to say, 'My granddaughter is such a good girl, but it would be better for her to marry Giannis and stop studying stupid bacteria in a foreign country.' Kalliope then added that Poppy would be much happier if she settled down with Giannis and had children.

The very notion that anyone would consider it stupid to study bacteria, or that bacteria was anything less than fascinating, was a complete anathema to me. Moreover, it went against everything Poppy had just relayed to me regarding how much she enjoyed her studies and how proud she was of some recent breakthroughs that pointed to a greater understanding of Streptococci. It occurred to me that it was Kalliope rather than Poppy, who would be happy if Poppy returned to Greece and settled down in marriage.

My supposition proved to be correct when Kalliope's ruse soon became clear, her whole demeanour changing from that of a sweet-looking elderly granny to that of a relentless interrogator with a steely-eyed stare. To say I was a tad taken aback by the grilling Kalliope subjected me to, would be an understatement: it certainly wouldn't have surprised me to learn she had trained as a KGB operative as she relentlessly dug for information about Giannis, demanding to know what he was up to these days and, more importantly, if he was courting someone new.

It became evident that Kalliope had high hopes that the romance between her granddaughter and Giannis could be reignited and that Poppy would give up all that nonsense about studying in a foreign country, instead returning to the bosom of her family, complete with Giannis in tow as her husband. Kalliope's tenacious desire to meddle put Marigold's matchmaking ambitions to shame; the doting grandmother clearly bent on getting her own way.

Twigging what Kalliope was up to, I felt it was not my place to provide her with the information she was bent on acquiring, nor had I got the impression from Poppy that she would be happy to give up her studies in order to settle down in the village. With that in mind, I played the only card at my disposal by pleading ignorance of the Greek language, repeating the phrase, "*Den katalavaino,*" meaning 'I don't understand', even though I had understood the gist of most of Kalliope's questions. Considering I had participated in the earlier three-way conversation in Greek, Kalliope looked rightly suspicious of my sudden lack of comprehension. Throwing in a couple of exaggerated yawns to indicate tiredness was affecting my brain, I maintained my pseudo-ignorance, having no wish to become the wooden spoon to the elderly woman's stirring.

When Poppy returned to the table, Kalliope's whole demeanour went through another transformation as she morphed back into sweet granny mode. Using the need to meet Doreen as an excuse to leave, I made my escape, more than a little disturbed by the way Kalliope was essentially plotting behind Poppy's back in defiance of the younger woman's ambitions. Knowing I was somewhat out of my depth, I decided to shelve my concerns for now, until I could confide in Marigold.

Speed was of the essence as I dashed to an electronics

store to purchase a new laptop. With no time to browse the models, I simply snapped up one that was identical to the one that gave up the ghost the night before. Fortunately, my good friend Gordon Strange was a bit of a whizz when it came to computers if I needed any help setting the new one up.

Arriving back at the police station, there was no sign of Doreen. Fortunately, the female police officer who had assisted us earlier spotted me hanging around like a lemon and came to my rescue.

"You want to see your lady friend? She pass the written test." The officer winked at me. Unsure how to interpret the gesture, I didn't ask her if she'd provided any of the answers. "Come with me. The testes are to almost finish the practical test."

About to jump in and correct her English, I thought better of it: I may well end up embarrassing both of us if I explained the meaning of testes.

Guiding me through the ground floor of the police station, the officer opened a side door, leading to an outdoor area used for the practical test. After consulting with the instructor, the officer advised me the test had just finished: it seemed I was too late to witness Doreen's prowess in riding a moped, skilfully manoeuvring it between the traffic cones laid out on the course, though I'd arrived just in time to see her taking a helmet off and handing it to an athletic young man.

A group that appeared to be primarily comprised of teenage boys, high-fived each other as they jubilantly celebrated passing the test. Spotting me, Doreen waved and made her way towards me. As the buoyant group of lads parted to make way for her, one of them let out a piercing whistle before good-naturedly shouting, "Go Doreen," the rest of them taking up his call. Blushing furiously, Doreen's cheeks matched her sting-reddened nose as she responded, *"Efcharisto mou..."*

"Agoria," I prompted Doreen, telling her the word for boys.

"Efcharisto mou agoria," Doreen cried out. I had never seen her so exhilarated. "Victor, can you believe it? I passed the test."

"Bravo," I praised, stepping backwards in case Doreen had any ludicrous notion of kissing me.

The female police officer moseyed over, telling Doreen, "Well done. You pass."

"Thank you so much for all your help," Doreen gushed, double kissing the police woman's cheeks. "I was so nervous but you put me at ease."

"Ride carefully," the officer advised as she bade us goodbye.

Making our way back to the car, Doreen was still on a high when she suggested treating me to lunch. "I could eat a horse. I was too nervous to eat a bite this morning."

Recalling that I'd been forced to lob a perfectly decent *spanakopita* out of the window earlier, I gladly accepted Doreen's invitation, suggesting we stop for lunch on the outskirts of town where parking would be easier. Opting for a traditional taverna opposite the sea, we took our seats in the shade of a glorious pink bougainvillea. Since Doreen had a fancy for the *sardeles psites*, freshly grilled sardines, she suggested we share them. I agreed, thinking they would go well with the *gigantes*, giant white beans cooked in the oven with spinach and herbs. A serving of *tzatziki* dip with warm *pita* bread completed our choices. As Doreen was celebrating, she ordered an *ouzo* to accompany the sardines whilst I, as the designated driver, stuck with sparkling water.

"Considering how nervous you were earlier, you seemed to take the test in your stride," I observed.

"I felt as though I stuck out like a sore thumb, especially with this ginormous pimple-style sting on my nose. Walking into the test room, it was full of teenage boys: I felt very conspicuous being the only foreigner, the only female, and the only person over forty..."

Doreen paused as I snorted, grudgingly admitting, "Okay, over sixty. But everyone was so friendly. I suppose they were so excited at the thought of being able to legally ride their bikes."

"How did you find the written test?"

"To be honest, most of it was quite a doddle. Some of the questions were so ridiculous that I was sure they must be trick questions."

"How so?"

"Well, one that stands out in my mind asked, 'How tight should the helmet be?' The options were 'A: It should fit without squeezing the head, and B: It should be very loose so the head does not sweat uncomfortably.' I was convinced that one was a trick question because no one wants a sweaty head, but I realised one must sometimes be uncomfortable when safety is involved."

"Quite so," I agreed. "You must always wear a helmet, Doreen, no matter how uncomfortable it is nor how much it messes up your hair."

"I do know that, Victor."

"Well, I was just reminding you..."

Adroitly changing the subject, Doreen said, "I wasn't prepared for a question about riding at night..."

"What was the question?" I prodded, genuinely curious.

"It asked, 'If you are dazzled by oncoming headlights at night, should you, A: Close your eyes, or B: Slow down or stop.'"

"I'm guessing you didn't opt for 'close your eyes.'"

"Of course not. There were a couple of questions involving technical parts of the bike, such as exhausts and brakes, but if ever I wasn't sure of the right answer, that lovely police lady popped up by my side and pointed to the correct multiple-choice option."

"I have to say, I'm quite amazed that the police were willing to help you out with the answers."

"I must get Norman to bake one of his cakes so I can drop it in at the station next time I'm in town..."

"That might be considered bribing a public official," I cautioned.

"What tosh. A cake is hardly the same as one of those infamous brown envelopes. Oh, here's the food. It looks quite wonderful," Doreen gushed as the waiter brought a platter of perfectly grilled sardines glistening with sea salt.

"Lemon?"

"Definitely. I'm getting quite the taste for it. Manolis puts it on everything," Doreen said as I squeezed the fresh lemon over the fish. Holding a sardine to the light, Doreen bit the head off before crunching her way through the body, a look of appreciative delight on her face.

"How did the practical test go?" I asked before sampling the *gigantes*. The dish was cooked to perfection: the beans, fluffy and almost creamy in texture, absorbing the garlicky lemon flavours of the tomato and spinach sauce.

"It was quite funny," Doreen surprised me by saying. "One of those teenage boys had ridden his motorbike to the police station even though he didn't have his diploma yet. The instructor said he would overlook it if we could all use his bike for the practical part of the test since someone taking the test last week had driven the usual one into a wall and dented the handlebars. It was bigger than the one Manolis bought me but my diploma will allow me to ride anything up to 125 cc."

"What's yours?"

"Fifty cc. Manolis didn't want me to have anything too powerful."

"Well, yours is a perfect size for whizzing around Meli on. Just keep your speed down and watch out for any stray cats leaping into the road. They can be an absolute menace. My mother has come a cropper more than once when a feral has appeared out of nowhere."

"I really don't know how they've got the nerve to unseat Mrs Burke," Doreen quipped.

Chapter 23

A Draught Down Under

After dropping Doreen back at her place, I returned home to the Bucket residence where I discovered Marigold sprawled out on a sun-lounger in the garden under the shade of a parasol, her nose buried in what I guessed was yet another moving abroad book. She retained an insatiable appetite for the genre, rarely finding a book that didn't comply with her expectations regarding excessive exclamation marks, despite my explaining that adding a pling didn't automatically turn a dull sentence into something worthy of exclaiming over.

"Did you have a nice trip to town, dear?"

"It was a tad hot but I got everything I needed done," I told her.

Plucking a fuzzy-skinned apricot from the tree, I used Marigold's bottle of water to rinse it off before sinking my teeth into the delicious fruit and joining my wife on the adjacent lounger.

"You really should be more discreet," Marigold chided, peering at me intently over the top of her sunglasses which had slipped down her nose. Marigold's dazzling smile and twinkling eyes belied her scolding tone.

Rather baffled by her comment, I queried her choice of words. "Discreet? About what?"

"It's the talk of the village that you were spotted in town canoodling with a very attractive younger woman. It was all anyone could talk about at the hairdressers."

Hedging my bets that Marigold's hair had been done, I jumped in with a compliment. "Your hair looks lovely, darling."

"That's the second time you've complimented my hair when I'm wearing a sun hat."

"Yes, but bits of your hair are poking out. It's not as though all your hair is invisible. You look quite lovely. I must say, I'm a tad bemused to be the talk of Athena's kitchen."

Marigold's lilting tone dripped in amusement when she said, "I very much doubt the gossips were referencing Doreen."

"I ran into Poppy in the bank," I told her, wondering who had seen me and blabbed about my innocent encounter. It wasn't as though I would have kept Marigold in the dark about my chance meeting.

News tended to spread like wildfire in a small Greek

village, the finer details of what one had been up to in town relayed to the village by mobile phone before one had even started the drive home. It wouldn't surprise me if someone with a malicious tongue had painted me as having a full-blown affair. Fortunately, my darling Marigold would simply laugh off any such rumours as utterly nonsensical.

"Ah, Poppy. How is she? It must be an age since I've seen her. Such a beautiful girl." As she spoke, Marigold leaned forward to wipe a dribble of apricot juice from my chin. "I remember how gullible you and Barry were, mistaking her for a supermodel."

"She's visiting her family for a couple of weeks before returning to her studies in Edinburgh. Poppy wasn't alone. She was with her grandmother, Kalliope. I had coffee with both of them."

"Why the frown, darling?"

"Kalliope deliberately engineered it so that the two of us were left alone…"

"You and Kalliope?" As I nodded in the affirmative, Marigold continued, "Isn't it funny how the gossips didn't mention a third wheel?"

"I doubt any gossip about my having coffee with an elderly granny would have the same provocative appeal…but listen. It was clear why Kalliope wanted me alone when she started quizzing me about Giannis. Kalliope thinks that her granddaughter should give up her studies. She seemed determined to reunite Poppy and Giannis."

"Well, they did make a lovely couple…"

"That's as maybe, but Giannis is with Yiota now…"

"And they make a lovely couple too," Marigold said. Despite her usual obsession with meddling match-making, my wife's next words were at odds with Kalliope's interference. "I think it's wrong for Poppy's grandmother to put any pressure on Poppy to give up her studies. I remember how Poppy always spoke of how her parents were so supportive and encouraging about her studies."

"The study of the Streptococci bacteria is an important field..."

"You and your germs, Victor. Still, it was Poppy's decision to part ways with Giannis to pursue her studies. She had too much ambition to willingly give up a glittering scientific career..."

"I never thought you'd refer to anything germ-related as glittering," I said with a chuckle. "There wouldn't be any opportunities locally if Poppy gave it all up to marry Giannis."

"And Poppy is as clueless in the kitchen as Giannis. I really think Yiota is a better fit for Giannis. The two of them both gave up life in a city in favour of a simpler rural life and they both enjoy working outdoors and with their hands."

"My mother's not too keen on Giannis at the moment..."

"That's true. And your mother is no fool, Victor. She can be pretty astute. Perhaps you should sound Giannis out, see if he's still carrying a torch for Poppy..."

"You can leave me out of it," I said firmly before filling Marigold in on the rest of the day.

My wife, delighted that Doreen had passed her

moped test with flying colours, paled just a tad. "I hope she doesn't have any ideas about expecting me to ride pillion."

"Just tell her you don't want a helmet messing up your hair. I'm off for a shower, darling. Tell me there's plenty of water..."

"There certainly is."

Before jumping in the shower, I took my new laptop into my study and placed a call to Gordon Strange. Since he was something of a computer whizz, I hoped he could give me a hand setting up the new machine. Explaining that my trusty laptop had given up the ghost after being fried in the previous night's storm, I told Gordon I would very much appreciate his help in getting the new one operational.

"It sounds as though you neglected to use protection," Gordon said.

"Protection? Something in the line of a laptop prophylactic..."

"A what?"

"A laptop condom."

After duly laughing along at my pathetically lame joke, Gordon clarified he was talking about a surge plug. Annoyed that it had never occurred to me that the laptop needed surge protection, I voiced my irritation in neglecting to pick one up in town earlier.

"I've a spare one I can lend you," Gordon offered, promising to pop over the next evening to help me get set up. "I've already made plans for during the day tomorrow. That young couple who are renting one of your apartments..."

"Toby and Flick..."

"They're the ones. They were keen on joining me for a spot of twitching. I'll be free in the evening though..."

"I can't say how much I appreciate your help with the new laptop." Without mentioning anything about the tremendous ordeal of having the book I'd written being cataclysmically wiped out, I told Gordon that I had lost some important documents stored on the computer.

"I might be able to retrieve them from the hard drive," Gordon suggested. "It's certainly worth a shot."

"Really? That would be amazing. Oh no, I binned it this morning." Without further ado, I hung up on Gordon and raced to the village bins, desperately hoping the laptop I had dumped that morning was still there.

Reaching the bins, I couldn't believe my bad luck when I discovered they had been emptied. Half of the time, the bin men were on strike, leaving the rubbish to fester for days on end. On the one occasion I yearned to see them overflowing, I was thwarted. My last hope to salvage the book was to telephone the *Dimarcheio* when they opened the next morning and try to find out where the rubbish had been taken. Recalling that I still had the printed copy of 'Bucket to Greece,' albeit covered in purple corrections courtesy of James Scraper, reminded me that not all was lost. Even though I had duly mastered the art of touch typing, it would be no small task typing the whole thing up all over again.

If it wasn't for the certainty that Marigold would make a mockery of my work by inserting unnecessary exclamation marks in place of periods, I might have tried to persuade her to help out with the typing. Thinking prudently, I realised the prospect of thousands of plings littering the pages was a risk too far. Plings and V.D. Bucket simply didn't go together.

By the time I had returned home again and finished my shower, Marigold had moved from the sun lounger to a cool air-conditioned spot in the bedroom. Rummaging through my underwear drawer, I thought I was losing my sanity when I discovered my reliable pile of neatly folded white Y-fronts had mysteriously vanished, every last pair replaced with red boxer shorts. The culprit was obvious: Marigold had taken it upon herself to restyle me. No doubt, she had got carried away on her recent trip to town with Athena, waiting until I was out for the day to make the switch.

"Marigold," I said, approaching the subject with a hint of caution. "What have you done with my underpants?"

"I thought it was time for a change, darling. Your usual tighty-whities..."

Cringing at Marigold's choice of words, I interrupted, "I do wish you wouldn't refer to them like that...it sounds so vulgar."

"As I was saying, your usual tightie-whities had a whiff of old man about them..."

"Excuse me. The only thing they whiffed of was washing powder."

"Must you take everything so literally, Victor? I was referring to whiff in the appearance sense."

"A whiff is a pong, not a pose..."

"Boxers are much more flattering, dear..."

"You know perfectly well that red is not my colour..."

"Not to mention, healthier. Did you know they improve male fertility?"

"Are you deluded, Marigold? Why on earth would you want me more fertile when your child-bearing days are well behind you?"

"Well, your skin will thank me."

"How so?"

"The looser fit means the fabric won't chafe your skin…"

"My old ones didn't chafe. I was more than happy with them," I protested. Holding a pair of boxers aloft to more closely examine them, I added, "And look, this loose style means I could well get a draught down under."

"Oh, for goodness' sake, Victor. Only you could worry about draughts in the searing heat of a Greek summer. These boxers are much more modern, Victor, not to mention sexier."

Knowing my wife as well as I do, something about her words just didn't ring true. "Spit it out, Marigold. What's really going on?"

Unable to look me in the eye, Marigold spluttered, "I…"

"Just tell me. What's going on?"

"If you must know, I was putting your clean laundry away this morning when I came across that revolting jar of drowned ticks in your underwear drawer."

Wondering what she was talking about, I recalled that I'd stashed the jar in the drawer as the sight of it on the dresser was giving Marigold the ick factor.

"Without realising what it was at first, I picked it up," Marigold continued. "Once it dawned on me what

I was holding, it fell through my fingers. Landing on the top of the dresser, it smashed, all the rubbing alcohol and tick corpses spilling into your underwear drawer and soaking into your freshly ironed Y-fronts. Not to mention a million shards of glass. I dumped the whole lot in a bin bag...after giving your drawer a thorough scrub, it dawned on me that you didn't have a single pair of underpants left. Athina helped me out...when we were in town, she'd bought some new boxers for Vangelis...don't worry, he hasn't worn them...they were still in their packaging." There was no disguising the hint of a genuine apology in Marigold's tone.

"It's good to know that you don't expect me to wear used underwear," I said, struck by the look of contrition on Marigold's face.

"I'll stock up on your usual style next time I'm in town. You'll just have to adapt to boxers until then. I feel bad that I didn't warn you. I wouldn't like it if you replaced all my Marks and Sparks pants with granny knickers or uncomfortable thongs."

"You'd definitely feel a draught in thongs," I joshed. "Well, I suppose it would be churlish of me to dismiss these boxers out of hand. I'll give them a whirl. I just hope they don't make me so fertile that I start acting like Kouneli."

Chapter 24

The Postman Knocks

Strolling home from the shop mid-morning, I spotted the postman knocking on the door of Kyria Sofia Kompogiannopoulou's house. Sighting the postman in the village was a rarity since he only visited Meli once a month, the rest of the time leaving the mail at the nearest post office.

I should clarify that I am using the term 'nearest' in its loosest form since in this instance 'nearest' most definitely doesn't equate to near, the post office being a good forty minutes' drive away from Meli. When a villager needs to pop down to the post office, it is customary for them to pick up any post for their neighbours and either drop it off personally or leave it in the village shop for Tina to dole out to her customers.

The once a month trip the postman made to the village was to deliver the pensions. With most of the population of Meli being in receipt of a Greek pension, the postman was entrusted with a sizeable wad of cash which he personally delivered, going practically door-to-door. This method of distributing the cash was a world away from the electronic pension payments deposited directly into bank accounts, more commonly made in England.

Since I rarely stopped by the post office myself and didn't receive a Greek pension, I was on nothing more than nodding terms with the postman, now knocking on the door of the house which had stood empty since Sofia's death. With no one responding to his knock, the postman's face expressed frustration. Clearly, he hadn't heard the news of her sad demise, even though such news usually travelled at the speed of light.

A screech of brakes heralded the arrival of Kyria Kompogiannopoulou's daughter, Ekaterina. Like the postman, she was another person I was merely on nodding terms with because she had often visited the village to spend time with her mother. Marigold, acquainted with her from the beautifying the cemetery group, relayed that she found Ekaterina plump, personable and pleasant. Ekaterina looked like a clone of her mother, so similar in appearance that there could be no doubt about her parentage. I personally observed that her parking skills were beyond shoddy, the front wheels of her car mounting the pavement, creating a safety hazard and impeding the progress of any passing pedestrians, of which I was one.

Practically leaping out of her car, Ekaterina accosted the postman, telling him she would sign for her mother's pension. With a pen poised above the signature line, Ekaterina was about to get her hands on the envelope of cash when Dimitris called out from his doorstep next door, telling the postman that Kyria Kompogiannopoulou had passed away. The postman immediately snatched the paper back, asking Ekaterina if it was true. Clearly, the postman was having no truck with handing over a dead person's pension to a potentially grasping relative who appeared to be attempting to brazenly commit financial fraud.

I am sad to report that my Greek language skills weren't quite up to translating the nuances of the screaming match that broke out between the postman and Ekaterina, the pair of them shouting over one another, their words delivered at an excessive speed akin to a barrage of bullets fired from a machine gun. Holding firm, Ekaterina insisted that by law she was entitled to her mother's final pension payment, the postman adamant that he wouldn't hand any cash over until she acquired written permission from the Department of Pensions.

With minimal understanding of their garbled words, it was hard for me to assess which one of the pair was in the right. However, it could be construed as suspicious that Ekaterina hadn't mentioned her mother's death until Dimitris brought it up. Moreover, I was not unaware of the myriads of rumours that a not insignificant number of people across Greece lived high on the hog by claiming a dead relative's pension. In line with the general Greek belief that rules are made to be broken, I had not been too surprised to hear the rumours bandied around that a number of taxi drivers had registered as blind so they could claim a monthly compensation. Such shameful examples of corruption were the daily fodder of heated exchanges in the *kafenion* though I am happy to report that Meli harboured no visually impaired taxi drivers.

Sticking to his guns, the postman stalked off in the middle of one of Ekaterina's rants. Getting into his car, he drove the few metres to Kyriakos' house. Perchance he was worried that the still screeching Ekaterina might let the air out of his tyres or use her lipstick to deface his vehicle with obscene words in the manner of whoever was taunting Nikos with gratuitous graffiti. Sending a daggers-drawn look at Dimitris for interfering in her business, Ekaterina dug out a key and entered the house, still chuntering in anger.

"I should have kept my nose out," Dimitris admitted, visibly shaking. No doubt the din of the slanging match had upset his composure. "Ekaterina was adamant that Sofia was entitled to one final month's payment..."

"But would it have been just the one month if you hadn't interjected?"

Dimitris' reply to my question was drowned out by the sound of a blood-curdling scream emanating from Sofia's house, the timbre of said scream sharing nothing in common with the type of shriek Marigold emits at the sight of a random lizard in the Bucket residence. The pair of us didn't hesitate to rush inside Sofia's house to proffer our assistance to her daughter. As we charged through the door, I reflected that although neither Dimitris or I painted the typical image of heroes, it didn't prevent us from unselfishly running towards potential danger.

"*Ekaterina, ti einai afto?*" Demetris called out, asking her 'What is it?'

"*Kapoios itan sto spiti,*" Ekaterina replied, saying someone had been in the house.

"*Einai akoma edo?*" I said, asking if they were still there.

"*Den koitaxa ston epano orofo,*" Ekaterina replied, saying she hadn't looked upstairs.

"*O Victor kai tha koitaxoume epano toro,*" Dimitris said, telling Ekaterina that the two of us would look upstairs now. I have to admit that I didn't appreciate Dimitris volunteering my services but if I refused to accompany him up the stairs, I could well be labelled a coward. With no clue what possibly awaited us upstairs, I considered it out of character for Dimitris to be so rash.

Before we headed upstairs, I looked around the living room for any signs that would indicate an intruder had indeed been there, recognising that grief may have played havoc with Ekaterina's imagination. Since I was not familiar with the interior of Sofia's house, I wasn't in a position to gauge if the place was unusually messy, particularly as the living room curtains were closed, making the room gloomy. However, I reflected that Sofia would most surely have kept the house immaculate:

when we had worked at the shop together, Sofia had been an absolute stickler for keeping everything in its rightful place, fighting a constant battle to keep even a hint of dust at bay.

As Ekaterina threw the curtains open, the sunlight highlighted the less-than-pristine condition of the room. A sleeping bag had been dumped on top of the sofa, the floor around it littered with dirty clothes emitting a most unpleasant musty scent, with yet more clothes spilling out of a large rucksack.

Grabbing a large flannel shirt from the pile of discarded clothes, I read the clues, pronouncing, "Since this smelly shirt clearly belongs to a man, I would hazard a guess that the intruder was male."

"Talk about stating the obvious." Ekaterina's words took me by surprise since I had no idea that she was fluent in English.

"A male who like the beer," Dimitris added, pointing to the empty beer bottles lined up on the coffee table.

"A male with slobbish tendencies who didn't have the good sense to use coasters," I added, noting the rings of discolouration caused by condensation seeping into the wood.

Since Sofia's grandson, the rightful new owner of the house, was still a young child, I automatically ruled him out as the beer drinker. It didn't take a great leap to reach the conclusion that the intruder had been squatting in the house. Recalling that I had noticed the curtains twitching on several occasions, I felt a tad guilty that I hadn't investigated further.

As Ekaterina lifted the sleeping bag from the couch,

alarm bells rang in my mind when I spotted a large red footprint on the material. I felt confident that the footprint was dried on red paint. If my suspicion was correct, it logically followed that the squatter and the vandal with a vendetta against Nikos, were one and the same.

"Let's check the kitchen before you go upstairs," Ekaterina called out. Following closely in her wake as she pointed towards the open kitchen window, I concluded that the squatter must have made it his point of entrance. Since the window was still ajar, it was conceivable that the culprit intended to return: that is, if he wasn't actually lurking upstairs. Considering the number of empty crisp packets and chocolate wrappers littering the kitchen, it seemed that the squatter had been living on junk food rather than doing any actual cooking.

Dimitris told Ekaterina to look around and see if anything was missing whilst he and I checked upstairs. A quick recce of the upstairs rooms revealed, to my great relief, that the house was empty. To my untrained eye, it appeared as though nothing had been disturbed in Sofia's neat and tidy bedroom: however, it didn't take a genius to conclude that Sofia had not been the one to leave soggy towels strewn across the bathroom floor nor fail to clean up the globs of toothpaste dried onto the washbasin.

After returning downstairs, the three of us pondered what to do next. None of us wanted to be there if the squatter suddenly returned; for all we knew, he could be armed and dangerous. Calling the police seemed futile as the squatter wasn't on the premises and we had no idea when he would return: the police were hardly going to hang around indefinitely on the off-chance. When my idea that we phone Spiros for advice went down well, I placed a call to the undertaker, asking him to pop over before waiting on the doorstep for him to arrive.

Spotting Spiros crossing the square, I felt a tad guilty for dragging him out. As he was smartly suited and booted in his working garb, I guessed he had a funeral to arrange or a burial to officiate.

"Victor, I am the much glad you call." Spiros' words instantly wiped out my feeling of guilt. "I have the unfortunate situation."

"How so?"

"I am to arrange the funeral of an elderly man and his the daughter keep making the ears at me."

"Making the ears?" I queried before twigging, "You mean she's been making eyes at you."

"Eyes, ears, legs, head...it is all the same. In all the years of the undertaking, I never have had to deal with the bereaved to flirting with me over the coffin. It is the wrong. It is not the respectful."

"It's most definitely disrespectful," I agreed.

"I tell the daughter I am the marry, but she still to make the eye."

"You could try spilling some embalming fluid on your jacket. You've often complained that the smell of formaldehyde puts most women off."

"Bravo, Victor. That might to work," Spiros cried before enthusiastically dropping a double kiss on my cheeks. "Now, why did you need me to come to the Sofia's house? Is it more the twitching?"

Whilst I was duly giving the low-down to Spiros about the squatter and the likelihood that said squatter was probably the person who had been tormenting Nikos, his phone rang. Before answering the call, Spiros looked at the caller details in a cautious way.

"It is not the woman with eyes," he said, relief evident in his voice. "It is the Kyrios Alexandros."

"The chap with the cat…"

"Yes. I must to take it," Spiros said, answering the call.

After exchanging the usual pleasantries, Spiros delivered the bad news to the elderly man, telling him the cat had fallen off the roof. Oozing fake sincerity, Spiros added that the cat was with the vet but it was touch and go if the feline would live.

Terminating the call, Spiros told me, "That went the well. By spreading the bad news out, the Alex is now prepare for the worse. Tomorrow, I will to tell him the cat is dead. Because he is the primed to expect the worse, the news should not to give him the heart attack."

Although I had initially thought there was madness in Spiros' method, I could now appreciate why he had circled around the issue.

"It appears the end may well justify the means. Your approach to letting Alex down gently has spared him the shock he could have received if you'd simply blurted out that the cat was dead."

"I must to bury the cat before the Alex return to Nektar," Spiros said.

"But there is no cat to bury," I reminded him, thinking the deceased feline may well be lying in the dump next to my discarded hard drive.

"I bury the cat...how to say in the English...the figuratively?"

As we entered the house, Ekaterina and Dimitris joined Spiros and I. Mulling over our options, Spiros was adamant that the most important thing was to learn the identity of Nikos' tormentor and to find out why he had made Nikos the target of his vendetta. With a consensus reached, Spiros directed that we should stake out Sofia's house and catch the squatter red-handed on his return.

"You should go the home, Ekaterina. It could be too much the danger for the woman," Spiros advised. Considering the way Ekaterina had ranted at the postman earlier indicated she was no shrinking violet. Indeed, she probably had more pluck about her than either Dimitris or I. "I cannot to stay now. I must to make the bury. Victor, can you to stay here?"

"No, I have plans for the afternoon. I'm meeting Pelham, a fellow public health inspector from Manchester."

Tellingly, Spiros didn't ask Dimitris if he could stay. Most likely, Spiros recognised that Dimitris may well fall apart if he was left to confront the squatter alone.

"It would be the better to wait until the dark," Spiros decided. "I will phone the around and arrange the posset..."

"The posset. That makes no sense, Spiro...ah, are you thinking of a posse?"

"Yes, the posse, the same as in the American cowboy movies. We hide outside in the dark and watch the house...when the vandal return, we to pounce."

"It would certainly help to have strength in numbers," I agreed, wondering if I was actually nimble enough to do any pouncing. I was still feeling a tad stiff after a bout of strenuous gardening the previous weekend.

"We have the three," Spiros said, his gesture incorporating me along with himself and Dimitris. "We need the more number…it would to make the sense to watch the house in shifts. Who else? Not the Nikos. The Barry, Vangelis and Blat…"

"And Guzim. There's also Hal and Gordon Strange… and Apostolis and Mathias…"

"It is better we use just the young men, Victor."

"Well, that rules me out," I said, attempting to hide my relief.

"You are the spring nowt chicken, Victor."

"If you're going to quote Violet Burke, at least get it right, Spiro. It's nowt but a spring chicken."

Since Spiros was adamant that I make up the numbers, I gathered that the term 'young men' applied to anyone under eighty. Whether I liked it or not, I resigned myself to spending my evening staking out Sofia's house, my assigned shift running from nine to midnight. It would be worth it to unmask the cretin that had been making Nikos' life a misery and drum him out of the village.

Chapter 25

Just Big-Boned

"Darn. It's a complete bureaucratic nightmare attempting to deal with those jobsworths down at the *Dimarcheio*."

After leaving Sofia's house, I had spent the last hour attempting to find out where the village bins had been emptied in the feverish hope that I could recover my hard drive and get my hands on my lost copy of 'Bucket to Greece.' Running out of patience with me, the woman on the phone had resorted to telling me that the location of the dump was a state secret. At least, I think that is what she claimed. I certainly hadn't missed the desperation in her voice as she tried to get rid of me. It wouldn't surprise me to hear my telephone number had been blocked by the *Dimarcheio* staff.

"I can imagine," Marigold sympathised. "It might help if your telephone Greek was better. I couldn't understand half of what you said."

"You know how my Greek goes all to pot when I'm staring down a telephone line," I admitted.

"Usually, I find it easier to understand a foreigner speaking Greek than an actual Greek."

"I'm the same, darling. I think it's because non-native speakers tend to be less confident in Greek, thus more prone to speaking slower whilst enunciating every syllable," I agreed. "Much as it pains me to say it, I can always understand John Macey when he speaks Greek in that pompous manner of his, even though his tenses are all to pot. Conversely, I can be left baffled when some of the elderly local men just sound as though they're speaking gibberish."

"They talk too fast and some of them are missing half their teeth," Marigold pointed out. "It's very difficult to enunciate clearly if a crucial tooth is missing. I suppose it's the equivalent of a foreigner trying to make sense of some of the things your mother comes out with. She's a great one for northern patter."

"At least her patter doesn't translate." Returning to the matter of the binned hard drive, I said, "With the *Dimarcheio* being so uncooperative, it seems my book is well and truly gone. I have no choice but to retype it from the copy I printed."

"Look on the bright side, Victor. A bit of typing is much less onerous than picking your way through a smelly rubbish dump. Just imagine how many bins have been emptied there...the stench must be horrendous. Perhaps you could try to find it when winter rolls around. The dump won't be as stinky in the cold."

"By winter, the binmen will have probably dumped another few tonnes of rubbish on top of my hard drive..."

"Well, retyping the book will give you another chance to edit out the boring bits..."

"You think my book is boring?"

"Considering that you refuse to let me read it, I can only imagine. No doubt it reads like one of your hygiene reports."

"James Scraper enjoyed it, at least the bits he didn't label pretentious..."

"Pass me the icing sugar, Victor," Marigold requested, bending over to take a tray of cookies out of the oven. "I need to top off these *kourabiedes* with a good dousing."

"What possessed you to bake almond Christmas biscuits in June?"

"I wanted to perfect the recipe before the holiday season."

"But it's months off..."

"It always pays to be prepared. There's no law against eating *kourabiedes* during the summer. It's a pity you didn't save some of those Jammy Dodgers instead of giving them all to Tonibler and Ana. If I could have taken them along to the Weight Loss Club, it would have saved me from having to bake in this heat."

Holding my tongue about the absurdity of taking

sweet treats to the inaugural meeting of the Fat Club, I simply reminded Marigold that she was running late. "Shouldn't you be on your way?"

"I'm just waiting for Athena. We arranged to walk over to Sherry's together."

"I thought you were having the Fat Club at Doreen's house since it was her idea."

"Must you call it that? I've told you countless times that it's a Slimming Club. And yes, it was Doreen's idea. At the last expat dinner party, your mother told Doreen she was getting quite chubby so Doreen is determined to do something about it."

"I think the extra weight suits her and Manolis loves Doreen's curves."

"I agree but Doreen really took your mother's words to heart."

"Pot and kettle come to mind. My mother could never be described as sylphlike. So, if the club was Doreen's idea, why are you all traipsing over to Sherry's house?"

"To avoid Norman getting under our feet. Doreen says he just sits around drinking for most of the day. She's very worried about him."

"Doreen suggested we do an intervention but the idea doesn't appeal to me. It's not really our business."

"I'm with you, Victor. I mean Norman's only part of our circle because he's married to Doreen…"

"Does that mean we can drop Norman if Doreen ever gets round to divorcing him?"

"I think it's a given that he's already dropped if he can't stay sober." I knew I could rely on Marigold to put forward a rational argument on the ridiculous notion of an intervention.

"Doreen's going over to Sherry's house on her new moped."

"I'd better warn Pelham to stick close to the verge when he walks over." I was looking forward to my arranged catch-up with Pelham, feeling quite thrilled at the prospect of a chat about the latest hygiene violations Pel had detected back in Manchester.

"Doreen can't be that bad on her moped," Marigold said. "After all, she did pass her diploma with flying colours."

"I reckon you must be talking about your ditzy friend." I nearly jumped out of my skin at the intrusive sound of my mother's voice. How anyone so bulky could be so light on her feet when it suited, amazed me.

"Must you sneak up on us like that, Mother?"

"You're the one that gave me a key so I can let myself in to clean the place. Had you forgot I was due?"

"Of course not," Marigold said.

It was no coincidence that the timing of the Fat Club meeting deliberately coincided with my mother coming up to give the place a good going over. Marigold always tried to have something arranged away from home when Vi was due in her professional capacity, my wife having a low tolerance threshold when it came to being labelled lazy and slovenly by her mother-in-law.

"Anyhow," Vi continued. "If you were talking about Doreen, she's a bloody menace on that new scooter of hers. How much did she have to bung in a brown envelope to pass the test?"

BUCKET TO GREECE (VOL.17)

"There was no bribery involved. Doreen studied hard for the written test. Moreover, she didn't knock a single traffic cone over during the practical," I said.

"Make your mind up, Victor. You've just said you need to warn Pelham about Doreen passing him on her scooter which implies she's a danger on the roads, and now you're defending her."

"I made a joke, Marigold. Don't tell me you've lost your sense of humour."

"Really, Victor. Perhaps if your jokes were funny, I'd appreciate them."

As she spoke, Marigold piled the *kourabiedes* into a Tupperware box. As they were still warm, the icing sugar which Marigold had sieved over the top of the biscuits bled into them in a clumpy mess, the visual result most unappealing. In contrast, the Jammy Dodgers I'd knocked up with my two young charges had looked as though they had been made by a professional. "I know you've come over to clean, Vi, but you could give the place a miss if you've changed your mind about joining us at the Slimming Club."

"I'd rather stick to charring, lass. I could do with the cash. I'm saving up for something right special to wear to Benjamin's wedding."

"It's not a wedding as such. It's a civil union," I reminded her.

"Close enough, lad. It's not every day my only grandson ties the knot."

"I can help you find something really fabulous, Vi," Marigold offered, no doubt hoping to avoid the embarrassment of my mother turning up in something wildly unsuitable. "Now, are you sure you won't join us at Sherry's?"

"I've already told you a hundred times, I haven't got any fat to lose. I'm just big-boned." Vi's assertion triggered a dramatic eye roll from Marigold. "There's not many folk my age could hold down a cleaning job which is exercise in itself, or pedal their way through the village. Look at that Doreen. She'd have been better off getting on a push bike to keep her fit like me, rather than whizzing around on that polluting moped. 'Appen she's just too lazy to pedal."

"Nonsense. Doreen has an exercise bike..." Marigold argued.

"You told me she never uses it as the saddle is too hard and pointy," I pointed out.

"Whether she uses it or not is beside the point. I said she has one," Marigold persisted.

"Maria would be right chuffed if you invited her to join you," Vi said.

"Maria? Surely you can't mean Kyria Maria from next door? She has about as much surplus flab as a skeleton," Marigold said.

"Aye, that's as maybe but she heard that it's a party with wine and cakes."

"Where on earth did she hear our meeting is a party?"

"'Appen it might have been something I said," Vi admitted. "Maria's always right keen to try out foreign food treats. She can't get enough of my Warrington eggs and she's right partial to my spotted dick."

"She'll be disappointed then as Marigold has made

authentic Greek *kourabiedes* to take along, rather than anything foreign."

"What? You mean them Christmas biscuits. I can't say I'm keen on them. The way they stick to my teeth puts me in mind of wet cement." Vi's words were accompanied by some rather odd gurning. Pushing her tongue against her cheeks as though trying to rid her mouth of said wet cement provoked a ridiculous image of a hamster on the loose in her mouth: or maybe a hoglet.

"Goodness knows why you're going to that Fat Club, Marigold. You're thin as a rake."

"Thanks, Vi," Marigold said, a genuine smile on her face as she chose to take her mother-in-law's sarky dig as a compliment.

"A bit of padding wouldn't kill you, lass. A couple of mucky fat sarnies would see you right."

Choosing to ignore Vi's comment, Marigold extended another invitation for my mother to go along to the Fat Club.

"Are you really sure you won't join us? You're most welcome."

"These mucky floors of yours won't wash themselves," Vi pronounced, rolling up her sleeves and adjusting her head scarf, ready to get stuck in. "I ran into Cynthia and she was telling me you'd had a jam crisis, Victor. It must have been a right bugger scraping jam off them cats of yours."

"Singular, Mother. Only one cat was involved. Tonibler did an excellent job of giving it a bubble bath."

"Now that I'd have liked to see."

"Marigold. *Eimai edo.*" Athena called up from the street below to say she was there. My wife responded by patting her hair and grabbing the Tupperware box of Christmas biscuits.

"If you change your mind, Vi, you know where we'll be," Marigold said, surprising me by giving her mother-in-law a peck on the cheek.

Despite the petty bickering the two women regularly engaged in, there was no disputing that Marigold had grown genuinely fond of Vi, her sentiments reciprocated.

"I'll walk down with you, darling. Pelham is due any minute."

"Will you and your mate be fancying a pot of tea in the garden?" Vi enquired.

"That would be lovely, Mother."

"Rightio. I'll fetch it down when it's brewed."

By the time Marigold and I met Athena on the street, Kyria Maria had joined the hairdresser. Clad in her usual black widow's weeds, she was apparently determined to join the other women at the Fat Club, whether they wanted her there or not. She certainly didn't need to lose weight, her angular bones pointy enough to do some serious damage. Despite her fragile appearance, she was as tough as a mountain goat.

Using one hand to squeeze Marigold's arm with bony fingers, Kyria Maria used the other to swing a carrier bag.

"*Echo ftiaxei keftedakia kai makaronia gia tous chontrous,*" Maria said. Mentally translating her words, I had to hide my laughter as Maria announced she had made meatballs and spaghetti for the fat people. My mouth began to water when Maria added, "*Kai loukoumades.*"

I had tried a multitude of *loukoumades* in Greek homes and tavernas, the honey-drenched, deep-fried crispy balls, the Greek equivalent of doughnuts. None surpassed the perfection of Maria's light and fluffy version.

Explaining to Maria that the women were off to a group focused on losing weight, I managed to convince her the *loukoumades* would most likely be shunned by conscientious dieters. My meddling achieved my goal, Maria willingly handing the box of honeyed treats over to me. I was sure that Pelham would appreciate the *loukoumades* as much as I would.

Watching as Kyria Maria firmly linked arms with Marigold, I chortled: the elderly woman's dogged insistence on joining the ladies had clearly paid off.

Chapter 26

The Joy of Grubby Kitchens

Loitering by the gate waiting for Pelham to arrive, I caught my first glimpse of Doreen on her shiny new moped as she puttered by. As the moped moved along at a snail's pace, I reflected that despite Doreen's wheels and the awesome power of the moped's fifty cubic centimetre capacity, she may well trail behind the elderly Kyria Maria in arriving at Sherry's.

I was pleased to notice that not only had Doreen adhered to the law by wearing a helmet, she was also kitted out in motorcycle goggles, a biker's leather jacket and a pair of sturdy boots. Clearly, she was taking the issue of safety extremely seriously.

Calling out, "*Bravo* Doreen," and giving her a cheery

wave, I felt a tad affronted when she completely ignored me. I had no idea what I'd done to fall out of her good graces: we'd got along perfectly fine over lunch in town: indeed, we'd enjoyed a pleasant time.

Pelham arrived, his attire more suited to a day at the office than vacationing. I was pleased to see he was protecting his balding scalp with a smart wide-brimmed Panama hat. I would have hated for him to succumb to sunstroke whilst sitting around in my garden.

Next to Pel, I felt positively underdressed, having once again chosen to throw caution to the wind and go tie-free, replacing my slacks with shorts because of the heat.

Ushering Pelham through to the garden, I gave him a tour of the outside space, pointing out the bountiful vegetable patch, the fruit trees weighed down with summer fruit, Marigold's scented herbs and her glorious flowering pot plants, my outdoor spa and the chicken house. I deliberately kept a safe distance from the Albanian shed dweller's home. Even though Guzim was most likely working on Yiota's farm, I didn't want to risk him interrupting us with his typical nonsense whilst we were enjoying a good chin-wag about flagrant hygiene violations. After all, Guzim himself might be considered a flagrant hygiene violation.

Leading Pelham to the outdoor seating area, I was happy to see that Violet Burke had left us a pot of tea as promised, though less delighted to see a plate of Warrington eggs. I could only hope my mother hadn't fried them in my kitchen. Marigold would not only have a fit if she returned home to the smell of deep-fried food but

I would face an inevitable lecture about eating such unhealthy fare.

On the plus side, my mother must have slunk away back to her charring, rather than hanging around to meet Pelham. Despite being an absolute stickler for hygiene herself, she did hate to receive a lecture on the subject, something she believed all public health inspectors were primed to do.

Despite my disquiet about the Warrington eggs stinking the kitchen out, the temptation to dig in was too great to resist. Marigold had laid the law down, decreeing Vi's pickled Scotch eggs coated in black pudding, dipped in beer batter and then deep-fried, a banned food not to be tolerated in the Bucket household. On occasion though, sometimes I found them tantalisingly good and hard to resist. Deciding that the ban Marigold had imposed did not cover what I chose to eat in the garden, I risked her disapproval by tucking in. In my defence, it was at least six months since a Warrington egg had passed my lips, probably even longer since I'd tucked into a Fray Bentos.

"Are those a Greek delicacy?" Pelham asked, eyeing the still-steaming eggs warily.

"Well, they came out of my kitchen which is in Greece," I quipped.

"Excellent. I have no qualms about eating anything that came from your kitchen. Even though you've retired from the profession, I'm confident you keep an immaculate kitchen."

"Of course," I replied. "Actually, my mother made the eggs and she's an absolute stickler for cleanliness."

"I expect that's where you get your high standards from."

Having no wish to acquaint Pelham with the grim details of my mother abandoning me in a bucket at the railway station and only making an appearance in my life during her seventh decade, I didn't bother disillusioning Pelham: let him think that my fastidious hygiene standards had been instilled in me by my mother.

Once we'd polished off the Warrington eggs, I encouraged Pelham to tuck into the *loukoumades*, happy to let him assume they had come out of my own spotless kitchen.

Admittedly, I kept my fingers crossed, knowing that Kyria Maria gave free domestic rein to her eponymously named tortoise, Maria.

On more than one occasion, I had personally witnessed the plodding mammal taking a leisurely stroll across her owner's preparation area. On balance, Maria's doughnuts were so deliciously moreish, they were worth the slight risk of a dicky tummy courtesy of the tortoise.

Introducing the glorious treat to Pelham, I told him, "*Loukoumades* are Greek doughnuts drizzled in honey and cinnamon."

"Oh, my goodness. They taste like heaven on a plate," he gushed, already spearing a second doughnut with his fork. "Are they a local delicacy?"

"You can't really get more local than my neighbour's kitchen. It is claimed that *loukoumades* were the first sweet dessert to ever be recorded. The Ancient Greek poet, Callimachus, wrote about them, but back in his day they were referred to as honey tokens."

"Why honey tokens...beyond the obvious use of honey?"

"They were awarded as tokens to the competitors at the Olympic Games of 776BC."

"Edible medals?"

"Exactly. The ball shape originated later. The BC version was just pieces of fried dough dipped in honey."

"This honey is the best I've ever tasted."

"It is produced by the local bee man, Giannis. In Greek, honey is known as *meli*..."

"The same name as this village. How fascinating. You're very up on your stuff, Victor."

"I need to be. In my role as a holiday rep, I lead guided gastronomic walking tours."

Batting a number of persistent pesky wasps away, I spooned some of the honey onto a saucer before putting the lid on the now-empty box of *loukoumades*. Placing the saucer on the ground at a distance, I hoped that my attempt at a wasp trap would prove to be as successful a deterrent as burning coffee grounds. I would hate to blight Pelham's holiday by doing nothing to stop a wasp from stinging him in my garden. Doreen's nose was still red and blotchy despite applying copious amounts of vinegar.

"So, tell me, Pelham. Have you detected any unusual health violations lately?"

My question prompted Pelham to launch into an intriguing catalogue of some of the most memorable horrors he had uncovered in grubby kitchens since I'd hung up my hairnet.

"There is one particular incident that really stands

out and takes the biscuit. So, this one restaurant kitchen was teeming with roaches."

I shuddered. Harbouring an aggregation of cockroaches in a kitchen is one of the most serious hygiene infractions one can commit. Not only are roaches beyond disgusting, they also contaminate food and transmit disease.

"Although it was clear the place had a nasty cockroach infestation, the restaurant owner tried to convince me the cockroaches were his children's pets, even calling them out by name. I was pretty convinced he was taking the mickey but didn't fancy challenging him: he had an aura of danger about him. Most definitely an unsavoury type," Pelham continued. "When the owner left the kitchen for a moment, one of his staff fessed up that the owner kept the roaches to use in races, a vile gambling habit he had picked up in prison."

"That must have made your hackles rise…"

"It certainly did," Pelham agreed. "Curious what he'd been inside for, I asked the staff member if the owner had been convicted of giving food poisoning to his customers."

"Had he?"

"No. He was sent away for attacking a sous chef with a machete. I don't mind admitting that I was too intimidated to confront him about the cockroaches until I had backup."

"I imagine you retreated until the police turned up…"

"It was the wisest move. Too many knives and sharp objects in close range. Although the owner was not exactly pleased when I told him I was shutting the restaurant down, he seemed relieved that the police were only there to help me to enforce the order to close his doors until he had rectified the blatant hygiene violations. I rather imagine he thought the cops were onto him about some sort of criminal activity. He was clearly a shady character. Can you believe he vented his anger at the police presence I'd summoned by stomping on a load of roaches..."

"Imagine murdering your children's pets," I joshed.

"The next one reminded me of something you once faced with pigeons, Vic."

"Do tell," I encouraged.

"On a recent inspection of a takeaway, I discovered a load of dead pigeons crammed in the refrigerator."

"Pigeons are definitely popular with some of those dodgy takeaways," I said.

"It's quite ironic..."

"How so?"

"Well, it's ironic that the odd Chinese place will try and pass pigeon off as chicken which is more expensive, yet some upmarket restaurants charge an absolute fortune for a plate of squab," Pelham observed.

"Indeed. But cultivated squab is quite pricey for restaurants to purchase whereas random pigeons can be successfully lured into a back alley to meet their fate and become a free ingredient."

"Would you eat it?" Pelham asked.

"Squab? I can't say I would. I've always considered pigeons to be flying vermin. I've yet to see pigeon on a Greek menu but I can't say definitively that Greeks don't eat it. During the hunting season, some of the hunters take the *tsichlas* they've shot into the tavernas to be cooked."

"*Tsichlas?*"

"Thrushes. It also means chewing gum."

"Have you tried it?"

"No, I loathe the stuff. Too much chewing involved." Belatedly realising that Pelham was referring to thrushes rather than chewing gum, I confirmed I had tried the birds a couple of years back when Kostis gave his father a mews of thrushes he'd shot and Nikos grilled them.

"Vangelis, a friend of mine, just loves pigeons. Not as food, I hasten to add, but rather he admires them as a fine specimen of bird, considering them to be beautiful doves. Although we have two distinct words for pigeons and doves in the English language, in Greek the word *peristeri* applies to both. Whenever I'm with Vangelis for coffee and a cheese pie, he orders an extra pie to feed to the pigeons."

"Now, that's what I call peculiar behaviour," Pelham said. Whilst agreeing it was indeed bizarre, it didn't quite top Vangelis' obsession with using shoe polish to dye his chest hair.

"I suppose in his defence, I have observed that Greek pigeons do tend to be more attractive than English ones."

With the last of the tea drained, Pelham and I opted to take a walk through the village to walk off the sinful treats we'd indulged in. As we meandered at a leisurely pace, Pelham stopped to admire a delicate pink wild flower, its creamy petals wide open atop a glistening green hairy stem.

"I don't recall seeing that flower before," Pelham said, asking if I knew what it was.

"Flowers are Marigold's purview rather than mine," I replied, trying to remember the name of the bloom. "It's silene something; I don't believe it has a common name. I'm your man if you want to know the names of any vegetables or fruit."

"I'm pretty well up on my carrots and spuds," Pelham quipped.

"But have you ever tried the prickly pear fruit from the *frangosyka* plant?" I asked, pointing towards a forest of huge wild cacti with an abundance of spiky yellow fruit.

"I didn't realise fruit from a cactus was edible."

"Oh, yes, but it's a tricky one to pick and peel, and a bit of an acquired taste. Marigold isn't too keen but that's got more to do with her slicing her finger open the first time she attempted to peel one, rather than the actual taste of the fruit. Our neighbour, Maria, slices them up and adds them to a *feta* salad. There's a huge *frangosyka* plant at the apartments. Feel free to pick the fruit and sample it."

"I'll do that. Bill is planning to knock up a salad this evening…"

"Then I must give you some of the salad things from my garden before you head back."

After pausing to admire some young goats gambolling in an olive grove, our conversation reverted to hygiene violations.

"I had an unsettling experience recently in the kitchen

of a somewhat upmarket restaurant. We received a tip at the agency that the chef 'slash' owner had taken to cooking in nothing but his boxer shorts," Pelham confided.

"Surely, he didn't leave his head uncovered? Customers abhor nothing more than finding hair in their food." The very thought of a chef failing to wear a toque on his head, or at the very least a bandana or cap, left me cold.

"Except cockroaches. I'd say a roach in the food is even more disgusting than a hair," Pelham opined. "This particular naked chef left his head uncovered, but he was completely bald. Unfortunately, his lack of hair did not extend to his chest and back. The kitchen was so hot that he was sweating profusely, the sweat from his hairy chest dripping into the food he was preparing."

"Perhaps he was influenced by that young chef, Jamie Oliver," I said, referencing a television programme named 'The Naked Chef' that first aired before we left England."

"That Oliver chap didn't actually cook in the buff," Pelham told me.

"Didn't he? I never saw it. I only discovered the joy of cooking when we settled in Greece. So, this chef who was cooking in his underpants...was it a regular thing?"

"It was a relatively new habit. The tip came in from a couple of waitresses who considered having to interact with an almost naked chef to be nothing short of sexual harassment."

"I can see that. There's inevitably a lot of brushing against bodies in the confined space of a professional kitchen."

"When I arrived to inspect, the chef claimed he had

only stripped down because the kitchen was so hot and he had no idea of the hygiene implications," Pelham said, his tone indicating he gave no credence to the chef's lame excuse.

"Being ignorant of the regulations is no mitigation. Surely, they must have taught him that at culinary school."

"It turned out he was one of those amateurs with more money than sense. With no training, he opened the restaurant on a whim and thought he could do whatever he fancied..."

"Such arrogance. Just crazy," I said. "Opening a restaurant is hardly a sound business venture for someone with no culinary experience. Consider the amount that go under every year. The television show, 'Masterchef' has a lot to answer for, convincing budding home cooks they are cordon bleu chefs."

"Well, he's gone under now," Pelham said.

"I sometimes felt guilty that staff lost their jobs because they'd done the decent thing and reported their boss."

"Fortunately, in this instance, I was able to advise the two waitresses who'd drawn attention to their naked boss, of a couple of job openings in a restaurant that always passed our inspections with flying colours."

"A restaurant where the chef kept his clothes on?"

"Of course."

"Bravo, Pelham. That's what I call a satisfactory outcome all round."

"One of the best tips you ever gave me, Victor, was how to read the room when I turn up in my professional capacity."

"Do elaborate."

"If the kitchen staff look worried when I turn up unannounced, it could be perceived as a good indicator they consider hygiene to be a serious issue. If they appear nervous, it might be because they are worried about having unwittingly overlooked some important detail such as failing to scrub all the grouting on a tiled floor in the customer toilet. On the other hand, if they come over as cocky and defiant, it could indicate they're on the defensive, knowing full well there's all sorts of disgusting stuff going on in the kitchen."

"I'm pleased to hear my tip has stood you in good stead, Pelham."

"Only a couple of weeks ago I encountered a defiant sous chef. Whilst I carried out my inspection, he carried on working, preparing the meat for the evening shift. Right in front of my eyes, he handled raw chicken before dicing the beef."

"Not with the same knife?" My stomach churned at the very thought. One of the most dangerous things in a kitchen is allowing cross-contamination, especially if chicken is involved.

"Actually, he used a different knife. But he failed to wash his hands after handling the chicken. When I ordered him to stop and bin all the meat he had touched, he argued that he didn't need to wash his hands because he was wearing disposable gloves…"

"Which he'd failed to dispose of."

"Exactly. He'd been wearing the same pair the whole time I was there."

"Well done, Pelham. It sounds as though your quick thinking averted a nasty outbreak of food poisoning."

Having circled back from the track we had followed around the perimeter of an olive grove, we headed to the church wall to take the weight off.

"Tell me, Victor, do you miss it?"

"Health inspecting?"

"The job, the country, the whole shebang."

"I can't deny that if I had the professional qualifications and the language skills to inspect here in Greece, I could well be tempted. It's all moot though since not only are my English credentials non-transferable, I'm also not related to anyone in the Greek civil service."

"So, it's true what they say about nepotism being rife over here?"

"It certainly is. As for missing the job, even though I have retained a keen interest in my former profession and like to keep up to date on any new regulations, I'm happy to have given up the daily grind of the old nine-to-five. Saying that, I really enjoyed hearing about your work this afternoon. It made me feel as though I was inspecting vicariously, through you."

"What about missing England?"

"That's a definitive no. I do believe that we made the best decision ever when we chose to up-sticks from Manchester and make our home in Meli."

"I think I'll follow your example when I retire."

"Move abroad?"

"No, that's too drastic for me. But I'd love to get out of the city and perhaps move to a small cottage in the Lake District. I often head up there on a weekend with my tent."

"I can see you enjoying the country life."

BUCKET TO GREECE (VOL.17)

"A life in the countryside with a lake view would really suit me. I'll leave the challenges of adopting to a foreign culture with a sea view to you."

Chapter 27

A Recipe for Disaster

"You're looking particularly svelte, darling," I complimented my wife on her return from the Fat Club.

"I feel terribly bloated. I rather overindulged on Kyria Maria's meatballs and spaghetti."

As she stumbled a little over her words, I wondered if Marigold was just a tad squiffy.

"So, no actual dieting was involved?" I asked, putting the kettle on to make my wife a vat of strong coffee.

"That's not true, Victor. Doreen made us all stand on the scales to record our weight. That is, all excepting Kyria Maria who refused to be publicly weighed."

"No doubt you were the lightest," I flattered, recalling the other supposed dieters were Sherry, Doreen and

Athena, the three women having a little more padding than my wife.

Marigold's tone hit a sharp edge as she revealed, "I would certainly have been the lightest if Cynthia hadn't made it." Her words indicated there was still some residual tension between the two sisters-in-law.

"Well, spending so much time running around after a two-year- old, keeps Cynthia trim. I'd swear I lost a couple of kilos just taking care of Anastasia the other day," I reassured Marigold. "Was the weigh-in before or after the meatballs?"

"After. We couldn't leave the meatballs to go cold."

"I'm guessing wine was involved," I ventured.

"You sound very judgemental, Victor. Anyway, the spaghetti soaked up the alcohol nicely."

"It's a good job that Kyria Maria gave the *loukoumades* to me. They would probably have added another kilo to your weight."

"Everyone brought along something sweet. Doreen brought one of Norman's cakes but it was utterly disgusting, only fit for the bin. Instead of adding sugar, he'd added salt," Marigold said with a sigh. With her sweet tooth, she was always quite partial to Norman's patisserie treats, at least the ones he created when sober. With her nose visibly twitching, Marigold's voice adopted an accusatory tone as she stated, "It smells dreadful in here, Victor. Have you been deep-frying?"

"Of course not." My words had a genuine ring of honesty since I was innocent of any charges that I'd had anything to do with frying the Warrington eggs. "I expect my mother got peckish and made herself a snack."

"Well, I wish she'd limit any frying to downstairs. By the way, Doreen sent you a message. She wanted you to know that she wasn't deliberately ignoring you earlier when she passed you on the moped..."

"She totally snubbed me," I griped.

"Doreen said she was just too afraid to take her hands off the handlebars to wave and her teeth were too gritted to even call out a greeting. She may have passed her diploma but nerves got the better of her at the thought of sharing a road with actual vehicles. She's still lacking experience."

"Did Kyria Maria enjoy the gathering?"

"She seemed to, though she may have had a glass of wine too many. It was a good job that Cynthia was able to be there, even though she turned up late. Ever since Cynthia borrowed that beautiful bridal veil from Kyria Maria, she's had a soft spot for our neighbour. Without Cynthia there, Athena and I would have been the only ones able to converse with Maria. You know how I like to mingle rather than being stuck with one person."

"That's true. You always enjoy a good mingle."

"Cynthia was telling me how Barry has gone out of his way to be more romantic," Marigold confided. "At first, when he came home with flowers and wine, she suspected he may have another woman. Desperate to allay her unfounded fears, Barry confessed that you'd been quizzing him about the state of his marriage and he'd decided to up his game."

"It's a pity you made me embarrass myself over nothing."

"Nonsense, you did the pair of them a favour,"

Marigold insisted. "Talking about embarrassing yourself, Kyria Maria certainly enjoyed telling everyone about your very public display of stripping off in the garden and showering under Guzim's hosepipe," Marigold said, the twinkle in her eyes indicating she found it all terribly amusing.

"Do tell me you didn't translate for the others..."

"Of course not, darling. I knew it would embarrass you. Fortunately, only Cynthia and Athena could understand what Maria said," my wife assured me.

I felt a sinking feeling. "You do realise that Athena will likely tell everyone who pops in for a haircut. She can be a bit of a gossip."

"Athena needs to keep abreast of everything going on in the village so she has something to chat with her clientele about."

"Can't she just stick to talking about holidays like any normal hairdresser rather than revealing what I get up to in the garden?"

Changing the subject, Marigold told me, "Just before Maria nodded off in the corner, she told me how much she really misses Harold's swimming pool." I couldn't help smiling at the memory of Kyria Maria refusing to leave Harold's pool.

"Did you walk Kyria Maria home?"

"No. We thought it better to let her sleep it off."

"So, you left her at Sherry's," I confirmed, thinking it was a tad drastic. "When she wakes up, she won't be able to communicate with Sherry."

"What nonsense, Victor. You forget that Sherry has a brand-new English to Greek dictionary. She said she was eager to try out her Greek on Maria once she wakes up. Sherry has totally immersed herself in the Greek language. There were yellow Post-it notes stuck everywhere, emblazoned with the Greek words for things: wine, glass, kettle..."

"I get the picture."

"She'd even slapped a label on Henry the hoglet."

"Well, it certainly sounds as though she's making an effort."

"She hopes to be able to manage the odd sentence on her next date with Vasos..."

"So, they've lined up a second date?"

"Yes. Sherry's terribly excited about it."

"Do you fancy salad for dinner? I've already picked some salad stuff from the garden," I said.

"I think I'll pass on dinner. I'm still stuffed with meatballs."

"If you're sure, darling. I'll need to eat early as I have plans for this evening."

"Oh, not again, Victor. Surely Dina can manage without you tonight."

"I'm meeting up with Spiros, Barry and Blat. We're taking the first shift staking out Sofia's house. I was quite relieved I didn't end up on the second shift. That one will be covered by Vangelis, Hal, Guzim and Dimitris."

"A stakeout. What on earth are you talking about?"

Realising that we had agreed to keep our plans quiet in case word got back to the stalker, I swore Marigold to secrecy when I told her, "Whoever has been terrorising Nikos with graffiti, rubbish, and decapitated pigeons, has been holding up in Sofia's house."

"Squatting?" A look of alarm crossed Marigold's face.

"Indeed. We hope to catch him red-handed when he returns to the house."

"What makes you think he will return?"

"He left a sleeping bag and some clothes there."

"I'd rather you didn't get involved, Victor. It could be dangerous. You really should leave it to the police."

"They don't have the manpower to stake the house out. There's no telling when the squatter will return."

"Well, promise me you'll be careful, darling."

"Of course. I'm not exactly known for acting in a reckless manner."

Our conversation was interrupted by someone pounding on the door.

"Are you expecting anyone?" Marigold asked.

"No. I'll go and see who it is…"

"Do try and get rid of them, Victor. I'm not in the mood for visitors."

"Rightio."

The last thing I expected to see when I opened the door was the Albanian shed dweller, struggling to hold a very inebriated Norman upright. Grim-faced, Guzim dripped with sweat as he told me that my friend fell over in the street, adding the blindingly obvious observation that Norman was drunk. "*O filos sou epese sto dromo. Einai methysmenos.*"

"*Den einai filos mou,*" I retorted, saying he was no friend of mine. I really had no patience for Norman when he was plastered: even sober he was a pain in the backside but under the influence he made an insufferably maudlin drunk.

Marigold appeared at my side. "What's going on, Victor?"

"For some reason that escapes me, Guzim has brought it upon himself to deliver a drunken Norman to our doorstep. I was just about to tell him to take him away."

"We can't just disown Norman, Victor. Look at the state he's in. And he's hurt. His chin is bleeding." Marigold's words drew my attention to Norman's bloody chin. So sozzled he could barely control his head, Norman was indeed in a sorry state.

"Guzim said he saw him fall over...he's so wasted, he can barely stand."

"Give Guzim a hand to bring him indoors." Marigold's authoritative tone brooked no argument. "Take him through to the kitchen. I don't want to risk him throwing up on the sofa."

Slinging one of Norman's arms over my shoulder, I managed to help Guzim half-drag the paralytic drunk inside. Failing to understand why Guzim had seen fit to bring Norman to the Bucket residence rather than take him home, I questioned the Albanian. I found his reasoning very weak when he told me that Kyria Doreen could never understand his Greek.

"*Tha katalavaine oti einai methysmenos,*" I snapped at Guzim, telling him Doreen would have understood Norman was drunk.

"There's no need to bark at Guzim, Victor. It's not his responsibility to deal with an intoxicated Brit."

"Nor is it ours."

"So, you'd be happy to leave Norman passed out on the street..."

"We could put a handful of traffic cones around him to warn any passing pedestrians not to stand on him..." I suggested.

"That really is the most pathetic joke, Victor.

"Who said I was joking?" I mumbled under my breath.

After steering a stumbling Norman into a kitchen chair, his head slumped down on the table. He seemed pretty much out of it. "Victor, find the first aid box and patch up Norman's chin, then try and get some black coffee down him. I'll give Doreen a call to come over."

"Theleis na meino?" Guzim asked if he should stay.

Just as I was telling Guzim he could leave, Marigold contradicted me, telling him to wait in case we needed a hand getting Norman home. Her use of the word 'we' made me roll my eyes, certain that Marigold would contribute zilch if it came to taking Norman back to his house. That task would surely land on me.

I will relay the rest of Guzim's words in English, his guttural speech growing ever louder since he had to compete with the unwelcome din of Norman suddenly breaking into song. Sounding like a scalded cat, no one could ever accuse the traffic cone man of being able to carry a tune, his hideous warbling sending Catastrophe and Clawsome running for cover.

"Do you want me to help you carry Mr Norman into the spare bed?" Guzim asked.

"Certainly not. The bed isn't available for just anyone found on the street..."

"You let me stay in the bed," Guzim reminded me.

"I didn't have to scrape you up off the street. Anyway,

you were a special case, Guzim." It was true. Although the Albanian shed dweller could be beyond exasperating, I felt a certain responsibility for him and his burgeoning young family, whereas I would have no qualms about happily washing my hands of Norman.

Watching Guzim swell with pride, I realised my words had clearly touched him. I could, however, have done without Guzim prostrating himself on my kitchen floor and declaring we were family.

"Do get up, Guzim. You're going to wear the knees out of those horrible jogging trousers."

Wielding a plaster to stick on Norman's graze, I was tempted to use it to zip up his mouth. Fortunately, Norman stopped singing. His attempt to focus on me with a pie-eyed gaze was thwarted by his head flopping forward and landing on his chest: he clearly had no control over his flailing head.

"*Kyria* Doreen deserves better," Guzim said, as though oblivious to the fact that Doreen and Norman had separated despite living under the same roof. "*Kyria* Doreen is very kind. She made the frilly thing to go on my bed."

"From my old curtains," Marigold reminded him.

"Can you try and get some coffee down Norman's gullet, Guzim? It may help to sober him up," I said. "Here, take some kitchen roll to wipe him up if he dribbles."

"Doreen and Manolis are on their way over now," Marigold told me.

"The sooner they take Norman away, the better," I said.

"You could try and be a little more compassionate," Marigold chided.

"The condition Norman is in is entirely self-inflicted. He needs to pull himself together and knock the drink on the head. I would hazard that he drinks out of boredom because his life has no purpose. Being stuck out in the sticks in a foreign country where he couldn't be bothered to learn the language, coupled with having nothing to do in retirement, is a clear recipe for disaster."

"You're right, Victor. Doreen has said much the same. It's lucky that we both keep so busy in retirement that we don't have time to get bored."

"Indeed," I diplomatically agreed. It would serve no purpose for me to point out that whilst I actually held down a job in our new homeland, Marigold was as free as a bird.

"You have your little job as a rep and I have my beautifying the cemetery group," Marigold said. "I seem to be forever organising something for the expat dinner club. Then, of course, the garden demands lots of work and there's always housework to be done…"

"We have a gardener and a cleaner, darling," I pointed out.

"Yes, but Guzim doesn't do flowering plants…"

"*Ti?*"

Ignoring Guzim's inevitable 'what', a question raised whenever he heard his name, Marigold continued, "And Vi doesn't do the laundry or cooking. Ah, this must be Doreen now."

Manolis walked into the kitchen with a purposeful stride, Doreen trailing behind him. I was happy to see

Manolis since he seemed sturdy enough to cart Norman home without my assistance.

"I can't believe the state Norman's got himself into," Doreen said apologetically. "I'm so sorry the two of you got stuck with him."

"That's down to Guzim scraping Norman up off the street and bringing him here," I told Doreen.

"*Ti?*"

Drawing level with Norman, Manolis put a comforting hand on the British man's shoulder. "I hate to see you like this, Norm. We're going to sort this out, once and for all. It's time for you to go to rehab."

A groan was Norman's only response.

Taking charge, Manolis said he was going to ring around and find a rehab place that would take Norman that night.

"Doreen, can you go back to your house and pack a bag for Norman?"

"I'll do it now," Doreen agreed. Making for the door, Doreen added, "Rehab is long overdue."

"It must be a burden on you, Manoli, having to deal with Doreen's husband when you took up with Doreen," I said.

"You know, I really like Norman and I don't mind going to bat for him. I can understand why he's turned to drink," Manolis said, his expression serious. "Imagine, it must be intolerable losing a woman as wonderful as Doreen. It's hardly surprising that Norman's life went to pot when he lost her. When I see him like this, I feel much guilt. I have even thought about calling things off with Doreen so the two of them can have a second chance, but I can't bring myself to do it. I am head over heels in love with Doreen. I want to marry her."

Manolis' words brought a definite twinkle to Marigold's eyes though her words were practical.

"Manoli, even if you did leave Doreen, she wouldn't go back to Norman. Although it wasn't common knowledge, she's been unhappy with him for years. With you, she's a new woman."

Whilst I wouldn't go quite as far as Marigold in extolling Doreen's transformation, there had certainly been many changes since she took up with Manolis, all for the better. Doreen appeared lighter, less weighed down with worry, happier for sure, certainly less irritating. Being in love suited her and she never hid how proud she felt to be walking out with Manolis.

Manolis made several telephone calls before finding a rehab clinic in Athens that was willing to take Norman that very night. Doreen returned with Norman's bag just as Manolis was confirming all the details.

"It is a one-month programme. I hope that will be long enough for Norman to embrace being sober."

The cynical side of me couldn't help wondering if it was self-serving for Manolis to attempt to find a rehab clinic that would take Norman. After all, with Norman out of the way for a month, Manolis and Doreen would be able to meet whenever they liked at Doreen's house without Norman putting his foot down.

"How much is this all going to cost, Manoli *mou*?" Doreen asked with a look of worry.

"Don't worry about it, Doreen. I will sort it out." Taking Doreen's hand, Manolis kissed it. "Hopefully, once Norman is sober, he will pay me back. The main thing is getting him well."

Manolis' words made me feel somewhat ashamed that I had mentally questioned his motives in packing Norman off to rehab. He appeared to genuinely like Norman and want the best for him.

Tears coursed down Doreen's face. Dabbing her eyes with a tissue, she said, "It is such a relief to know Norman is going to be getting some help. It has been such a strain having to live in the same house as him when he's drunk. I've been on tenterhooks the whole time."

"We should make a move," Manoli urged. "We've a long drive ahead of us." My admiration for Manolis grew: not only was he prepared to foot the bill for Norman's rehab, he was going to personally drive him there. Catching sight of the enormous suitcase which Doreen had wheeled over, Manolis questioned why Norman needed so much stuff.

"I only packed a few changes of clothes, and some toiletries," Doreen said defensively.

"So, why such an enormous case?" I asked.

"I squeezed a couple of Norman's traffic cones in," Doreen said. "I thought he should have something with him to make him feel at home."

Chapter 28

Ripping the Balaclava off

Dressed all in black to better blend into the darkness that had descended, I strolled through the village towards Kyria Kompogiannopoulou's house, Marigold's entreaty to be careful ringing in my ears. I don't mind admitting that I felt a tad apprehensive about the stakeout mission; the vandalising squatter could well be armed and dangerous, even an aerosol can of paint capable of doing some damage. Still, it was vital to take the risk and unmask the culprit, to finally put a stop to the petty antics despoiling Meli.

Approaching the village bins, I halted abruptly in my tracks when I spotted a dark-clad figure rooting about in the rubbish. Taking cover behind a conveniently placed plane tree, my senses were heightened as I silently observed, afraid to bat a persistently annoying mosquito away in case the sudden motion drew attention. The figure could well be an innocent villager simply disposing of his household rubbish, or he could be up to something more sinister.

Alarm bells clanged in my head as I realised the figure was hauling a bulging bin bag out of the bins, rather than depositing one.

Keeping a suitable distance, I watched as the figure started heading in the direction of one of Nikos' olive groves. Even with a safe amount of space between us, I could tell the figure was male, tall and well-built; alas his identity was concealed by a balaclava pulled over his face, the sweat-making encumbrance hardly natural attire in the heat of a June evening. With a jaunty spring in his step, he swung the rubbish bag in a happy-go-lucky fashion as though he didn't have a care in the world.

His action of climbing over the stone wall surrounding the olive grove was illuminated by the glow of the outside light coming from an adjacent house. Time stood still when my mobile phone rang. Immediately disconnecting the call, I watched with bated breath as the figure turned around and stared suspiciously in my general direction. Although confident he couldn't see me sheltering behind the tree, I practically quaked in my boots at the prospect of the vandal crossing the road and discovering me. Relief coursed through me when the man shrugged and focused his attention on emptying the bin bag into the field. To my utter disgust, he pulled a couple of headless pigeons from his pockets and chucked them on top of the unsightly heap.

Cursing under my breath when my mobile trilled again, I once again disconnected the call, but not before the man turned in my direction to scour the horizon. Hearing a rustling in the undergrowth at my feet, I doubly worried that whatever it was may draw further unwanted attention in my direction.

Looking down, I saw a pair of green eyes staring malevolently up at me. The shock of seeing Cynthia's mutant cat, Kouneli, in my vicinity, almost made me exclaim aloud. Controlling the urge to wring its neck, I held my breath as the vile feline stealthily sprang away.

Tearing across the road and leaping over the wall, Kouneli landed in the mound of festering rubbish at the feet of the suspicious dark-clad figure. Even with the distance between us, I heard the figure loudly exhale, saying, *"Apla mia gata,"* meaning 'Just a cat.' Although I remained clueless to the man's identity, his words revealed he was Greek. When Kouneli emerged from the pile of rubbish with a headless pigeon clamped between its teeth, the man swung a leg and kicked the cat, revealing he was no cat lover.

I could hardly believe that Kouneli had saved my bacon, the squatting reprobate obviously thinking the noise he had heard from my direction was the cat. Without further ado, the man concentrated on emptying the final remnants of rubbish into the olive grove. Not bothering to lower his voice, he proclaimed, 'Take that,' followed by an expletive: *"Parto afto. Bastardos."*

Although I had the culprit in my sights, I considered

it much too rash to attempt to tackle him alone. Things could get violent: at the very least, I might end up like Kouneli, the unfortunate victim of a good kicking. I reflected there was definitely strength in numbers: the three other posse members waiting for me were all younger than I, and, I would hazard, more skilled with their fists.

The suspect was soon on the move again, walking in the direction of Sofia's house. Straining to keep him in my eyeline as I followed at a discreet distance, I felt my mobile vibrate in my pocket. Ducking behind another tree, I took the call.

"Victor. Where are you?" Spiros hissed in an exaggerated whisper. "You should to be here on the stakeout."

"I am on my way, Spiro. I'm following him now…"

"Him. Who is the him?"

"I don't know. He has a balaclava over his face."

"You make no sense. The *baklava?*"

"No. Not the honeyed dessert. A balaclava. The same thing my mother wears when it's cold."

"You follow the Violet Burke?" Spiros was getting more confused by the minute.

"No," I hissed in exasperation. "This is a terrible line, Spiro. I daren't speak any louder in case I attract his attention. Put Barry on."

"Victor, what's going on?" my brother-in-law asked.

"I'm following the culprit now. He's heading to Sofia's house."

"Who is it?"

"I don't know. He's wearing a balaclava. He's definitely Greek; I heard him speak."

"You've spoken to him?"

"No. Just listen. I watched him dump a load of rubbish in one of Nikos' olive groves."

"Well, we're all in position here. Spiros is inside the house. I'm with Blat in the courtyard at the back of the house. We plan to jump him if he tries to get inside through the kitchen window."

"Excellent. He should be there in less than a minute."

"I'm hanging up, Victor."

"Good luck. And, Barry, do be careful," I exhorted.

Hurrying my pace, I continued to follow the miscreant. Although pretty confident where he was going, I was anxious not to lose sight of him just in case his destination changed. Drawing level with Kyria Kompogiannopoulou's house, the vandal did a quick recce of his surroundings before disappearing down the side alley leading to the courtyard at the back of the house. Rushing forward as fast as I could, I heard the sound of a scuffle as I reached the alleyway.

Hearing Barry shout out, "Got you," I felt a huge weight lift. Dashing into the courtyard, I saw a pair of raised legs pointing upwards, sticking out of the kitchen window, Barry and Blat each holding onto a squirming limb. On the other side of the open window, Spiros grasped the man's shoulders. Stuck between the three of them, the squatter was well and truly wedged in place. Ripping the balaclava off, Spiros exclaimed in shock. "It's Kostis!"

With the identity of the squatter uncovered, Spiros told him to give it up, *"Kosti, parata to."* Spiros added a few more choice words which went over my head. I definitely heard him say, "*Se echoume,*" meaning 'We've got you," but I couldn't swear that his Greek words translated to bang to rights.

Releasing their grip on Kostis' legs, Barry and Blat pushed him head-first through the window, the three of us using the door to join Spiros in the kitchen. Directing Kostis to take a seat, Spiros passed Blat a length of rope that had been used as a washing line, telling him to tie Kostis to the chair. The look of defiance on Kostis' face began to fade when he realised the very real predicament he'd landed in. When Spiros started to interrogate Kostis, demanding to know why he had been terrorising his father, Kostis avoided his eye. I wasn't buying the look of servile submission on Kostis' face.

"*Giati? Mila, pes mas giati?*" Spiros shouted. Demanding to know why, Spiros urged Kostis to speak, insisting he tell us why.

"*O pateras mou me petaxe exo apo to spiti,*" Kostis told us, saying his father had thrown him out of the house.

"*Giati chtypises tin Eleni.*" Spiros reminded Kostis that he had been thrown out for hitting Eleni, adding that it was wrong to hit his wife. "*Einai lathos na chtypas ti gynaika sou.*"

"*I Eleni den mou edose agori, mono achrista koritsia.*" Kostis' look of defiance returned when he responded by complaining that Eleni did not give him a boy, only useless girls, spitting on the kitchen floor to emphasise his contempt for his wife. Kostis continued to make pathetic excuses for his abhorrent behaviour, blaming Nikos for making him homeless.

Spiros rounded on Kostis, telling him he had certainly made himself at home in Sofia's house, defiling the home of a woman Spiros had only recently buried.

"*I Sofia einai nekri kai to spiti itan adeio,*" Kostis fired back, showing absolutely no respect for the recently deceased when he said Sofia was dead and the house was empty. Although I had never really liked Kostis, considering him a lazy weak man content to let his father provide for him, I'd never realised just how despicable he was.

"I'm very tempted to punch him," Barry said.

"You'd be more than tempted if you'd seen the way he kicked Cynthia's cat earlier."

"Kouneli? Are you saying that this lowlife piece of cheating scum kicked Cynthia's beloved cat?"

"He most certainly did."

Watching as Barry's hands balled into fists, I put a steadying hand on his arm. "Perhaps we should leave this for the police to deal with."

"*Astynomia. Ochi astynomia.*" Kostis voice trembled as he begged for no police, the first time his emotions seemed genuine.

"We must to tell Nikos and let him to decide what to do," Spiros said. "I call him now."

Spiros stepped out to the courtyard to telephone Nikos. Returning inside, he told us Nikos was on his way.

"Did you tell him it was Kostis?"

"Not on the phone. The Nikos will to see for himself when he get here."

Thanking Blat for his help, Spiros asked him to leave, telling him that Nikos would likely feel shame at his son's actions. I was touched when Blat assured us the events of the evening would remain private. Wondering if we should leave too, Barry and I exchanged glances, deciding to stay when Spiros reminded us that Nikos thought of us as family.

"I think I'll wait for Nikos outside and break it to him gently," I said. "I don't want the shock of his son's betrayal to give him a coronary. And it will be a shock. A couple of times Kostis' name was bandied about as the culprit but Nikos dismissed even the possibility out of hand. This is going to knock him for six."

Waiting for Nikos to arrive, I decided to follow his lead in any decisions he took. I could only imagine how heartsick and despondent he would feel when it was revealed that Kostis had been the one to deliberately terrorise his father. Intercepting Nikos on the street, I pulled him to one side to break the news about Kostis.

"No." Nikos cried. "It cannot be my son."

"It is, Niko. I personally witnessed Kostis emptying a bin bag full of rubbish in one of your fields earlier."

"No."

"It's true."

"How can the son to do that to the father?"

"I think he's a very troubled man."

"If he do it, he is not the man."

"Do you want to come inside and confront him or would you rather I ask Spiros to call the police to deal with him?" I asked.

"No police," Nikos' tone was emphatic. "If the police involve, word will get back to the Dina. We must keep his shameful actions a secret to protect her feeling.

It would break the Dina's heart if she find out. Who else to know?"

"Just Spiros, Barry and Blat. Blat won't say a word."

"The Blat is the good man. His father must be proud to raise such the son. I feel only the humiliate when I think of Kostis and what he has done."

Entering the kitchen of Sofia's house, Nikos ignored Kostis whilst accepting Spiros' embrace. Neither Barry nor Spiros mentioned the provenance of the fresh swelling Kostis was sporting on his face, his right eye almost closed, the skin around it already turning black and blue. Whilst I abhor violence, I had no sympathy for Kostis: I highly doubted he would have spared me the same treatment if he'd caught me spying on him earlier. Marigold would never believe me when I told her how Kouneli had come to my rescue and the treatment the mutant cat had received from Kostis' foot. I made a mental note to drop off a packet of cat treats at Barry's place.

Sinking into a chair facing the one his son was tied to, Nikos planted his legs apart. Putting his hands on his thighs, he leaned forward, examining Kostis with disdain. Nikos looked as though he'd had all the stuffing knocked out of him, his usually sharp eyes dull and rheumy, worn down by the stress of it all. He only had one question for his son, asking, *"Pos tha borouses na to kaneis afto sti mitera sou?"* meaning, "How could you do this to your mother."

Refusing to meet Nikos' eye, Kostis hung his head in shame. The mumbled words he uttered cast himself in the role of victim. It was a sorry state of affairs to hear a grown man with a wife and two children refusing to take any responsibility for the mess he had made of his life, even though he'd had everything handed to him on a plate by two loving parents. His pathetic whining was the sort of thing one might expect to hear from an entitled teenager yet to chart his path through life.

As Nikos listened to Kostis' self-pitying diatribe, his resolve visibly hardened. Cutting his son off mid-sentence, he told him to leave the village and stay away, and to keep his distance from Eleni and his two daughters. Nikos warned him that if he ever showed his face in Meli again, he would personally hand Kostis over to the police. Gesturing towards myself, Barry and Spiros, Nikos gave Kostis notice that he had witnesses to his breaking into Sofia's house and to his spate of criminal graffiti, his deliberate despoilation of the natural environment, and his sick spree of decapitating pigeons.

Telling Barry and I that he'd like a quick word in private, Nikos guided us through to the courtyard. Speaking in hushed tones, he reiterated that Dina must never know what had happened, neither the details of Kostis' shameful behaviour nor Nikos' banishing his son from the village. Assuring him that we would keep his confidence, we slipped away into the darkness, relieved that the matter was finally closed.

Chapter 29

A Kokoras with an Extra K

Lounging around with Barry the next evening beside his ecological pond where we were serenaded by croaking frogs, I badgered him to tell me, "Was it you or Spiros?"

"I suppose I might as well fess up. It was me," Barry admitted. "It was hearing that Kostis kicked Cynthia's cat that did it for me. I can't abide cruelty to animals."

I thought it best not to mention how many times I'd been tempted to kick the mutant feline, though of course I'd never acted on it. The nearest I'd come to acting out my violent fantasies was to brush Kouneli away with a broom when I caught him trespassing.

"It was surprisingly satisfying to give Kostis a thump

but my knuckles don't half hurt now." Barry studied his bruised hand with a rueful expression as he spoke.

"*Bravo*, Barry. I must confess, I was delighted to see Kostis get his comeuppance." Although I had missed the action itself, it had been impossible to miss Kostis' shiner.

"I honestly thought you would disapprove. You're usually so strait-laced."

"I can make an exception in this instance."

"I just hope Dina never hears about any of this." Barry held a couple of crossed fingers in front of his face. "Nikos went out of his way to shield her and protect her feelings. Kudos to him for being such a thoughtful husband."

"Well…" Pondering whether or not to fill Barry in, I hesitated before blurting out the truth. "Dina knows."

"No…"

"She does."

"No…"

"She popped over earlier with a jar of *glyka tou koutaliou vyssino*…"

"Sour cherry spoon sweets. My favourite."

"I'll save you some. They were a thank-you gift for my helping her out in the taverna kitchen…we're straying off the point though. The syrupy fruit was just an excuse for Dina to confide in me. It turns out she knew about the graffiti and the rubbish all along, ever since the first word was spray-painted on a wall, but she didn't tell a soul."

"She knew even though Nikos went out of his way to keep it from her?"

"Well, you know as well as I do that it's practically

impossible to keep anything under wraps in this village, particularly something as visible as bright red and green graffiti," I said. "Dina put two and two together and worked out that Kostis was the guilty party long before we did...even though she dotes on her son, she knows all Kostis' weaknesses. The real giveaway that confirmed it for Dina was Kostis' atrocious spelling..."

"His spelling?"

"Dina said he's always had a problem with it. When he spray-painted *kokoras* on Nikos' walls, he put an extra K in it. Even though Dina was convinced it was Kostis, she was adamant that Nikos not find out that she knew all about the vandalism or that she was convinced her son was the culprit. She didn't want Nikos to think he'd let her down by failing to shield her from Kostis' criminal and disrespectful behaviour. Also, she had no idea where Kostis was hiding out."

"Well, you could knock me down with a feather," Barry declared.

"A feather from a misspelt cockerel," I quipped.

"So, does Dina have plans to talk Nikos into taking Kostis back?"

"No. She's finally done with him; all this upset was the last straw. She hated that Kostis' actions put such a heavy burden on Nikos' shoulders. Knowing Kostis went too far, her priority is making the taverna a safe haven for Eleni and the girls, whenever they want to visit. Dina wants to protect Nikos from heartache just as much as he wants to protect her."

"I would do anything to protect Cynthia and Anastasia. And Marigold, of course."

"That's my job as Marigold's husband…"

My words were cut short when Cynthia's vile cat sprang out of nowhere, taking me by surprise. Landing on my lap, Kouneli dug its sharp claws into my thighs. "Get away, you vile mutant."

"I thought the cat was your new best friend since it saved your bacon last night."

"It did," I grudgingly admitted. "If Kostis had cottoned on that I was following him, he might have disappeared into the night, free to continue tormenting Nikos. As a gesture of appreciation, I left some Lidl cat treats in your kitchen."

"Thanks, Victor. Cynthia will be chuffed…" Barry's words faded away and his brow furrowed into a frown. "Flipping heck…"

"What is it, Barry?"

"We never got to the bottom of what was going on with all those headless pigeons…"

"You're right. How could we be so remiss? I suppose it will just have to remain a mystery."

"Cheers to pigeons," Barry toasted, clinking his bottle of Amstel against mine.

"And cheers to all those pigeons that lost their heads."

"I've been meaning to say how grateful I am, Victor, for the way you stuck your oar in my marriage."

"I was just doing Marigold's bidding…"

"Yes, but I wouldn't have taken it so well if it came from my sister. It made me realise that I needed to put the spark back into our marriage and start romancing Cynthia more. It wouldn't do for things to become stale."

"Women love being romanced," I mused, thinking it wouldn't hurt for me to up my game and use some romantic moves on Marigold.

"Indeed. How would you feel about taking Anastasia overnight so that I can dim the lights and reignite the spark…"

"We'd love to have Ana…"

"That's marvellous. And just one other thing, Victor…"

"Anything for you, Barry."

"Can you take Kouneli home with you too? He's got a habit of sneaking up on me at very inappropriate moments. One day, I'll show you the claw marks."

A Note from Victor

I hope you enjoyed the latest volume of the Bucket saga.

All Amazon reviews gratefully received, even a word or two is most welcome

Please feel free to drop me a line if you would like information on the release date of future volumes in the *Bucket to Greece* series at vdbucket@gmail.com or via Vic Bucket on Facebook.

I am always delighted to hear from happy readers.

Printed in Dunstable, United Kingdom